Identity Studies in the Social Sciences

Series Editors

Margaret Wetherell
The Open University
Milton Keynes, United Kingdom

Valerie Hey
University of Sussex
Brighton, United Kingdom

Stephen Reicher
School of Psychology and Neuroscience
University of St. Andrews, St. Andrews
United Kingdom

Identity brings together work on core social categories such as social class, race, ethnicity, gender, disability and sexuality. This series investigates the ways in which social and personal identities are lived and performed in spaces and contexts such as schools, work places, clinics, homes, communities, streets, politics and public life, and explores a range of theoretical, methodological and epistemological debates over, for example, the demise of essentialist models, the rise of 'identity politics' and the relationship between psychological and social processes. Identity research has been the vehicle for some profound reflections on the nature of new and emerging social and cultural forms and the impacts of globalization, transnationalism, postcolonialism and multiculturalism. This series welcomes critically and theoretically-informed work in a variety of areas including nationhood, family, gender and class, as well as on issues of identity and space, media representations of identity, social inclusion and exclusion and social identity theory.

More information about this series at
http://www.springer.com/series/14859

Guy Elcheroth • Stephen Reicher

Identity, Violence and Power

Mobilising Hatred, Demobilising Dissent

Guy Elcheroth
Institute of Social Sciences
University of Lausanne
Lausanne, Switzerland

Stephen Reicher
School of Psychology
University of St Andrews
St Andrews, United Kingdom

Identity Studies in the Social Sciences
ISBN 978-0-230-27260-6 (hardcover)
ISBN 978-1-349-59129-9 (softcover)
DOI 10.1057/978-1-137-31728-5

ISBN 978-1-137-31728-5 (eBook)

Library of Congress Control Number: 2016962652

© The Editor(s) (if applicable) and The Author(s) 2017, First softcover printing 2019
The author(s) has/have asserted their right(s) to be identified as the author(s) of this work in accordance with the Copyright, Designs and Patents Act 1988.
This work is subject to copyright. All rights are solely and exclusively licensed by the Publisher, whether the whole or part of the material is concerned, specifically the rights of translation, reprinting, reuse of illustrations, recitation, broadcasting, reproduction on microfilms or in any other physical way, and transmission or information storage and retrieval, electronic adaptation, computer software, or by similar or dissimilar methodology now known or hereafter developed.
The use of general descriptive names, registered names, trademarks, service marks, etc. in this publication does not imply, even in the absence of a specific statement, that such names are exempt from the relevant protective laws and regulations and therefore free for general use.
The publisher, the authors and the editors are safe to assume that the advice and information in this book are believed to be true and accurate at the date of publication. Neither the publisher nor the authors or the editors give a warranty, express or implied, with respect to the material contained herein or for any errors or omissions that may have been made. The publisher remains neutral with regard to jurisdictional claims in published maps and institutional affiliations.

Printed on acid-free paper

This Palgrave Macmillan imprint is published by Springer Nature
The registered company is Macmillan Publishers Ltd.
The registered company address is: The Campus, 4 Crinan Street, London, N1 9XW, United Kingdom

Preface

An Invitation to Perplexity

This book was not written in a day. The idea of writing a joint book which examined intergroup relations through the prism of collective mobilisation (or else demobilisation) first crossed our minds in the spring of 2008. This was a period that we spent together in the seemingly timeless environment of St Andrews—a small, beautiful and ancient town perched on the far edge of the European continent which was at the epicentre of the Scottish religious wars of the sixteenth century, where the wars have been largely forgotten since but nothing else seems to have changed much.

We were meeting about once a week to compare patterns from our respective research on ethnic violence in the former Yugoslavia and in India, and to design a new study on the local repercussions of a global event—the rise of the Scottish independence movement in the aftermath of the Iraq invasion. Early on in our discussions, it appeared to us that these cases are telling examples of dynamics that do not yet receive the full attention they deserve in social psychology texts. Both in the former Yugoslavia and in India, there is a striking contrast between, on the one hand, grand narratives of entrenched ethnic or religious conflict, and, on the other, the reality of fluid social relations and malleable identity constructions on the ground. But it also struck us that we need to beware of making too stark a distinction between fixity and fluidity. There are periods when social categories and social relations do indeed remain constant over extended periods and periods where they go through rapid changes. Which one discovers is a matter of timing. In general terms, it would be wrong to treat either as the norm. Rather, we need a more historicised approach which allows us to identify and analyse the turning points where social relations lose (or gain) their fluidity and where identity constructions become frozen (or unfrozen).

When we do take an historical view—whether in relation to our own studies of the former Yugoslavia and of India, or indeed of elsewhere—it becomes abundantly clear that, at different times, the cleavages in social relations have been based on different social categories: sometimes people confront each other in terms of nation and sometimes in terms of class, or caste, or religion or ethnicity. Multiple differences have therefore to be forgotten and multiple conflicts have to be put on hold before a critical mass of people can think or act together in terms of any one of these, still more before one can take it as self-evident that there is a long history of conflict between Hindus and Muslims, Serbs and Croats, or whatever other groups are seen as trans-historical entities.

So how are categories reconfigured? How could social relations become frozen along ethnic lines and ethnicity become a matter of life and death—as they did in Vukovar or in Sarajevo, in Ayodhya or in Gujarat, or in many other places at different times in history?

Back in 2008 an impression arose which evolved into a critical thesis that led us to re-assess the existing evidence and re-analyse our own. Such dramatic disruption of the normal fluidity of collective identities cannot just happen spontaneously. It requires such a violent shock to the system that the fundamental ways in which we are able to relate to others are changed and hence we begin to think and talk of the cleavages between self and other, 'us' and 'them', in new ways. And not only must the shock be violent but also violence is a powerful means of achieving such a shock. Even if you never previously saw yourself and others in terms of, say, religious identities, if you are attacked as a Muslim—or even hear of others attacked as Muslims—can you afford to ignore the possibility that you, your family, your friends might be positioned as a Muslim in future encounters? Can you therefore afford to avoid acting as if you were a Muslim, thereby confirming others view of you as such and hence fuelling a vicious spiral? Unwillingly, perhaps, but no less effectively, the awful realities of violence affect the identities through which we organise our everyday world.

This insight might seem relatively modest and mundane. But the more we thought about it and the more we considered the implications, the more the fabric of received wisdom on conflict and intergroup relations began to unravel. Traditionally, conflict is seen as an output of identity processes. There are two broad variants of this. On the one hand it is argued that longstanding identities generate animosities that, given the power to act, will result in violence. So, notably in the former Yugoslavia, it is argued that the state may have temporarily suppressed the ancient hatreds between groups in the region. But once that state dissolved, people could express their hatreds in ways that still haunt the imagination. On the other hand it is argued that those with power and influence deliberately invoke antagonisms between groups and deliberately incite violence which ordinary people are incapable of resisting.

The three terms here—identity, violence and power—are ones that we retain and which are central to our analysis. But we reconceptualise their relationship. Instead of putting either identity or power at the start of the process—as inbuilt features of our psychological make-up which all too easily generate antagonism towards outsiders or conformism towards cynical leaders—we also treat them as outcomes. Equally, instead of putting violence at the end of the process we also place it at the start. Instead of conceptualising a simple linear relationship between terms, we examine the multiple configurations of identity, violence and power. Violence thereby becomes much more than the tragic end of the play. Above all, it is the shock that serves to create and consolidate identities and thereby to transform power relations during the next act.

However, one cannot alter the way in which identity, violence and power relate to each other without rethinking these core constructs themselves. Our approach to each construct lays much more stress than usual on meta representation and communication. That is, who we are, what we think and what we do is as much a matter of what we think others are thinking as of what we think ourselves, and also of what we think others will allow us to do. It follows that reconfiguring identities may be best achieved by altering our knowledge of others' thoughts and intentions rather than trying to change our internal beliefs. Our ability to gain that knowledge—the relations of communication between people—thereby gains centre stage.

We thus understand and analyse identities, violence and power as social facts. That makes them no less real for those who experience them and no less consequential in their effects. But it does mean that they arise out of human activity and they shape human activity from the inside. Indeed, identity, violence and power are the most powerful of tools for crafting our social worlds. By occluding old identities, violence makes it impossible to mobilise people on the basis of those erstwhile constituencies. By creating new identities, violence makes possible new forms of mobilisation and thereby creates the power to sustain new social worlds.

One way of seeing our model, then, is as a psychological example of a mobilisation approach to intergroup relations and social conflict (something that may be common in other social sciences, but which is something of a departure for psychologists). It is a model that recognises the importance of manifold forms of social practice and of social communication (not only from leaders to followers). As many scholars before us, we don't presuppose that ingroup identities and outgroup hatreds are stable realities and we examine how and why people are mobilised around particular identities to hate particular others. But we also examine the processes whereby, under extraordinary circumstances associated with specific historical periods, these identities and these hatreds evolve towards a more stable form. While we argue that these hatreds arise within a contingent social order, we hope to elucidate how sometimes they come to be seen as part of an inevitable order.

Writing While the World Goes By

We have described how we set out to write in 2008. Back then, we thought that our argument might be pushing at an open door. Our focus was to be on a set of intriguing conundrums that arise once one follows through a constructivist view of identity: How can such fluid and malleable things as collective identities sometimes become hard social facts? Why do people sometimes actively support leaders whose politics have disastrous effects on their own interests? What makes political violence such a dreadful vehicle to re-pattern collective identities, impacting even on those who under normal circumstances would forcefully resist? Our assumption was that establishing a critique of essentialist approaches to identity would be the easier and less original part of the work. It could function as a discrete backdrop to the main stories of the book. After all, who in the early twenty-first century could still seriously believe that differences in language, religion or culture are sufficient to explain why people who are different from each other would violently clash with each other?

But much has happened in the ensuing years, and looking back, early 2008 seems almost an age of innocence. It was before the financial crash, the ensuing recession, unemployment, austerity and chronic global sense of economic insecurity. It was before an explicitly ethnic party—the Bharatiya Janata Party (BJP) and its leader, Narendra Modi, who promote the notion of India as a Hindu nation—won power in the world's largest democracy. It was before the Arab Spring, the ongoing violence in Egypt, the conflict in Yemen, the collapse of the Libyan state, the civil war in Syria, the rise of ISIS and the return of ISIS militants to their European countries of origin. It was before people displaced by these and other conflicts began to flee to Europe, before the spectacular rise of anti-immigrant populisms in even the most liberal of democracies, and before the resurrection of borders and barriers between European nations. It was before the return of war to European soil in the clashes between Ukrainian forces and Russian-backed separatists, and before the Russian annexation of Crimea.

In today's more fractious world, it is all too easy to believe that that ghosts of ancient and ineradicable conflicts have come back to haunt us—or even that we are being punished for our temerity in denying their existence. As we write now, in the spring of 2016, even the Eurovision Song Contest (ordinarily that most innocent frippery) has become politically and ethically charged. The winning song, entitled '1944', is about the deportation of Crimean Tatars by Stalin with obvious reference to the annexation of 2014. The lyrics begin "When strangers are coming/ They come to your house/They kill you all/and say/We're not guilty/not guilty." More prosaically, the notion that conflict arises out of a clash of engrained identities has gained renewed legitimacy in public discourse and policy decisions concerning war and peace. It has become a readily available grid through which to understand and respond to contemporary conflict.

Accordingly, what we had thought to be easily dealt with in terms of a background to our studies has now become far more controversial. What might once have been an open door has become stiff with age and far more effort is needed to shift it. We could no longer just state a set of assumptions about the constructed nature, and hence the contingency, of identity, violence and power. We were in danger of using a language to explain the world just at the point that the world was moving beyond that language. The fear that our words would not even speak to a new generation of students and scholars, for whom the book was primarily intended, began to haunt us.

This fear led us to revise our manuscript to be more explicit about the problems with fatalistic conflict theories. Accordingly, the first part of the book spells out our criticisms of models that treat group identities as immutable, conformity within groups as natural, and hostility between groups as unavoidable. As we have already intimated, there are two variants of this view and we devote a chapter to each: Chapter 1 looks at the idea that ordinary people are doomed to hate those from different groups and leaders can, at best, mitigate the worst excesses; Chap. 2 looks at the idea that ordinary people are doomed to follow leaders who incite them to hate those from different groups.

The second part then provides a systematic outline of our own position based on three key constructs: identity, violence and power. This involves rethinking both how each of these relates to the others and also how the construct itself should be understood. So, in Chap. 3, we start with identity as something that is created through shared social practices and hence is transformed through the disruption of existing practices. In Chap. 4 we turn to violence as a particularly potent means of achieving such disruption and hence of reconfiguring the map of social identities and social groups. Finally, in Chap. 5, we address power—more specifically, the role of leadership and power politics in managing violence and identity.

In the third part, this conceptual model is applied to three case studies. In Chap. 6 we dissect the dynamics of religious violence in parts of India. In Chap. 7 we examine ethnic violence in the former Yugoslavia. In Chap. 8 we analyse anti-war protest in the UK, and more specifically in Scotland, in reaction to the military invasion of Iraq. Since parts of these case studies have been published before as journal articles, we were able to present the findings here without disrupting the flow of the book with too much methodological detail. We also opted to integrate each case study with new, so far unpublished, material that extends both the empirical and the conceptual reach of our analysis.

Beyond the Prophet Motive

The changes of recent years have led us not only to alter the structure and stress of our argument but also to reconsider its impact and implications. As lines of public debate shifted so that discourse that had been perceived as extremist became normalised, we were led to become more reflexive about the way that we—as social scientists—refer to the mainstream and to the margins in public controversies. As, like everyone else, we were continuously taken by surprise by the new givens and developed an ever more uncomfortable feeling of running behind events, we were forced to confront a foundational question: What exactly is our analysis for? After all, the conventional justification of scientific analysis is that it allows us to predict what will happen. If we (like everyone else) so obviously fail in prediction, then what on earth is the point of what we are doing?

To address such deeply troubling questions, let us consider a further case which is, as we write, still unfolding. We refer to Burundi, whose past and present plights are largely ignored despite the fact that something like a quarter of a million people were killed in past atrocities, culminating in 1972 and 1993, and that, over the last year alone a further quarter of a million people have fled the country in fear of further violence.

At one level, the latest bout of violence was clearly foreseen. When the first author travelled to Burundi in early 2014, the country seemed safe. It was perfectly possible to talk in a relaxed manner with local researchers, aid workers and activists. Many people spoke openly. Some of them were happy to air their differences about the challenges facing Burundian society in its attempts to deal with a legacy of violence. It was easy to travel around the country and to visit commemoration sites, each of which told a different story about the nature of this past violence. But among well-informed locals, few expected this to last. With surprising consistency and great precision many conversations alluded to the prospect that the current period of calm and tolerance would come to an end within 18 months, to be replaced by a new period of heightened tension.

They were right. After President Pierre Nkurunziza decided to ignore the two-term limit on office and, in April 2015, announced his intention to seek a third term, there were massive protests in the streets of Bujumbura (the Burundian capital), a radio crack-down, a failed coup attempt, and, eventually, vicious repression of the anti-third-term opposition. That is also when the flow into exile began. But if many people foresaw these tensions starting from a long way off, there was a limit to their prophetic powers. Once conflict had started, no one could tell how it would develop. Everyone was perplexed as to how the next day might turn out.

It was as if an understanding of the simple power calculus between the main actors, a glance at the electoral calendar, and an awareness of past events (elections in Burundi have repeatedly been tainted by violence) was enough for well-informed observers to predict that a crisis would occur, and even when it would occur. Just like clockwork, the president would try to cling on to power, his rivals would cry foul and an almighty stooshie (to use an evocative Scottish word for conflict) would break out. But once events were in motion—once social forces had been moved out of a stable equilibrium into a state of volatility—then the smallest of causes could produce the largest of effects. It then became all but impossible to spot what was coming and where things were going.

Strangely enough, as knowledgeable locals became more perplexed, international observers became more certain about the focus of concern. They had one question: Would the crisis lead to an outbreak of ethnic violence? So, on 13 May 2015, while the coup attempt was still unfolding, CNN splashed the headline "Amid fears of ethnic violence, coup attempt reported in Burundi". Meanwhile, the *International Business Times* announced, "Africa watches Burundi coup to see if conflict spreads, reignites Hutu-Tutsi ethnic conflict". The following day the UK *Daily Telegraph* newspaper entitled its report: "Burundi shares ethnic balance that led to Rwanda genocide—but this conflict is different".

Here was prophecy. At the time these and suchlike headlines were written, they didn't describe the reality on the ground. If anything, they were ahead of that reality. A Hutu general was leading a coup against a Hutu president, with whom he previously fought together in the rebellion movement, built up the powerful CNDD-FDD party, and served as his head of intelligence services until a mere two months before. Both loyal and putschist army factions were ethnically mixed, as was the state administration and the protest movement in the streets. It was only after the failure of the coup that things began to change. Some members of the ruling party started to spread rumours that opposition to the president was a Tutsi plot against a Hutu ruler and they combined this with fierce repression against various Tutsis alongside their alleged anti-presidential 'sympathisers'. Would this ethnic frame succeed? Would it reignite past horrors? Many Tutsis were not prepared to take the risk that it wouldn't and so started to flee. This exodus in turn seemed to validate the ethnic frame. It certainly broke the back of the protest movement. As people became afraid to gather together, many returned to the private sphere of their homes. An uneasy calm returned to the streets combined with anxious expectations of further violence in the neighbourhoods of Bujumbura.

This crisis has taught us two important lessons. The first concerns the radical inadvisability of making predictions. In part, this is because of the likelihood of getting things wrong. Beyond being able to posit in general terms that a conflict might occur, we can see how, without the benefit of hindsight, it is hard to know what forms a conflict will take, how the conflict might develop or how it will turn out. We are not dealing with mechanistic or deterministic processes here. The nature and course of events depend upon how critical actors make sense of them, and sense making is a non-deterministic, slippery, infinitely variable and infinitely malleable process. So, by posing as prophets and by making predictions we run a serious risk of making fools of ourselves.

But there is another, and possibly greater, problem: occasionally, our predictions could turn out to be right, not because they were particularly clear-sighted, but because they feed into an interpretation of events that increases the odds of the predicted outcome. Our prophecies may end up as self-fulfilling in themselves or, more plausibly and more problematically, condoning the prophecies made by the most powerful conflict actors (those who are in the best position to make their prophecies become true). The underlying issue here is that, if we accept that identities and conflicts are constructed and contingent rather than natural and inevitable, and if we also accept that identities can be rooted in the way we will be seen by others as much as in the way we see ourselves (like those who fled for fear of being apprehended as Tutsis) then we can never be certain of providing an innocuous definition of events. We are not like taxonomers defining reality from the outside. We are, whether we like it or not, insiders who are part and parcel of the conflict process. If we take ethnic categories as givens, and if anyone takes us seriously, then people will increasingly expect to be seen in ethnic terms and act accordingly.

One reaction is to insist that no one takes academics seriously or even notices our obscure scribblings. Quite apart from the ironic nature of a defence of academia based on the fact that academics are useless, the claim tends to deny certain historic realities. Over the last two centuries, social scientists have been at the very core of various national projects and certain disciplines—history, of course, but also anthropology, archaeology and others—arguably arose precisely in order to sustain such projects. But also, as we shall see at various points in the book, politicians have explicitly drawn on academic analyses (e.g., ethnic conflict is inevitable) to draw policy conclusions (e.g., there is no point in intervening to try and stop it).

The second lesson we learn from Burundi takes us from the war of words to the war on words and on those who spread the word. Much of the early conflict surrounded control of the radio, the country's only mass media. Indeed mass protests in Bujumbura were triggered when the government decided to close down the privately owned station, *Radio Publique Africaine*, which had been supporting opposition to Nkurunziza's third-term presidential bid.

The subsequent 13 May coup against Nkurunziza began with an attempt to seize the capital's main radio station, where the rebellious soldiers were met by loyalist troops. The two army factions exchanged gunshots before the rebels, realising their inability to take control of the station, decided to surrender. The radio station was damaged during the short bout of fighting. State forces then took advantage of the resulting confusion in order to destroy Bujumbura's remaining four main radio stations. While the domestic media were forcibly silenced, the international media remained silent out of disinterest. Little space for collective discussion remained. Burundians were left without appropriate means of coordinating their understanding of the new realities. Because the government had declared that there was no crisis, it became difficult even to talk about the events without being open to accusations of treason. In terms which we will develop further in due course, people were left in a state of epistemic isolation.

The situation brings to mind Foucault's use of Bentham's panopticon as a metaphor for the operation of power. This refers to a structure whereby an authority at the hub can see all those arranged around the rim, but these people cannot see each other. They are therefore held in the gaze of that authority without being able to draw upon their fellows for support. In such a situation, where communication between people is excluded, it becomes impossible to counter the voice of authority. Authority thereby retains the unique capacity to define events, to construe identities and to shape collective action. If only it were possible to break down the partitions between those around the rim, things would be very different.

And with these thoughts in mind we can begin to return to the point of writing this text. The first purpose of any words should be to open up conversations—in this case concerning the nature of conflict. If there is one thing we would hope to achieve with this book, it would be to bring people together in new configurations to address received truths and consider new perspectives. It is for this reason that we have deliberately written our book in a way that transcends traditional disciplinary boundaries. We have also sought to make the book as clear and as lively as possible in order to be accessible for those outside the academy who have to handle and live with the many conflicts which cleave our world: practitioners, politicians and the interested public. We have tried to avoid jargon where possible, to define it where not, and to use theory only as far as it sheds light on phenomena of broader interest. Our hope is that, even if readers disagree with some of our analyses, they will feel that they have at least found out something about conflicts in the world and something that helps them in questioning the available explanations of conflict.

That leads on to another—central—reason for our book in particular, and for critical new theory in general. More and more, psychologists tell us that human beings have an engrained craving for a world that is known and certain. The academic enterprise is often justified in terms of answering that call: by promising to increase our certainty about the world, how it works and how it will work out. However this is a dangerously one-sided perspective, because sometimes the value of academic work is (and should be) to disrupt existing certainties, to provide new ways of seeing and thinking, to raise questions where there were none before. Indeed one of the main purposes of new theory is to raise new questions and not simply to provide new answers. That is certainly how we want our own contribution to be judged.

Back to Perplexity

To be more concrete, our ambition for this book is as follows. Having listened to the news in print, on television or online, and having heard about Sunnis fighting Shias, Kurds fighting Turks, Hutus fighting Tutsis or whatever—and maybe even having heard some pundit explaining that, back to time immemorial, Sunnis have always fought Shias, Kurds have always fought Turks, and Hutus have always fought Tutsis—we hope that our readers will experience a heightened sense of dissatisfaction.

More specifically, we hope that readers will be left with two niggling questions. The first is to ask 'Why Sunni and Shia, and why right now'? Since it obviously cannot be true that every Sunni has hated and aggressed against every Shia at every point in history (or does so today), how has reality come to be seen in terms of these groupings in a specific time and place? Why have these particular categories been chosen over possible alternatives—who is promoting these categories and why are they doing so? In the same way that a word, endlessly repeated, can come to sound strange to the ear, so the categories endlessly repeated in the media may eventually begin to sound absurd—and reading this book might speed up the process. How mad that, out of a huge range of possibilities, we should have ended up dividing and treating people in this specific way. And how much more absurd to suppose that this must ever be so.

The second question is how did we get from 'Sunni and Shia' to 'Sunni against Shia'? Is a mention of identity sufficient to account for conflict? Is invoking identity and past conflicts between those of different identities enough to trigger present violence—at least when there was sufficient power to turn malevolent intentions into actions? Is violence a tragic but unintended outcome of identity dynamics or is it a critical component of those dynamics?

In sum, our aim (like the court jester or the poet) is principally to provide new angles for looking at the familiar and making it seem surprising. Where there was complacency we wish to bring unease. Where there was certainty, we wish to bring perplexity. It is not simply that we have no aspiration to play prophets. If anything, we aspire to escape from an age of prophecy. Certainty closes down the future. It keeps us on the straight and narrow. We prefer to think about the future as open, to envision multiple possibilities, to facilitate debate and, hence, extended choice over which of these possibilities are worth pursuing. To the same end, we aim to expose the means by which academics, activists or autocrats seek to close down our options. Violence, we contend, is prime amongst these.

Lausanne, Switzerland   Guy Elcheroth
St Andrews, UK   Stephen Reicher

Acknowledgements

One of our core arguments in this book is that human understanding and action derive more from what happens between us than from what happens within us. Who we are, what we think and what we do are all functions of what others think of us and act towards us, and, yet more recursively, what we think others think of us and will do to us. Our own ideas are inextricably intertwined with those of others. They are impossible to separate out. And what is true of the argument in the book is equally true of the book itself.

Although there are parts of the text which derive more clearly from the concerns from one or the other of the two authors, over time the conversations between us have shaped and reshaped these thoughts to the extent that we can no longer draw clear lines and claim 'this is mine' and 'this is his'. It is truly a collaborative enterprise which neither of us could have completed alone and both of us have benefited immeasurably by those many conversations with each other.

But the web goes wider. Many people, both wittingly and unwittingly, have contributed to this project. We have gained immeasurably from their work and from our dialogues with them. As with each other, it is impossible to determine exactly which idea belonged to whom. In this way, although the book was actually written by the two of us (and we take full responsibility for all the arguments it contains) it is also a collective accomplishment.

Of those others who contributed, first and foremost come Sandra Penic and Rakshi Rath. The Croatian case study wouldn't have been possible without Sandra and the Indian case study wouldn't have been possible without Rakshi. The two relevant chapters (6 and 7) largely draw on material that Sandra and Rakshi collected as part of their thesis work. We are grateful to both of them for allowing us to reuse this material here and also for their subtle and fine-grained insights. It was only through these that we were able to understand the material and appreciate its significance for our broader argument. Another person who provided invaluable practical assistance is Nicole Repond, who checked and completed the references.

More broadly, many of our colleagues in both Lausanne and St Andrews have been generous with their criticisms, their comments and their suggestions both on our general arguments and on preliminary drafts of the chapters. And there are colleagues beyond our home institutions who have played an equally valuable role. The material on obedience and leadership in Chaps. 2 and 5 and also the Indian research in Chap. 6 comes out of many years of productive collaboration with Alex Haslam and Nick Hopkins. The research presented in Chap. 7 is rooted in a long and fruitful collaboration with Dario Spini, and several concepts introduced in Chap. 3 originate in joint work with Willem Doise.

Without doubt, the book would have been different and poorer without regular, tough but cordial exchanges over the last three years with friends and colleagues from all five continents gathered within the Pluralistic Memories Project. These exchanges were an invaluable tool in tempering our ethnocentrism and for helping us to consider how the problems discussed here might look from different parts of the worlds. Visits to Sri Lanka, Burundi and Palestine have been eye-opening in many regards. They provoked a whole set of revisions. They also generated the seeds for what we hope to become the next generation of case studies.

Finally, we could not have completed this book without generous material support. The Universities of Lausanne and St Andrews provided time, space and stimulating environments for us to write. The UK Economic and Social Research Council (ESRC) funded two separate research projects—one on Milgram and obedience and the other on collective action in India—which fed much material into our text. The Swiss

National Science Foundation (SNSF) provided financial support at the start of our journey, through a fellowship which, in 2007–2008, allowed the first author a one-year stay as a visiting research fellow in St Andrews. Towards the end of the journey, the SNSF has helped again, through the research for development scheme (r4d), by funding the Pluralistic Memories Project since 2014.

Contents

Part I   Critique   1

1   Hateful Groups and Weak Powers?   3

2   Evil Leaders and Obedient Masses?   39

Part II   Model   71

3   Identity: The Group as a Collective Performance   73

4   Violence: How Collective Shocks Transform Social Practices   99

5   Power: The Role of Leadership at Critical Junctures   129

Part III   Case Studies   153

6   Riots, Religion and the Mobilisation of Communal Hatred in India (with-Rakshi Rath)   155

7	**Ethnic Violence in the Former Yugoslavia: From Myth to Reality (with Sandra Penic)**	183
8	**British Warriors and Scottish Voters: When 'Rallying the Nation' Backfires**	215

Conclusion 243

Index 261

List of Figures

Fig. 8.1　Moral principle positions and the timing of debates (*above*) as well as social cleavage positions (*below*) according to their coordinates along two dimensions defined by an MCA of their joint occurrences within parliamentary interventions. Arguments related to the 'home front' appear in *bold*.　223

Fig. 8.2　The positions of individual interventions (marked by party affiliation) according to their coordinates along two dimensions defined by the MCA (see Fig. 8.1) of the joint occurrences of moral principles, social cleavages and the timing of debates. Interventions from members of separatist parties appear as filled grey triangles.　225

List of Tables

Table 7.1	Rates of acceptance of mixed marriage before and after the war, across eight political entities (sorted by decreasing level of pre-war ethnic diversity)	185
Table 7.2	Perceived sources of inter-group inequality in pre-war Yugoslavia	188
Table 7.3	Popular support for future institutional scenarios in pre-war Yugoslavia	189
Table 7.4	Perceived ethnic conflict in pre-war Yugoslavia	189
Table 7.5	Affiliation to different territorial entities, before and after the war	191
Table 7.6	Estimate of the population share for three types of identification in Croatia and Serbia; with group means of attachment, glorification and collective guilt acceptance	195
Table 7.7	Summary of the results of the thematic coding of the parliamentary debate held on 13 and 14 December 2005	202
Table 8.1	A structured inventory of moral arguments: generic moral judgements and nested concrete arguments invoked by the 'external front' and the 'home front' as well as frequencies before and after the invasion	221

Table 8.2	A structured inventory of categorical arguments: generic social cleavages and nested concrete arguments invoked by the 'external front' and the 'home front' as well as frequencies before and after the invasion	222
Table 8.3	Multivariate predictors of the separatist opposition (above) versus the Labour majority (below) vote: partial logistic regression coefficients	235

Part I

Critique

1

Hateful Groups and Weak Powers?
Ancient Hatreds (And Other Fables)

In the Orson Welles film *Mr. Arkadin*, the eponymous hero recounts a fable:

> And now I'm going to tell you about a scorpion. This scorpion wanted to cross a river, so he asked the frog to carry him. No, said the frog, no thank you. If I let you on my back you may sting me and the sting of the scorpion is death. Now, where, asked the scorpion, is the logic in that? For scorpions always try to be logical. If I sting you, you will die. I will drown. So, the frog was convinced and allowed the scorpion on his back. But, just in the middle of the river, he felt a terrible pain and realized that, after all, the scorpion had stung him. Logic! Cried the dying frog as he started under, bearing the scorpion down with him. There is no logic in this! I know, said the scorpion, but I can't help it—it's my character. Let's drink to character.

This fable applies well to the topic of our book. The simplest story about violence between groups is that violence is just what groups do. It might not be palatable. It might not seem logical. Often, indeed, those who attack others are themselves consumed by the ensuing violence. But groups can't help it. It is in their character—the dark side of humanity divided into groups—whether we want to 'drink' to it or not.

The simple story does not imply constant violence between groups, and is therefore immune against refutation by the historical reality of extended periods of peace. Groups will not always act on their hatreds, especially when there is a powerful centre to counteract such centrifugal tendencies from spiralling out of control. But take away such dampening forces and the violence will once more flare into the open. Such positions have gained contemporary momentum in two subsequent waves: first, since the fall of the Berlin Wall and the ensuing bout of conflict both within the old Soviet Union and the former Yugoslavia; second, in the wake of the post-nine-eleven wars in Afghanistan and Iraq, the subsequent rise of the Islamic State group and the ideological framing of the wars fought against them all in terms of 'clashes of civilisation'.

When, after the end of the Cold War, conflicts arose between such groups as Armenians and Azeris, Bosniaks and Serbs, Kyrgyz and Uzbeks, an often expressed view was that Communist rule may have suppressed fundamental ethic identities and ethnic antagonisms—but it never did eradicate them, nor could it have. As the authoritarian regime crumbled, so the identities and the conflicts re-emerged—if anything, more virulent than ever for having been suppressed for so long. From this perspective, after decades of the iron rule of 'ideology', the stage was finally cleared for the historic revenge of 'ethnicity'.

As illustration, one only has to turn to two statements made within months of each other in 1993 by the leaders of the USA and the UK. On 20th January, in his Inaugural Address, President Clinton warned that:

> Today, a generation raised in the shadows of the cold war assumes new responsibilities in a world warmed by the sunshine of freedom but threatened still by ancient hatreds and new plagues.[1]

On 23rd June, Prime Minister Major addressed the British House of Commons, referring specifically to conflict in the former Yugoslavia, but spelling out the argument subsumed in Clinton's brief statement:

---

[1] The full text is available at http://www.presidency.ucsb.edu/ws/?pid=46366.

The biggest single element behind what has happened in Bosnia is the collapse of the Soviet Union and of the discipline that that exerted over the ancient hatreds in the old Yugoslavia. Once that discipline had disappeared, those ancient hatreds reappeared, and we began to see their consequences when the fighting occurred. There were subsidiary elements, but that collapse was by far the greatest. (Hansard, 23rd June 1993, col. 324)

Both comments were made against the backdrop of the war raging in Bosnia–Herzegovina, whose atrocities alarmed Western public opinion and urged Western intellectuals to re-work their analytic concepts. The year following the end of the war, 1996, Samuel Huntington published his famous article on the *Clash of Civilizations*, to which we shall return in detail later in this chapter. The language used in this article has provoked much controversy since its publication, in academic and non-academic circles alike. But despite all sceptic voices, Huntington appeared to have generated a widely available frame, to which many have come to refer again in more recent years, in a global context of mounting tensions. Prominent voices have come to claim that the clash of civilisations is now materialising.

Following the shooting of French cartoonists in Paris in January 2015, and the subsequent international stigmatisation of religious censorship in the name of Islam, Turkish President Tayyip Erdogan issued the following warning: "Despite all our efforts to prevent it, the clash of civilisations thesis is being brought to life". The year before that, a Huffington Post essayist had argued that "We should have seen it all coming", alluding to the sombre prophecies spelt out in Huntington's article: "The future (the article) describes has become our present and the challenges it raises will continue to define the global order for decades to come" (Johnson, 2014).

The same year, former French Minister of foreign affairs Dominique de Villepin gave an address at the World Cultural Forum. He took this opportunity to comment on the way reality had surpassed the fears he had prominently expressed more than a decade earlier, when France did not follow the United State's call to invade Iraq. In February 2003, Villepin had warned against the consequences of an invasion of Iraq in a resounding speech given at the UN Security Council, wondering whether "such intervention (would not) be liable to exacerbate the divisions between societies, cultures and peoples, divisions that nurture terrorism?" The title of De Villepin's 2014 talk—"Will the clash of identities consume us?"—was as evocative as its opening phrase: "Since 2001, we have entered a vicious clash of civilizations. We have not seen the bottom of it yet". His description of the calamitous state of Iraq a decade after the invasion names a clear culprit, the *cult of identity:*

> In Iraq today, the national feeling almost disappeared behind ethnic and religious identities. But such identities exist only as differences from each other. They become hysterical, incompatible and intolerant of all diversity. The cult of identity is a selfish and brutal vision of the world than can lead to the most terrible crimes.

Epistemologically, the most troubling aspects of the clash of civilisations debate are the thin lines between comment and warning, between prediction and prescription, along which it evolves. These ambiguities are well illustrated by the following words used by *New York Times* editorialist Roger Cohen in a controversial opinion piece, published in February 2015:

> To call (the Islamist) movement, whose most potent manifestation is the Islamic State, a "dark ideology" is like calling Nazism a reaction to German humiliation in World War I: true but wholly inadequate. There is little point in Western politicians rehearsing lines about there being no battle between Islam and the West, when in all the above-mentioned countries tens of millions of Muslims, with much carnage as evidence, believe the contrary.

There are actually two remarkable things about Cohen's argument. The first is that it introduces a notion of "inadequate truth": the idea that even when complex accounts are analytically accurate, it can still be morally wrong to utter them. The second lies in the implied logic that *their hate* constrains *our reality*. Cohen perceives (on whatever basis) "tens of millions of Muslims" who believe there is a battle between Islam and the West, and he therefore infers there is no other choice left than to accept the battle as a fact. Doing so, the editorial appears to call for a self-imposed restriction of epistemic freedom, elevated to the status of a moral duty. The rationale seems to be that complex truths are a dangerous luxury in a world where many angry people believe in simple stories.

It is rather easy to see how such calls, were they followed diligently, can lead to a vicious spiral of rapidly reducing freedom of interpretation and, thereby, of options for action. If whenever you anticipate that certain others see the world in a black-and-white fashion you need to adopt the same view, then the imagination of a few will fatally end up in leading all to see the world in black and white, and act accordingly.

What is explicit in all these quotes is the Hobbesian notion that people have an inherent tendency to violence which will inevitably manifest itself once state structures dissolve and people return to a state of nature. Moreover, this bestial nature is tied to collective identities: it is pursued and legitimated in the name of collective interests, not personal gain; it is targeted against collective enemies, not personal foes. However, what is perhaps more telling, precisely because it is taken for granted rather than stated explicitly, is an assumption that these collectivities will be organised around deep-rooted communal (ethnic, religious or cultural) fault lines. This presupposition that there is a primordial manner in which people define themselves down the centuries is what ensures continuity between the past and the present, why people see events of many hundreds of years ago relevant to them currently, and why ancient battles remain a matter of what 'they' did, and continue to do, to 'us' in the here and now.

Whether those who take on board this assumption are right or wrong in arguing that present conflicts reproduce past history, what is undoubtedly true is that their explanations of conflict reproduce past accounts of history. Indeed, the quoted depictions of ethnic violence following the break-up of the Soviet empire eerily echo accounts of similar violence following the break-up of the Ottoman and Austro–Hungarian empires. Take, for instance, the words of the Nobel Prize-winning author Ivo Andric, who wrote about the violence which erupted in Visegrad in 1914:

> That wild beast, which lives in man and does not dare to show itself until the barriers of law and custom have been removed, was now set free. The signal was given, the barriers were down. As has so often happened in the

history of man, permission was tacitly granted for acts of violence and plunder, even for murder, if they were carried out in the name of higher interests, according to established rules, and against a limited number of men of a particular type and belief ... (1945, pp. 282–283)

There are very different ways, however, of explaining the rise in ethnic or religious violence since the end of the Cold War. The same year as Huntington published his *Clash of Civilizations* article, Brubaker and Laitin (1998) published a theoretical paper that identified as the key factor the disappearance of macro-political cleavages between capitalism and communism. This removed any political incentive to frame conflicts ideologically and consequently enhanced the relative payoff of ethnic conflict frames. After 1991, a rebellion fought in the name of communism would no longer recruit international allies to the side of the insurgents. However, if one fought in the name of overturning ethnic repression or in order to achieve national self-determination, then it might be possible to recruit the support of ethnic 'kin groups' in other states and of members of the ethnic diaspora. It might also win the support of third-party neutrals and international human rights organisations.

There is much to recommend such an approach. First, it doesn't treat conflict as inevitable, nor does it treat the framing of conflict in terms of particular group memberships as inevitable. Rather, it sees such categories as resources, which are actively invoked for the purposes of mobilising support. It therefore points to the importance of leadership. It also looks to the importance of the contemporary context (and not only events of the past) in determining which categories are employed, and, more to the point, which categories are successfully employed. It therefore opens up an investigation into why and when the appeals of leaders succeed in mobilising the masses. The question, then, is not whether a culture provides tales in which an evil ethnic foe is set against a virtuous ethnic ingroup. Such tales are indeed widely available. The question is rather why and when these tales are taken up, woven into political rhetoric, and why they momentarily work (cf. Nirenburg, 1996).

But we are getting ahead of ourselves. We shall discuss such questions in detail in later chapters. For now our point is that approaches such as that of Brubaker and Laitin, for all the respectful recognition they have gained among peers, appear not to have decisively shaped the way most people, policymakers and media commentators think about conflict, or at least about how they talk about conflict in public. They are still eclipsed, in political communication and public debates, by those who read the present as the eruption of a long and troubled past. While constructivist thinking over the past decades undoubtedly had a profound impact on the social sciences, and on conflict studies in particular, it does not appear to have had a similar impact beyond academia.

At first glance, this might be understood as a consequence of academics' lack of ability, perhaps of motivation, to get the more complex stories out and make them relevant to those interested in dealing with real-world problems—the ivory tower cliché. But, as many examples throughout this book will illustrate, the problem might as well reside in a form of ambiguity within the academic field itself. While very few social scientists at present would enthusiastically self-declare as 'primordialists', or argue in their theoretical writings that identity is immutable, many do adhere to research practices that treat their research subjects *as if* they had one overarching and stable group belonging, which orients their perspective on the world—one that informs the research design and data analysis.

In our post-Cold War world, where the loudest and most powerful voices describe conflict in ethnic terms, it therefore becomes ever more critical for social scientists to ask why there has been such a turn rather than to follow it ourselves. That is why, in what follows, we treat the three prevailing narratives of collective identity formation as *metaphors*. In so doing we express our understanding that they are better seen as frames which guide and limit the evidence collected about the nature of identity, rather than as a reflection of the evidence itself.

1.1 Metaphors of Identity

In this section, we shall examine three broad metaphors, which are used to explain how people divide into different and antagonistic groups. The first likens group identities to kinship, the second to civilisations and the third to games. We do not suggest that these cover the full range of understandings of identity that have been developed in the social sciences. Indeed, the main goal of Chap. 3 will be precisely to show that alternative understandings are available, and in Chaps. 4 and 5 we will discuss their implications for the study of collective violence and of struggles over power. For the moment, our goals are more restricted. We seek to highlight how common sense metaphors frame and constrain the way social scientists look at group identities and the way they link to violence. We also seek to draw attention to the social and political consequences of these understandings.

1.1.1 Identities Defined by Descent: The Kinship Metaphor

Descent is central to most definitions of ethnicity. For example, Fearon (2008, pp. 852–853) states that "In ordinary English usage, the term 'ethnic group' is typically used to refer to groups larger than a family in which membership is reckoned primarily by a descent rule [...] That is one is or can be a member of an ethnic group if one's parents were also judged members". In this view, markers of ethnic identity such as 'common language, religion, customs, sense of a homeland, and relatively dense social networks' might describe the group as a whole, but they don't define who belongs to it as an individual. In Fearon's words, "Becoming fluent in the language, manners, and customs of Armenia will not make me 'ethnically Armenian'. The key constitutive feature is membership reckoned by descent".

If people are born into ethnic groups, it is only a short step to argue that ethnic identity is also something that derives from birth—from biology rather than social experience. Primordialist conflict theorists readily make this step. As Harvey (2000) explains, not all group affiliations are equal. Rather, "from an 'evolutionary' perspective [...] ethnic ties are inherently more potent (and fit) as an organizing force than, say, ties based on class or occupation. Individuals are bound to their ethnic group by virtue of some 'absolute import attributed to the very tie itself'". In evolutionary language, social markers of identity, like 'language, dialect, customs, diet', are relevant only in terms of 'phenotypic matching'.

They are mere cues to biological relatedness. In more technical terms, they serve as a 'kin recognition mechanism for humans'.

The significance of this mechanism is that it informs us with whom we share a common reproductive interest, and hence who will be on our side (and who won't) when push comes to shove. This, so the evolutionists claim, is universally true, but they do acknowledge that the types of situation which invoke kinship categories vary across time. Melotti, for instance, quoted by Harvey (2000, p. 51), asserts: "when man had more or less mastered the inimical forces of his … environment (such as hunger, cold, and predatory animals), war became the main selective factor in human evolution".

Harvey helpfully puts the various steps of the argument together: "humans tend to bond for evolutionary reasons, primarily to enhance reproductive success, and enhancing kin survival through reproductive success is the key to evolutionary explanation for ethnic conflict" (p. 41). This is effectively the fable of the scorpion and the frog all over again, but this time taken a step further. It is not just that groups conflict because that is the nature of groups. It is that humans conflict along ethnic lines because that is in the nature of human beings. Whether we like it or not, and however much we try to work against it, in the end our racist nature will out and ethnic mayhem will ensue.

1.1.2 Identities Defined by Opposing Worldviews: The Civilisation Metaphor

Not everyone who explains conflict in terms of inevitable categories sees these categories as a matter of descent. Indeed, one of the most famous such explanations—Huntington's (1993) 'clash of civilizations' thesis—takes what seems at first glance to be a very different approach.

For Huntington, identities are not rooted in biology. He makes no reference to evolutionary processes or to reproductive instincts in order to explain why categories form. For him, categories relate to 'civilisations'—what one might call 'ways of seeing'—rather than set forms of being. Moreover, he sees these civilisations on a very large scale. There are, Huntington contends, no more than seven or eight such civilisations in total, whose boundaries largely overlap with those of the main world religions: "Western, Confucian, Japanese, Islamic, Hindu, Slavic-Orthodox, Latin American and possibly (sic) African civilisation" (p. 25).

One might think that such an approach would open the way to a rather more flexible approach to categories. After all, our biology and our biological relatedness to others may be fixed, but, especially in an increasingly globalised world with massive movements of populations from continent to continent, one's 'civilisation' would seem more open to change. But that is not Huntington's own view. He suggests that we can no more overcome barriers based on civilisation than those based on biology. This is because of the very long history that produced them—a history that reaches back much farther than particular political belief systems which prioritise alternative categories—such as class. In part because of this history, civilisational identities act as fundamental filters which affect all aspects of the ways in which people perceive and experience social reality. Huntington provides a long list to underline his point:

> The people of different civilisations have different views on the relation between God and man, the individual and group, the citizen and the state, parents and children, husband and wife, as well as differing views on the relative importance of rights and responsibilities, liberty and authority, equality and hierarchy. These differences are the product of centuries. They will not soon disappear. They are far more fundamental than differences among political ideologies and political regimes. (1993, p. 25)

Such unbridgeable differences make agreement and co-operation across civilisations difficult, if not impossible. They make misunderstandings, disagreements and conflicts likely, if not inevitable. But, as Huntington argues next, it is not simply that civilisational identities themselves are fundamental, fundamentally opposed and resistant to change. It is also that individuals cannot change their civilisational identity:

> In the former Soviet Union, communists can become democrats, the rich can become poor and the poor rich, but Russians cannot become Estonians and Azeris cannot become Armenians. In class and ideological conflicts, the key question was 'Which side are you on?' and people could and did

choose sides and change sides. In conflicts between civilisations, the question is 'What are you?' That is a given that cannot be changed. (p. 27)

At this point, for all their seeming differences, the civilisational and the kinship accounts of identity become all but indistinguishable. Although they use different means to do so, both essentialise identity as necessary, eternal and inescapable. In the end, the story is the same. You can mask them for so long, you can seek to replace them with more contingent categories, but in the end people will revert to fundamental cleavages. Hence, Huntington uses the past tense to refer to those 'class and ideological conflicts' which are now consigned to the dustbin of Soviet histories. He uses the present tense for 'conflicts between civilisations' which, because they have very old roots, are far more relevant for the present and future. On this basis he is able to present a map of Europe dating back to 1500, which marks the "eastern boundary of Western Christianity" (p. 30), and use it both to explain conflicts at the end of the twentieth century and also to prophecy that the "next world war, if there is one, will be a war between civilizations" (p. 39).

1.1.3 Identities Defined by Competition: The Games Metaphor

The third metaphor, the games metaphor, may seem to sit very oddly with the two we have just discussed: ethnicity as kinship and ethnicity as civilisation. To start with, whereas these others root conflict in the differences between groups (and the differences in what they believe in, care for or aspire to), the games metaphor roots conflict in *similarities* of belief, value and aspiration. It is because we want the same thing—but can't all have it—that we fight others for the commonly desired prize.

Moreover, whereas kinship and civilisation approaches explain intergroup relations in general, and conflict in particular, through the past, games approaches situate their explanations firmly in the present. It is not the trans-historical essence of the group that matters—it is the particular set of circumstances they find themselves in which matter. As circumstances change (and it is in the nature of circumstances to do so), a games approach suggests that group relations will change. Indeed, this was the core point that the classic 'games' studies sought to show. In effect, then, the core challenge we all face is not the primordial ethnic or cultural group but rather (to borrow the famous quote which Harold Macmillan may or may not have actually uttered) "events, my dear boy, events".[2]

According to the games metaphor, intergroup relations are essentially structured like sports competitions. The whole point of a football team in a football league, say, is to play against and to win over other teams. Players could try to get along with each other and avoid competition, but at that point they would cease playing football and being league teams. So, it is argued, once competition is part of the very definition of the group context, then rivalry and distrust and even hostility seem derived almost as a logical consequence. Such theories are often referred to as 'realistic' conflict theories because they assert that intergroup hostility is neither irrational nor accidental but rather based on an objective reality of conflicting interests. The only way our team can win the game is to make their team lose. We therefore want them to lose, we try to make them lose and we rejoice at their misfortune.

The foundational and prototypical studies in the 'realistic conflict' tradition are those conducted by Muzafer Sherif and his colleagues in the late 1940s and early 1950s using American boys at summer camps—most famously, the 1954 'Robbers Cave' study (Sherif, Harvey, White, Hood & Sherif, 1961/1988). The whole point of these studies was to use the camps as a blank canvas, creating groups that had never existed before, which had no history at all (let alone a history of antagonism), and then creating different relations between them to see what would ensue. So, in the 1954 study, the boys were divided into two groups: the Rattlers and the Eagles. At first, they didn't know of each other's existence, but then they were brought together in competitive games: baseball, tug-of-war and so on. This immediately created animosity. Friendship choices across groups were strikingly rare; the boys began to stereotype members of the other group in derogatory terms. They began to denigrate them and their

---

[2] For a history of the phrase, see http://www.telegraph.co.uk/comment/personal-view/3577416/As-Macmillan-never-said-thats-enough-quotations.html.

achievements. Most dramatically, they began to attack each other's huts, stealing and vandalising property.

Sherif's most fundamental message was that antagonisms between groups can be turned on and turned off by circumstances and, as a consequence, even the most peaceful people can be made violent. This is summed up in one of the most important quotes in the history of social psychology, written to describe the point at which the conflict reached its zenith:

> If an outside observer had entered the situation after the conflict began … he could only have concluded on the basis of their behaviour that these boys (who were the 'cream of the crop' in their communities) were either disturbed, vicious or wicked youngsters. (Sherif & Sherif, 1969, p. 254)

This work and these words have had considerable influence across the social sciences. Somehow ironically, they have been taken on board by ethnic theorists when they formulated ethnic competition models. These view interethnic conflict as grounded in objective conflicts of interest, typically over the share of economic rewards (e.g., Olzak, 1992). The scarcer a resource, and the more a resource is valued, so the more competition and the more antagonism there will be between ethnic groups. Hence, prejudice, hate crimes and interethnic violence flourish where there is economic scarcity and/or high immigration flows.

But even if these theories borrow the games metaphor to explain *when* groups conflict, they remain fundamentally at odds with games theories in explaining *what* groups conflict. So, whereas Sherif saw groups as defined and constituted by the game, ethnic competition theorists introduce a notion of groups as prior to the game, as defined long before any game has ever started.

That is, Sherif saw group boundaries, memberships, solidarities and antagonisms as essentially arbitrary. They are created by the ways in which people are put in competitive (or co-operative) relations within the situation itself. Thus, when the social structure is such that a gain for the Rattlers is a loss for the Eagles (and *vice versa*), people see themselves and others in terms of those groups. But when, later in the study, Sherif altered the structure such that the Rattlers gained when the Eagles gained (and *vice versa*), an inclusive group emerged and antagonism diminished.

By contrast, ethnic competition theorists presuppose that group boundaries, memberships, solidarities and antagonisms will always be along predefined ethnic lines. All competition does is determine whether relations between groups will be more or less toxic. But prejudice and conflict, when they do occur, won't be between any old (or rather, any young) groups, but, in the first place, between natives and immigrants or, more generally, between people born into different nations or culturally defined groups.

On the whole, such theories (unlike realistic conflict theories) don't explicitly address why co-operation and competition would operate on predetermined ethnic groups. They just take it as a given that this is the case. When the question is posed in practice, the answer falls back on assumptions about biological relatedness or about long-standing cultural processes. That is, in practice, the games metaphor tends not to be used in its 'pure' form, but in a more or less implicit amalgam with one of the other two metaphors that we have been discussing.

1.2 Why the Metaphors Are Misleading

Our previous discussion begins to touch on some of the unsettling implications of the various approaches to violent conflict that we have been discussing. To the extent that they present ethnic or cultural categories as fixed across biological or historical time, and to the extent that they suggest different groups are prone, if not doomed, to fight, then the pessimistic conclusion is that human beings are bound to be ethno-centric and group conflict cannot be avoided. Such conflicts will occur all by themselves. No intervention is needed. They might be suspended, but they cannot be stopped. In the long run, most intervention will be futile at best and may even make things worse.

We will discuss these matters in more detail in the next section. But first, we want to address the validity of the three approaches. After all, we cannot reject arguments simply because they are uncomfortable. If people were naturally ethno-centric, we would have to face up to the fact.

We can, however, reject arguments because they don't account for the evidence—either suggesting things we know not to be so or else denying things that we know to be the case. When it comes to the three metaphors, there are at least four such bases on which to express doubt.

1.2.1 Errors of Generalization

If one is looking for them, it is easy to find examples of conflicts between different ethnic or civilisational groups. Huntington, for instance, bases his argument on multiple examples of such conflicts. The examples are graphic and they make his position seem compelling. But the real test of an argument is not whether you can find examples to support it (hypothesis confirmation) but what happens when you try to find examples to undermine it (hypothesis disconfirmation). Billig (1987), for instance, counsels that if ever anyone makes a strong claim (ethnic groups are inherently prone to conflict), then consider the exact opposite (ethnic groups are inherently prone to co-operate) and run with that as hard as you can. Only if you get nowhere should you give credibility to the original claim.

In this case, it is as easy to find situations where different 'civilisations' co-exist harmoniously as it is to find examples where they conflict. To take just one of countless examples, consider Mazower's (2005) history of the co-existence of Jewish, Muslim and Christian communities in Salonica. So to claim that civilisations inevitably clash is simply untrue—or at least it is a dramatic over-generalization. Moreover, to make such a claim doesn't help us understand when such conflicts break out and when they don't. After all, even where there is a history of antagonism between groups such as Jews, Muslims and Christians, it remains true that most of the time people live together peacefully. Violence is always sporadic and requires close attention to the immediate context in order to understand how, why and when tolerance turns to violence and *vice versa* (see, for instance, Nirenburg's 1996 analysis of relations between the three religions in medieval Aragon).

Kaufmann tries to address this problem by arguing that, perhaps, not all ethnic groups clash in all circumstances, but once they do, the violence cannot be forgotten. Ethnic grudges last forever and hence peaceful co-existence between the relevant groups becomes impossible. Leaving aside the problem that this still leaves the question of why violence occurs in the first place unanswered, and also that it fails to explain when violence will and won't occur between the said groups, there are still two major problems with such an account. The first is that, even if it were true that a memory of past ethnic antagonism feeds into future ethnic antagonism, the very fact of memorising presupposes that one views oneself and others in ethnic terms. But sometimes it is possible that we entirely forget about past groups and hence the violence associated with them, such that both become entirely irrelevant to our past and future.

The great historian Ernest Renan made this point eloquently when he asserted that modern social forms, such as the nation, depend upon forgetting the older social categories which needed to be brought together to make a country. In his words:

> No French citizen knows whether he is a Burgundian, an Alan, a Taifale, or a Visigoth, yet every French citizen has to have forgotten the massacre of Saint Bartholomew or the massacres that took place in the Midi in the thirteenth century. (1990, p. 11)

If Renan is talking about forgetting over an extended historical period, there is evidence that one's sense of ethnic identification can also change in the shorter term. Thus, Bhavnani and Miodownik (2009) analyse the two first rounds of the Afrobarometer survey, in 1999–2001 and in 2002–2004. They show how, in post-apartheid South Africa, the proportion of people who answered that their 'first and foremost' identification lies with their ethnic group was almost halved within three years, falling from 42 % to 22 %. In neighbouring Zimbabwe, the decline was even more dramatic, going down from 47 % to a mere 13 % in the same period. Unlike diamonds, ethnic groups are not forever.

The second problem with Kaufmann's account is the converse of this. If ethnic categories can decline to irrelevance, hence removing the basis for ethnic conflict, so such categories can become important and lead to conflicts in contexts where none existed before. Many years ago, a young Bosnian woman was interviewed on the BBC's flagship morning radio news programme 'Today'. She explained how she had fled the violence in Sarajevo and now lived in London. Even so, she still always had a suitcase packed under her bed in case she had to flee. The interviewer expressed surprise. With the casual ethno-centrism of the English, he pointed out that London is not Sarajevo and we don't engage in barbarities such as ethnic cleansing here. The woman replied by explaining how, when she grew up, Sarajevo was a byword for cosmopolitanism. It was modern and vibrant and effortlessly diverse. Ethnicity meant nothing to her; she didn't even know if most of her friends and schoolmates were Muslim or Orthodox or Catholic. That is why, when the conflict and the divisions came, they were all the more devastating. They came as lightning from a clear blue sky. If it could happen in Sarajevo, she concluded, it can happen anywhere.

We will examine exactly how such ethnic division was produced in Sarajevo, seemingly out of nothing, in future chapters. For now our point is that the assumption that ethnic/civilisational conflict is inevitable—or at least, once it starts, it is bound to continue—leads not only to over-generalizations but also to under-generalizations. It breeds not only pessimism or even fatalism about the inevitability of conflict in some circumstances, but also complacency about the impossibility of conflict in other circumstances. It is hard to say which is worse.

1.2.2 Errors of Association

It is very rare to find unconditional relationships in the social sciences. There are always so many factors at play. So perhaps we are setting the bar a bit high. Perhaps it would be fairer to ask whether there is an overall association between ethnic or cultural divides and violence: where there is one, the other becomes *more likely*. After all, this is the sort of thing we usually look for. If one exception would damn a theory, no theory would ever last long in the social sciences.

But even when addressed in more moderate terms, the ethnic account does not fare well. In two independent analyses of *all* state dyads, by year, over most of the nineteenth and twentieth centuries both Henderson and Tucker (2001) and Chiozza (2002) reached the same conclusion:

violent conflict is more likely between two states of the *same* 'civilisation' (according to Huntington's criteria) than between two states of different civilisations. Remarkably, this relationship even holds when controlling for geographic proximity (Henderson and Tucker) or for the existence of a common border between the two states (Chiozza). The point is clear and deserves stressing: *throughout the era of nation states, a country is at less risk of becoming involved in a war with another state from a 'different civilisation' than with an equally remote state from the 'same civilisation'.*

This may seem decisive enough to justify scepticism about the civilisation metaphor, but there are data to buttress the argument more generally. If one turns one's attention from relations between states to relations within states, the kinship metaphor would suggest that increased ethnic diversity would lead to more conflict. But again, the evidence points in the opposite direction. Østby (2008) reports that diversity does not increase the risk of civil violence. It is only where there are social inequalities between ethnic groups that there is more violence. Wimmer, Cederman and Min (2009) make a similar point. Analysing data from all independent states of the world since the end of World War II, they show that, once one controls for the magnitude of exclusion from political power of certain ethnic groups, 'linguistic fractionalisation' (which is often used as an indicator of ethnic diversity in comparative analyses) is only marginally related to the outbreak of violence.[3]

Finally, the relationship between migration rates and anti-immigrant prejudice, central to the game metaphor in ethnic competition theories, appears to be inconsistent at best. It is true that Semyonov, Raijman and Gorodzeisky (2006) found cross-sectional evidence that anti-foreigner sentiment was higher in European countries with high rates of non-European immigration in 1988, 1994 and 1997. But in 2000 the relationship had disappeared. In the United States, Scheve and Slaughter (2001) looked at three different time points and found no difference in

---

[3] One could add that the indicator of ethnic diversity is less exogenous and the relationship more circular than it might look at first glance. If most people in France speak French today this is precisely an outcome of the fact that linguistic identities that were important until the nineteenth century have been forgotten together with the grievances that opposed the groups. In the former Yugoslavia, Serbo-Croat has been replaced by four new languages after the war, that is, violence and nationalism created the languages, and not linguistic diversity the violence.

attitudes towards immigrants between those living in areas of high immigration and those who did not. In Canada, Wilkes, Guppy and Farris (2008) conducted an extensive time-series analysis spanning the last quarter of the twentieth century and also found no relationship between immigration rates and attitudes towards immigrants in Canada.

So, whether one looks at international conflict or intranational conflict, whether one looks at settled ethnic populations or the flow of ethnic migrants, however much one gives them the benefit of the doubt, the evidence in support of the argument that ethnic or cultural diversity makes conflict more likely is, at best, hard to find.

1.2.3 Errors of Group Psychology

Let us turn, now, from the empirical evidence (or lack thereof) for conflict theories to their conceptual underpinnings. As we have seen, the three metaphors rest on the general claim that groups have an inherent tendency to conflict with each other. The point is actually often taken as so self-evident as to require no justification. However, on those occasions where the argument is warranted, two authors in particular tend to be referenced: Sherif for his boys camp studies and the resultant realistic conflict theory, and Tajfel for his minimal group studies and the resultant social identity theory (Tajfel, Billig, Bundy & Flament, 1971; Tajfel & Turner, 1979). In both cases though, there is a problem of partial findings being presented and of specific claims being extracted from the broader theoretical framework of which they form a part. This way, caricatures of the seminal studies and theories have replaced the real thing, and arguments are advanced in the name of these theories which are at odds with their original intentions.

In the case of Sherif, the focus is so exclusively on how competition produces conflict that it is forgotten how his key point was to show that conflict is contingent, dependent on how people are set against each other in particular social systems and how conflict can therefore be overcome. It is also forgotten that, even where there is competition and conflict, Sherif didn't see this simply as a matter of relations between the two groups. He also examined how intergroup competition can create new opportunities and incentives for struggles within groups. In fact three out of four of Sherif's original research hypotheses regarding the stage of competitive games referred to the changing ingroup dynamics, and only one to intergroup orientations. Finally, it is forgotten that Sherif did not see competition between groups as a simple objective given. He was well aware that it is important to examine the frame of reference through which people understand social relations, the nature of their groups and the relations between them. Indeed, as he discovered at his own cost in an abandoned 1953 boys camp study, you can put groups in competitive games, but they won't always see themselves as in competition and fight over the spoils (see Reicher & Haslam, 2014).

Overall, Sherif's aim was to show that 'the dark side' of human conduct—hatred, war, genocide—was not inevitable. It didn't reflect some unchangeable essence of our social or biological nature. Rather, it reflected something about the ways in which we are put into competition within a contemporary market society (Kayaoglu, Batur & Asliturk, 2014). Ethnic competition theories, then, are not an application and extension of the realistic conflict approach. They are its nemesis.

Turning now to Tajfel, the use of his work to argue that 'discrimination between groups is inevitable' is, if anything, even more of a distortion and a sign of sloppy scholarship. In his minimal group studies, boys are divided into two groups on trivial or even random grounds. They then have to divide points between two individuals about whom all they know is that one is a member of their own group and the other is a member of the other group. The key finding is that they show a small but significant tendency to give more points to the ingroup member even if this comes at the cost of the absolute level of reward to the ingroup. Tajfel then explains this finding by arguing, first, that people define their identity in terms of membership of the group; second, that they then evaluate their group membership through comparison with relevant other groups; and third, that in order to achieve a positive evaluation (and the positive esteem that flows from it) they differentiate themselves from the other group, seeking to come out better in the relevant comparison.

In the minimal group studies, the only group one has to identify with is that to which one is assigned, the only group one has to compare with is the one to which one is not assigned, and the only dimension along which one can compare oneself positively is the number of points one's group is allocated. In the minimal group studies, then, differentiation necessarily means giving more points to one's own group. However, Tajfel has always been very clear about the dangers of generalising from the specific behaviours in a study rather than examining how the underlying process might operate differently in different settings:

> What is, however, important is a clear realization that the 'general' case is an impossible myth as long as human beings behave as they do because of the social expectations with which they enter an experiment—or any other social situation. If these expectations are shared—as they always are by definition to some degree in any social context—I shall obtain data from my experiment which are neither 'general' nor 'individual'. The observed regularities of behaviour will result from the interaction between general processes and the social context in which they operate. Without the knowledge of this context the data may be irrelevant to the confirmation or the falsification of a hypothesis. (Tajfel, 1972, p. 74)

In the case of the minimal group studies, this argument plays out at two levels. First, whereas the process of differentiation may play out as financial discrimination in the highly constrained setting of the experiments, it may play out in many different ways in different group contexts. Indeed, the substantive outcomes of the differentiation process will always depend on the natures of the groups involved, the things that they value and therefore the dimensions along which they seek to compare themselves. In some cases that might result in behaviours that bring the other group down (we want to be harder, stronger, richer), but equally, in other cases it might result in actions which benefit the outgroup (we want to be more generous, kinder, more loving). So whereas differentiation means discrimination in the minimal group studies, this will not always be so and groups will not always discriminate against each other.

At the second level, social identity theory does not suggest that members of groups always differentiate themselves from outgroups. Whether they do or not depends upon a series of structural and ideological factors such as the possibility of movement between different social groups (permeability), and the legitimacy and the stability of intergroup relations. Social identity theory, then, is definitely not a theory of (inevitable) intergroup discrimination. It is not even a theory of (inevitable) intergroup differentiation. It is actually a theory of how the differentiation process plays out in different social settings (see Reicher, 2004).

1.2.4 Errors in the Description of Conflicts

Now, let us consider still more closely the assumption that conflicts are driven by ethnicity, and that violence is motivated by ethnicity. Ethnic conflict accounts are fundamentally rooted in a way of representing the protagonists in a conflict as Serb and Croat, Hutu and Tutsi, Hindu and Muslim—whether or not they are, whether or not they see themselves as such, and whether or not this is relevant to what they do. Thus, when the conflict is between different groups it is often assumed that religious differences are the true underlying cause of conflict. When, say, a Muslim worker confronts a Hindu moneylender, it is assumed that it is the religious (rather than the economic) category that counts. When a Hindu attacks a Muslim, it is seen to be about the fact that they don't like that the other is of a different religion rather than about more immediate temporal concerns. Once you have found your generic Hindu and generic Muslim, enquiry can stop, for that in itself is enough to explain violence.

However, as our previous examples illustrated, people do not always view the world and themselves through ethnically tinted spectacles. We all have many group-based identities—as a Catholic, as Swiss, as a socialist, as a football fan, say—and these will become salient in different contexts. It follows equally that the way I categorise others will change according to context: the same individual who I may see as an outgroup Protestant in one context, I may see as an ingroup Swiss in another. No one can be classed as ingroup or outgroup in general terms. We can only make these judgements in specific contexts.

But even if people do see themselves in ethnic terms, and even if they were to feel antagonism towards each other because of ethnic differences, that still would not get us very far. It certainly would not explain any violence that occurred. This takes us back to a point we have made before. Even in the most extreme cases of ethnic conflict, violence is never a constant. It doesn't happen all the time; it doesn't happen in every place.

Simply invoking universal ethnic antagonisms doesn't tell us where violence happens, when violence happens, why it starts and how it stops.

Take India as a case in point, where so-called communal violence between Hindus and Muslims has claimed, and continues to claim, hundreds, thousands, even millions of lives (if one includes the events of partition). As Brass (2006) argues, with particular power, riots are not a simple chain of action and reaction. They do not simply repeat themselves without cease. Waves of rioting come and go. Any single wave lasts for a few days at most. It may be true that particular massacres, as in 1992 (following the destruction of the Babri Masjid and 2002 (in Gujarat), are so horrific and so command our attention as to make the time between them seem insignificant and make us feel that violence is going on all the time. But, in fact, most of the time passes without riot. So why did the dispute come to a head in 1992 and why was it reinvigorated in 2002?

The same questions can be asked spatially as well as temporally. Again, riots so command the field that we can fail to notice that even the most intense 'wave' of violence leaves most places untouched. Why, in particular, was the most intense rioting that followed the sacking of the Babri Masjid in Bombay—a city nearly 1000 miles away, one of Asia's most cosmopolitan cities and a most unlikely site for such carnage (Tambiah, 1996)? Once more, if one assumes that riots simply reflect the universal antagonism of all Hindus towards all Muslims, then there is no way of knowing except to invoke chance.

But there is still a last point to consider, in order to fully grasp the problem. Collective violence is never an inchoate explosion in which anything goes. However extreme the actions, they always have a pattern. Some targets are attacked. Some are left alone or even defended (e.g., Davis, 1973; Thompson, 1971). The Indian evidence tells a similar story. Violence is always expressed in culturally meaningful forms and patterns, and these are different in different events (e.g., Brass, 1997, 2006; Wilkinson, 2005).

Putting these various points together we reach the conclusion that the greatest problem with the three metaphors is not only that are they misleading, but even if they were right they wouldn't tell us very much. They are simply irrelevant to the explanation of ethnic (or any other) conflict. But this is not to say that they are irrelevant full stop. For what they lack in explanatory power they make up for in pragmatic impact.

1.3 Accounts and Accountability

Any account of any event necessarily has implications for whether and how the outcome could have changed, for who was responsible and hence for who should (either literally or metaphorically) pay the consequences. As discourse analysts remind us, accounts always manage accountability (Edwards & Potter, 1992). If, for instance, my car ploughs into the back of yours, was it 'just one of those things' which you can't get rid of without getting rid of driving, was it because you slammed your brakes on too hard, because I was inattentive, because the garage didn't service my brakes properly, because the council didn't maintain the road surface properly … each different account points the finger in different directions and opens (or closes) the door to different solutions.

What is true of everyday accounting is also true of academic explanations. And as the stakes grow higher, so the stamp of academic credibility on any particular account becomes all the more important. This is particularly relevant to our concerns here: how one explains deadly violence can itself be a matter of life and death. More specifically, accounts of conflicts as historic fatalities can serve to exonerate those who would otherwise be seen as war criminals—or at least accessories to murder. They can also serve to warrant policy options which, we shall suggest, at best leave existing antagonisms intact, and at worst reproduce the conditions that bred them. We shall address each of these concerns in turn.

1.3.1 Letting Leaders Off the Hook

In order to clarify our point about exoneration, let us ask the questions: Who according to the three metaphors, are the perpetrators? Who is responsible for doing the killing and for letting it happen? These seem like obvious questions, but actually they are rather hard to answer. If passionate hatreds and violence flow from ethnicity or civilisation, then all members of the ethnic group, or even civilisation, are responsible. But if all ethnic groups, let alone civilisations, are similar in their inbuilt hostility for others, then everyone is responsible—which is the same as saying no one can be picked out as responsible since we are all as guilty as each other. All we can do, in our more sanguine moments, is bemoan this critical flaw in our evolved human nature.

By contrast, there is a linked, but distinct, question that is much easier to answer: Who is *not* responsible? Who is off the hook? This is not to deny that many try to fudge or hide the answer. But political scientist Roger Petersen (2002) is more open. Following his bold aphorism that "it is better to be clear and wrong than to be unclear" (p. 35) he clearly argues in his influential treaty 'Understanding ethnic violence' that *leadership* was *not* necessary and not to blame for the ethnic violence that swept across Eastern Europe in the twentieth century.

Petersen asks, "How does a collective body, such a violent mob, come to act as a coherent unit in terms of specifying an ethnic target?" He instantly replies: "Emotion can coordinate motivations and effectively point a legion of individuals in one particular direction. *Emotion can substitute for leadership*" (p. 4, our emphasis). In other words, leaders did not form people into groups, they did not specify targets, they did not incite violence. In fact they did not—they could not—lead at all. All they could do was follow, echoing what the masses had already understood and done. In Petersen's own words, leadership elites were "responding to structural change and mass emotion rather than shaping it" (p. 252).

In such circumstances, these elites neither needed nor had any particular abilities or skills, and Petersen is accordingly scathing about them, particularly the political leader of the Bosnian Serb forces during the 1992–1995 Bosnian war, Radovan Karadzic: "it is difficult to see how this bad poet, average psychiatrist, and convicted embezzler could become a leader so easily if he did not tie into some existential motivational force among Bosnian Serbs" (Petersen, 2002, p. 35).

At the time when Peterson was writing these lines, Karadzic was Europe's most wanted fugitive. Eventually he was arrested, and from 2009 he has had to answer for his deeds during the war before the International Criminal Tribunal for the Former Yugoslavia (ICTY). To observers of his trial, it is intriguing to see how close his own line of defence sometimes comes to the analysis of scholars like Petersen.

In the hearing of 16 October 2012, Karadzic declared:

> In the 1990s, the Serb community in Bosnia-Herzegovina in 1992 became very anxious when the HDZ appeared in Croatia and when Izetbegovic made his announcement in Bosnia-Herzegovina. The Serbs were frightened of the Ustasha rhetoric and there were also suspicions that Mr. Izetbegovic, the author of the Islamic Declaration, would apply this Islamic Declaration as a political platform of his party. There is not a single Serb or any man anywhere in the world who could convince Serbs that there is or isn't a threat of genocide. It is only when they saw where things were going in Yugoslavia that they understood what's the writing on the wall before I even said a word.

The critical point of this defence is, of course, that the Serbian masses perceived that they were facing a "threat of genocide" before Karadzic himself "even said a word". They spontaneously "saw where things are going", when other ethnic groups supported 'Ustasha' (i.e., fascist) or 'Islamic' parties. They understood the dangers posed by these other groups, and acted to pre-empt those dangers without needing any guidance from Karadzic.

Far from being a war-monger or genocidaire, then, Karadzic presented himself to the court as a peace-loving group therapist, who had written poetry for children, and cherished personal friendships with Muslims and Croats. If there was any violence perpetrated by Bosnian Serbs, it occurred in self-defence against the threats and aggression from the other communities. It occurred despite, and not because of, Karadzic's leadership, so he was not responsible for his people's deeds. If one believes his words, collective violence did not occur as a consequence of the power that Karadzic exerted over his people, but as a consequence of the limits of his power.

A second example makes the relationship between social scientific accounts and (legal) accountability even more explicit. Before the ICTY turned its attention to Karadzic, Dario Kordij and Mario Cerkez (the former a Bosnian Croat political leader, the latter a military commander) were indicted for crimes against humanity committed against Muslims in the Lašva Valley in 1993. Part of the prosecution's case was a sociological report arguing that the Croatian leadership had promoted a climate of excessive nationalism supportive of war crimes. In response, the defence invited Stepan Mestrovic, a Croat-born American sociologist, to address the Tribunal. In the audience of 26 June 2000, he stated that:

> Contrary to the assertions made by Dr. Allcock in his expert report, who claimed that (…) Franjo Tudjman somehow single-handedly engineered or produced ethnic tension in Croatia, what the data suggests is that prior to Franjo Tudjman even being on the scene, the sense of ethnic distance arose of its own accord, from the bottom up, and whatever factors led to it certainly they were not and cannot be attributed to Franjo Tudjman.

Mestrovic went on to argue that, to the extent that the Croatian elites did have anything to answer for, it was a sin of omission, not commission. It was not that they communicated a nationalist vision, but rather that, as the old certainties were collapsing, they failed to communicate an alternative vision. As a result "a vacuum was created in which formerly communist nations were looking to the west that was not prepared to give them guidance and nationalism was, so to speak, the logical alternative. But my point is that this nationalism arose from a bottom up as a way to fill this vacuum precisely because there was no top down or centre guidance".

At the end of the trial, Dario Kordij and Mario Cerkez were found guilty of crimes against humanity. In this particular case the judges did not appear to be convinced by the attempt to shift accountability away from individual leaders and towards the masses. But the very fact that the attempt was made and that the ICTY had become a theatre of sociological controversy provides a telling illustration of how scientific debates can become a life-and-death matter for leaders.

If such bottom-up arguments serve to deny the immediate responsibility of local leaders in creating antagonism and violence, they also serve to absolve more distant leaders from the responsibility of doing anything to stop the violence. We have already shown how John Major and Bill

Clinton subscribed to the ancient hatreds narrative. Recall Major's speech to parliament in June 1993 where he claimed that conflict in Bosnia was the resurgence of ancient hatreds, no longer constrained by Soviet discipline. The key point about that speech was that it was used to refuse British intervention. Indeed, the passage we cited was preceded by the words "I do not envisage that any further British troops will be sent to Bosnia in the near future".

Clinton also drew the link between ancient hatreds and non-intervention, albeit less publicly, but even more explicitly. Journalist Richard Reeves recounts how Clinton had decided on a policy of actively siding with the Bosnian Muslims, dubbed 'Lift and Strike' (lift the arms embargo on Bosnian Muslims and strike at Bosnian Serbs). Then, one day, the President came to a meeting carrying Robert Kaplan's best-selling book *Balkan Ghosts*—a book which explicitly associates ethnic diversity and recurrent atrocity and which puts the ferocity of the conflict in Bosnia down to the nature of its ethnic patchwork. Reeves quotes Clinton as saying, "My wife read this and I read some of it too. And it says that we can't succeed doing anything in that society. They've been killing each other for thousands of years and they're going to keep doing it". Reeves then quotes the reaction of the Secretary of Defense, Les Aspin, who was in the room: "Aspin said later, he was sitting there thinking, 'He's going to go south on Lift and Strike' … And in fact the President did".[4]

1.3.2 Legitimating Ethnic Segregation

As should be clear by now, the question of *who* is responsible for starting violence or else for stopping it cannot be separated from the question of what can be done to ensure violence doesn't re-occur. If violent conflict is just part of the character of groups and an inevitable consequence of our natural tendency to prefer people from our own kind or civilisation, this implies a fatalistic pessimism, which does not just relieve leaders of responsibility, but also radically reduces the policy options open to them.

---

[4] Retrieved on 15th September 2015 from http://www.pbs.org/wgbh/pages/frontline/shows/choice/bill/reeves.html.

For if, as Huntington suggests, history is written in advance, and if, as a consequence, groups are doomed to fight, then, as Bill Clinton concluded, there is precious little one can do about it even if one wanted to.

However, just as there are more or less radical variants of theoretical fatalism, so there are weaker and stronger forms of policy pessimism. Thus, ethnic competition theorists, even if they assume that conflict necessarily occurs across ethnic lines, still argue that the level of conflict will be moderated by levels of competition. If there is enough cake for everybody, different ethnic groups can co-exist in the same society. But if the cake is not big enough (normally measured by looking at rates of growth and employment) or there are too many people (normally measured from the perspective of the majority by looking at rates of migration or minority birth rates), then there will be trouble. In particular, when there is an economic downturn and the cake shrinks, then one's options for stopping conflict reduce to clamping down on migration or even expelling minorities.

The argument is taken a step further by those who argue that ethnic diversity is doomed to remain an irreversible source of disharmony, once a first instance of ethnic violence has occurred. This is the position adopted by Kaufman, who asserts that "competition to sway individual loyalties does not play an important role in ethnic civil wars, because ethnic identities are fixed by birth" (p. 140). He does, however, suggest that ethnicity can vary in its significance. In particular, "war hardens ethnic identities" (p. 139) and also 'shrinks the scope for individual identity choices' (p. 143). Once this has happened, change becomes difficult. Ethnic groups become impossible to reconcile. Policies that might once have had a chance—power-sharing arrangements, state-building, reconstruction of ethnic identities—become redundant. "Even if ethnic hostility can be 'constructed'", states Kaufman, "there are strong reasons to believe that violent conflicts cannot be 'reconstructed' back to ethnic harmony" (p. 153). The only remaining means of breaking a cycle of ethnic violence then would be ethnic separation.

Kaufman retains a tactful silence as to whether ethnic diversity causes conflict in the first place. His call for segregation has been limited to situations where conflict has already happened. Lim, Metzler & Bar-Yam, however, have shown no such constraint. Natural scientists by training, these authors embarked on a slippery journey when they applied not only the analytic techniques but also the causal models of their own disciplines to nothing less than the explanation of ethnic violence in India and the former Yugoslavia. From an academic perspective, the journey appeared successful since their findings made it into a *Science* article in 2008. In this article, Lim, Metzler & Bar-Yam, used an analysis of concurrent spatial patterns between local ethnic mixing and ethnic violence to propose that conflict reflects "the natural dynamics of type separation, a form of pattern formation also seen in physical or chemical phase separation (p. 1541)". That is, with the same regularity as a stone falling through water, proximity means violence and separation means peace. There is as much sense in trying to fight this natural law as there would be in leaping off a cliff and hoping gravity will not work. Ethnic segregation is necessary to prevent violence and not just as a response to it.

We are not suggesting that any of these authors are cynical or politically motivated in what they propose. Indeed, our point is that their conclusions (which certainly are congenial to others who are politically motivated) are the logical conclusions which flow from the fatalistic premises inherent in the kinship, civilisations or games metaphors used to think about groups. If Kaufmann, Lim and others were right about the nature of groups, then they would also be right that we face a stark choice between endless ethnic war and apartheid.

If that was the choice, many might be tempted to choose apartheid, as the lesser of two evils. But let us not lose sight of the fact that ethnic separation in places such as the former Yugoslavia and India is a terrible evil in many different ways. It institutionalises the outcome of ethnic cleansing. It durably disrupts multi-ethnic social ties, including between close friends and relatives. It prevents the contacts between ethnic group members, which might otherwise reduce the prejudices between them. It grants no right of return to people who have been illegally and violently expelled. It officially endorses and structurally supports definitions of identity promoted by the architects of mass killing and persecution. It renders the presence of 'ethnic outsiders' intolerable.

This is a long litany, to which we need to add the fact that, even if the rhetoric of separation is 'separate but equal' we know from apartheid South Africa that, in practice, separation means consigning the less powerful to radically impoverished economic and social circumstances. The alternative therefore has to be truly awful for separation to have any justification. There can only be any moral grounds for separation if the consequences of a policy of ethnic mixing are quite literally MAD: mutually assured destruction. But what if—as we have argued—such assumptions are wrong? What if it is far from assured that diversity will lead to conflict? Then the balance shifts radically. When the kinship, civilisation or games metaphors feed into policies, they engender a series of negatives and mitigate against nothing. Indeed, they can only inspire policies which create the very things they claim to protect against: entrenched ethnic categories, unbridgeable civilisational divides, indelible fears and eternal resentments. Once such a fatalistic viewpoint spills over from analysts to actors, we really are in trouble.

1.4 Beyond Fatalism

In this chapter, we have been critically addressing the idea that violence is a product of immutable group processes based on immutable identities. We have seen that this idea can come along in slightly different guises: while some authors see us humans as programmed by our genes to stick together with those who are similar to us and compete with those who are different (the kinship metaphor), others see us as programmed by a long history that has divided us into cultures of incommensurable worldviews and values (the civilisation metaphor), while still a third set of authors sees hostility as rooted in zero-sum competitions for social and economic goods, which display the peculiarity that the competing teams were made in long-forgotten times and everyone since has had to play on the team of his remote ancestors (the games metaphor). For all the subtle nuances that separate them, one over-arching argument unites the three metaphors: *we cannot escape our past.*

What the proponents of all three metaphors have in common is a readily available, simple answer to the puzzle as to why (from a contemporary perspective) collective behaviour often looks so disturbingly irrational: it does not respond to the logic and stakes of current reality, because it is locked into the logic of an (imagined) distant past—when our genes formed, when civilisations emerged or when the teams were made. The notion of ancient hatreds typically expresses nothing else than the fact that the origin of conflict is projected into the same mythical era as the foundation of groups themselves. From that time on, groups are imagined to be prisoners of absurdly tragic spirals of violence, whereby each group sees itself as responding to previous offences of the other: 'we see our attack on you as a response to your attack on us and a way of pre-empting your future attacks, although we can anticipate that you might see our attack as an unwarranted provocation revealing our vicious nature and necessitating a defensive reaction …' Like Sisyphus rolling his rock up the hill, we are all fated to repeat this futile pattern forever.

Our arguments against such fatalistic conflict theories have been both analytic and normative. Analytically, we have shown how they only gain credibility by selectively focusing on the few cases where they seem to apply. But this ignores the fact that there are many more cases where they don't apply and that, overall, there is little to suggest that ethnic diversity makes conflict more likely. Moreover, even in the cases that are cited as support, fatalistic conflict theories explain very little about the phenomena—not when they happen, not where they happen, not the forms that violence takes, not even the choice of who is and who isn't targeted.

Normatively, we have shown how these approaches serve to limit responsibility for extreme crimes and how they point to policy options that are literally worse than useless—they make future crimes more likely. How do we deal with ethnic violence? By structuring the world ever more in terms of ethnicity and thereby creating the world that ethnic cleansers dream of?

One of the places where the analytic and the normative come together most obviously has to do with the issue of leadership. Leaders are in the business of guiding how we interpret the world and hence how we should act in it. So, by presupposing or obscuring the issue of how violence is interpreted, fatalistic conflict theories deny or obscure the role of leaders in violence. If we are programmed to see the world in particular ways, then leaders become simultaneously innocent and redundant.

As we will show in the next chapter, there certainly are those who do so emphasise the importance of leadership that they reduce followers to mere ciphers. But a stark opposition of leadership and followership—of the influence of the elite and the active choices of the population—still misses the main point. If we want to understand violence, we need to address *both* how leaders frame situations of violence and how the populations embrace, adapt or reject, and constrain what leaders do. There are active agents at all levels. Agency—and hence responsibility—is not reserved to one class of people.

Let us then conclude by summarising the key analytic constructs which underpin the fatalistic conflict approaches that we have critically examined in this chapter, and which need to be re-considered if we want to move beyond the position that conflict between groups is immutable and violence between groups a normal consequence of conflict. The first of these is identity. Fatalistic conflict theories assume that people see themselves and others in terms of fixed categories. They also assume that relations between those of different categories are bound to be fraught, prone to be violent, and that once violence has started there is no way back.

The second construct is power. This is seen as an exogenous factor. It is the ability of other groups to stop people acting according to their identity or expressing their hostility towards others. It can therefore dampen the expression of violent tendencies between people of different ethnicity or civilisation, but it can never remove them. When the power of the third group passes (as it always does), then 'nature' will reassert itself. That is why the end of empire is always a bloody affair.

The third construct, which we have already invoked, is violence. In the view of fatalistic conflict theories, violence is driven by identity, although its concrete occurrence can be moderated by the presence or absence of external power.

So, their argument is about identity, violence and power. So will ours be throughout the book—however, we will plead for a rather different way of articulating the three constructs. But before we can do that, we still need to take our critical review a step further and extend it to the theories that appear to claim or to imply the exact opposite of theories examined so far: that all evil comes from evil leaders, and that all we need to know about ordinary people is how easily they can be led to obey anyone on anything.

References

Andric, I. (1945). *The bridge on the Drina*. Chicago: University of Chicago Press.
Bhavnani, R., & Miodownik, D. (2009). Ethnic polarization, ethnic salience, and civil war. *Journal of Conflict Resolution, 53*(1), 30–49.
Billig, M. (1987). *Arguing and thinking: A rhetorical approach to social psychology*. Cambridge: Cambridge University Press.
Brass, P. R. (1997). *Theft of an idol: Text and context in the representation of collective violence*. Princeton, NJ: Princeton University Press.
Brass, P. R. (2006). Collective violence, human rights, and the politics of curfew. *Journal of Human Rights, 5*(3), 323–340. doi:10.1080/14754830600812324.
Brubaker, R., & Laitin, D. D. (1998). Ethnic and nationalist violence. *Annual Review of Sociology, 24*, 423–452.
Chiozza, G. (2002). Is there a clash of civilizations? Evidence from patterns of international conflict involvement, 1946–97. *Journal of Peace Research, 39*(6), 711–734. doi:10.1177/0022343302039006004.
Davis, N. Z. (1973). The rites of violence: Religious riot in sixteenth-century France. *Past & Present, 59*, 51–91.
De Villepin, D. (2014, August 19). Will the clash of identities consume us? *The Huffington Post (Worldpost)*. Retrieved from http://www.huffingtonpost.com/dominique-de-villepin/clash-of-identities-impact_b_5509538.html
Fearon, J. D. (2008). *Ethnic mobilization and ethnic violence*. In D. A. Wittman & B. R. Weingast (Eds.) (pp. 852–868). Oxford: Oxford University Press.
Hansard. (1993). *Commons Sitting of 23 June 1993—European Council (Copenhagen)* (Official Report Series 6, Vol. 227). Retrieved from http://hansard.millbanksystems.com/commons/1993/jun/23/european-council-copenhagen
Harvey, F. P. (2000). Primordialism, evolutionary theory and ethnic violence in the Balkans: Opportunities and constraints for theory and policy. *Canadian Journal of Political Science/Revue Canadienne de Science Politique, 33*(01), 37–65. doi:10.1017/S0008423900000032.
Henderson, E. A., & Tucker, R. (2001). Clear and present strangers: The clash of civilizations and international conflict. *International Studies Quarterly, 45*(2), 317–338. doi:10.1111/0020-8833.00193.
Huntington, S. P. (1993). The clash of civilizations? *Foreign Affairs, 72*(3), 22–49. doi:10.2307/20045621.
Johnson, T. (2014, October 6). The clash of civilizations: Our new global order. *The Huffington Post (UK edition)*. Retrieved from http://www.huffingtonpost.co.uk/tom-johnson/the-clash-of-civilizations_b_5656201.html

Kayaoglu, A., Batur, S., & Asliturk, E. (2014). The unknown Muzafer Sherif. *The Psychologist, 27*, 830–833.
Mazower, M. (2005). *Salonica, city of ghosts*. London: Harper Perennial.
Nirenberg, D. (1996). *Communities of violence*. Princeton, NJ: Princeton University Press.
Olzak, S. (1992). *The dynamics of ethnic competition and conflict*. Stanford, CA: Stanford University Press.
Østby, G. (2008). Polarization, horizontal inequalities and violent civil conflict. *Journal of Peace Research, 45*(2), 143–162. doi:10.1177/0022343307087169.
Petersen, R. D. (2002). *Understanding ethnic violence: Fear, hatred, and resentment in twentieth-century Eastern Europe*. Cambridge: Cambridge University Press.
Reicher, S. (2004). The context of social identity: Domination, resistance, and change. *Political Psychology, 25*(6), 921–945.
Reicher, S. D., & Haslam, S. A. (2014). Camps, conflict and collectivism. *The Psychologist, 27*, 826–829.
Scheve, K. F., & Slaughter, M. J. (2001). Labor market competition and individual preferences over immigration policy. *Review of Economics and Statistics, 83*(1), 133–145. doi:10.1162/003465301750160108.
Semyonov, M., Raijman, R., & Gorodzeisky, A. (2006). The rise of anti-foreigner sentiment in European societies, 1988–2000. *American Sociological Review, 71*(3), 426–449. doi:10.1177/000312240607100304.
Sherif, M., Harvey, O. J., White, B. J., Hood, W. R., & Sherif, C. W. (1961/1988). The robbers cave experiment: *Intergroup conflict and cooperation*. Middletown, Connecticut: Wesleyan University Press.
Tajfel, H., Billig, M. G., Bundy, R. P., & Flament, C. (1971). Social categorization and intergroup behaviour. *European Journal of Social Psychology, 1*(2), 149–178. doi:10.1002/ejsp.2420010202.
Tajfel, H., & Turner, J. C. (1979). An integrative theory of intergroup conflict. *The Social Psychology of Intergroup Relations, 33*(47), 74.
Tambiah, S. J. (1996). *Leveling crowds: Ethnonationalist conflicts and collective violence in South Asia*. Berkeley: University of California Press.
Thompson, F. P. (1971). The moral economy of the English crowd in the eighteenth century. *Past & Present, 50*, 76–136.
Wilkes, R., Guppy, N., & Farris, L. (2008). "No thanks, we're full": Individual Characteristics, national context, and changing attitudes toward immigration1. *International Migration Review, 42*(2), 302–329. doi:10.1111/j.1747-7379.2008.00126.x.

Wilkinson, S. I. (2005). Communal riots in India. *Economic and Political Weekly, 40*(44/45), 4768–4770.

Wimmer, A., Cederman, L.-E., & Min, B. (2009). Ethnic politics and armed conflict: A configurational analysis of a new global data set. *American Sociological Review, 74*(2), 316–337. doi:10.1177/000312240907400208.

2

Evil Leaders and Obedient Masses?

Let us now turn things around—in more senses than one. If, as we argued in the previous chapter, one cannot explain violent conflict in terms of the deep-seated hostility that members of groups have for each other, then perhaps it has more to do with people doing what others tell them to do. Perhaps conflict is a reflection of the will of elites as channelled through the masses, rather than the will of the masses themselves. Perhaps the perpetrators of violence are simply obeying orders, which only reflect the motives of those who *give* the orders—and do not reveal more about those who carry them out than their propensity to obey, albeit sometimes in a shockingly thoughtless way.

In such a perspective, the role of leadership appears under a radically different light to what we've seen so far. If most people are reduced to the role of subservient followers, leaders command the masses rather than accommodate to them. They do not merely adapt to the course of historical events, shaped itself by complex factors. They *make* history.

A strong version of history as a tale of either great or greatly evil leaders can be read in Stoessinger's (2007) *Why Nations Go to War*. In this book, Stoessinger discusses the reasons for many past wars, including the 1990s wars in the former Yugoslavia. Stoessinger's account is the exact opposite of the mass-level approaches discussed in the previous chapter: "The story of the dismemberment of Yugoslavia is the story of *one man's* destructive hubris: Slobodan Milosevic, who destroyed his country and died in a jail cell while on trial on charges of genocide" (XV, our emphasis). Such a view opposes the agency of decision-makers to the determinism of contingencies:

> (The) theme of inevitability is a haunting and pervasive one. Most of the statesmen who made the crucial decisions behaved like actors in a Greek tragedy. The terrible dénouement was foreseen, but somehow it could not be prevented (…). Historians too have been affected by this fatalistic attitude. As one leading scholar has summed up his analysis of the outbreak of the war (WWI): 'All the evidence goes to show that the beginning of the crisis (…) was one of those moments in history when events passed beyond men's control.' (…) such a view is wrong: Mortals made these decisions. (p. 4)

But if history is driven by a handful of leaders, what does that imply regarding the agency of armies of followers? If millions of people can be ordered into collective catastrophes like the two world wars, the most dangerous aspect of human psychology lies no longer in our ability to hate, envy or resent people different from us, but in our ability to obey our own leaders—even when their orders are bluntly misguided, morally outrageous or potentially calamitous in their consequences.

Over the last half century and more, this idea has exercised an extraordinary hold over social psychologists, social scientists and indeed our society at large. The notion that people are *natural conformists*, and that their conformity explains the worst excesses of human behaviour, has been used to explain all sorts of phenomena—most particularly the worst of the worst, the Nazi Holocaust. To a large extent, the prominence of this assumption originates in Stanley Milgram's studies on human obedience—studies that have become the most famous ever conducted in the discipline of psychology (Banyard & Grayson, 2000).

2.1 Stanley Milgram and the Study of Obedience

Before Milgram had started his studies in December 1961, the strong and simple assumption was that perpetrators must be peculiarly vicious people. They could not be just like the rest of us but rather had to have severely twisted profiles, idolising the powers above them and brutalising those below them; craving rigid order and hating ambiguity; demanding conformity and determined to eliminate deviance (and deviants). In the terms of the most influential such theory, they had to have authoritarian personalities (Adorno, Frenkel-Brunswik, Levinson, & Sanford, 1950).

Milgram's studies marked an irrevocable break with the previous common sense that extreme brutality must be related to extreme personalities. His studies showing how people with very ordinary personalities were led to disturbing levels of cruelty are amongst the few which have gone beyond the disciplinary boundaries of psychology to have influence across the academic world. They are amongst even fewer which have impacted on public consciousness, for even if people do not recognise Milgram's name, many do recall those studies in which people delivered massive electric shocks to innocent victims under the orders of an experimenter.

Being so well known, there is no need to provide more than a brief outline of the experimental set-up (see Milgram, 1974 for a full account, and Blass, 2004, for an account of the history leading up to the studies). Participants were invited to take part in a set of studies ostensibly about the role of punishment in learning. Once at the laboratory, they drew lots with another participant (actually a confederate of Milgram's) to determine who would be allocated the position of teacher and who that of learner—although the draw was rigged so that the real participant was always the teacher. After this, the learner was strapped into an electric chair. The teacher then read out a series of word pairs which the learner had to remember. Following this, the teacher gave the first word of a pair followed by four possible options and the learner had to respond with the correct match. Each time an error was made, the teacher delivered an electric shock, the level of shock escalating by 15 volts for each subsequent error, all the way up to 450 volts.

In fact, of course, the electric shock machine was bogus. But Milgram choreographed the studies to make them realistic. The learner responded consistently at different shock levels, expressing pain at first, then complaining of a heart condition and demanding to be released, then escalating these complaints and demands and finally falling into an ominous silence. Throughout, the experimenter impassively asked the participant to continue the study and, should the participant show resistance, employed a pre-scripted set of four 'prods' to try to get them to continue. Only if resistance continued after the fourth prompt was the trial terminated.

So would people deliver what they believed to be large and potentially lethal electric shocks to a victim whose sole offence was to make an error on a memory task? Certainly very few of those who Milgram questioned believed so in advance. Of a sample of 110 people (39 psychiatrists, 31 college students and 40 middle-class adults), none believed that they would go all the way, no one believed that they would go beyond 300 volts (labelled, on the 'shock machine' 'intense shock') and, on average, they believed that they would go up to around 135 volts (somewhere between 'moderate shock' and 'strong shock'). When questioned about the behaviour of others, they predicted that few people would go beyond 150 volts and only a tiny pathological fringe of about one person in a thousand would continue to the end point.

But when it came to the actual results on what came to be known as the 'new baseline study' (actually experiment 5 out of the 18 variants that Milgram describes in his 1974 book), fully 65 % of participants went all the way, and the mean shock level was between 360 and 375 volts. To invoke a much over-used metaphor, these were findings which shocked the world. But if Milgram had uncovered a phenomenon of great consequence, finding an explanation of that phenomenon proved altogether more troubling.

In the first publication of results from his studies in the *Journal of Abnormal and Social Psychology* (1963), Milgram discusses 13 possible contributory factors—and in later publications he adds yet more. This discussion acknowledges that the participant is conflicted, torn between two competing voices (the experimenter and the learner) and two competing obligations (to heed authority and to avoid harming our peers). He considers the various factors which increase the prestige of authority and our obligation to authority. He also notes the fundamental uncertainties surrounding the study and what can be demanded of the participant (something we will return to presently). Eleven years later, when Milgram published *Obedience to Authority* (his seminal summary of the studies: Milgram, 1974), he again notes all these various considerations. However, they are overshadowed by an altogether different approach: the agentic state account.

Milgram argues that when exposed to a legitimate authority people enter into an agentic state, a radically different state of consciousness which is underpinned by shifts in neural functioning. It is a state in which people see themselves "as an agent for carrying out another person's wishes" (p. 133). He then explains how entry into the agentic state affects the behaviour of his participants:

> the entire set of activities carried out by the subject comes to be pervaded by his relationship to the experimenter; the subject typically wishes to perform competently and to make a good appearance before this central figure. He directs his attention to those features of the situation required for such competent performance. He attends to the instructions, concentrates on the technical requirements of administering shocks, and finds himself absorbed in the narrow technical tasks at hand. Punishment of the learner shrinks to an insignificant part of the total experience, a mere gloss on the complex activities of the laboratory. (p. 143)

In this treatment, extreme abuses become a matter of unawareness. It isn't that participants uncritically endorse the harm done to victims—they simply don't consider it. It isn't that perpetrators unthinkingly endorse a 'morality' that allows harm, it is that morality is reduced to how well they have done the bidding of authority.

2.2 Entrenching Conformity Bias

There is probably only one other study in psychology that comes close to matching Milgram in terms of notoriety and impact. That is Philip Zimbardo's Stanford Prison Experiment, conducted a decade later in 1971. This experiment is again so well known that it only needs minimal introduction. Ordinary young college students were randomly divided into the role of Prisoners and Guards and incarcerated in a simulated prison environment (actually the basement of the Psychology Department at Stanford University), with Zimbardo himself acting as the 'Prison Superintendent'. According to the received account, to be found in virtually any psychology textbook, the Guards rapidly became so brutal, and the Prisoners so passive and disturbed, that the study—scheduled for two weeks—had to be terminated after only five days (see Haney, Banks & Zimbardo, 1973 or Zimbardo, 2007 for fuller accounts). Like Milgram, Zimbardo filmed much of his study, and the images remain shocking to this day (see Zimbardo, 1989). Guards wielding billy clubs can be seen abusing the prisoners, sexually humiliating them and imposing harsh physical punishments.

For Zimbardo, these events were eloquent testimony to the power of the situation over human behaviour. People simply cannot escape the demands placed upon them. Dress them in a uniform, put them in a role and they are virtually programmed to enact the associated role requirements. Or, as Zimbardo and his co-researchers had it, the aggression of the Guards was "emitted simply as a 'natural' consequence of being in the uniform of a 'guard' and asserting the power inherent in that role" (Haney et al., 1973, p. 12).

As Stanley (2006) recognised, this argument takes us a step further than the obedience studies:

> Zimbardo's prison study was even more shocking [than Milgram's research], if only because the students assigned to play guards were not instructed to be abusive, and instead conformed to their own notions of how to keep order in a prison.

We would take slight issue with this formulation. The suggestion is not that people simply enacted their idiosyncratic notions of Guard (or Prisoner) behaviour. Rather, they carried out socio-cultural notions of what the role entails. The point is that, according to Zimbardo, you don't even need an authority figure to stand over you and police conformity to the existing social order. Human psychology ensures that people will police themselves. We are all born conformists. We act in ways that reproduce the *status quo*. Human beings have an inner conservatism which keeps the social system going.

The view of people as inherently conservative goes hand in hand with a view of people as essentially passive—and the more conservative, the more passive. This is true both of masses and of elites. Thus, the whole point of Milgram's misleadingly named 'agentic state' analysis is that people lose agency. They simply enact the will of others. But, ironically, the fact that people are held to enter this state in the presence of authority means that the authority figure doesn't need to do anything in particular in order to secure compliance. The business of leadership is reduced to simply 'being there'. And, as we have just argued, Zimbardo's formulation extends the argument still further: people are driven by external forces even in the absence of authority, and authorities don't even need to be there in order for the systems and norms they represent to be upheld. In such a world, social change is rendered all but impossible.

When, over three decades later, Zimbardo (2007) published *The Lucifer Effect*, he re-asserted this perspective, and went even further in his stance to seek agency—and hence, accountability—elsewhere than among the immediate perpetrators. Interestingly, when Zimbardo explains the methodology underlying his book, he emphasises the need to build charges against "senior military officers" and their accomplices in the "civilian command structure" (rather than against low-ranked soldiers)—but mainly for pragmatic reasons pertaining to the "limits of our legal system", which demands that individuals and not situations or systems be tried for wrongdoings:

> it is time (…) to go up the explanatory chain from person to situation to system. Relying on a half dozen of the investigative reports into these abuses and other evidence from a variety of human rights and legal sources, I adopt a prosecutorial stance to put the System on trial. Using the limits of our legal system, which demands that individuals and not situations or systems be tried for wrongdoing, I bring charges against a quartet of senior military officers and then extend the argument for command complicity to the civilian command structure within the Bush administration. The reader, as juror, will decide if the evidence supports the finding of guilty as charged for each of the accused. (p. XIII)

In recent years, a number of models have emerged which extend this logic. These include system justification theory, which, as the name suggests, proposes an inherent bias, even amongst the disadvantaged, towards accepting and rationalising the *status quo* (Jost & Hunyadi, 2002). In a line of thought similar to Zimbardo's, system justification theory goes a step further in teaching us *why* 'the system' is so powerful: because we all want it to be powerful, almost regardless of whether it is functional or dysfunctional, just or unfair, beneficial or harmful to our own interests. There are particular implications for how people react—and why they react the way they do—in times of crisis and instability: by embracing conformity and respect for authority even more when the system is shaken:

> An additional hypothesis that may be derived from system justification theory is that people should be motivated to defend the existing social system against threats to the stability or legitimacy of the system. If there is a defensive motivation associated with system justification, then it should be more pronounced under circumstances that threaten the status quo [...] Thus, we hypothesized that situations of crisis or instability in society will, generally speaking, precipitate conservative, system-justifying shifts to the political right, but only as long as the crisis situation falls short of toppling the existing regime and establishing a new status quo for people to justify and rationalize. (Jost, Glaser, Kluganski, & Sulloway, 2003, p. 351)

In other words, people would generally oppose social change as long as it does not happen—a view which clearly does not locate the forces that (sometimes do) bring about social change in the agency of ordinary people.

But most influentially perhaps among the contemporaneous theories that see humans as generally more skilled in conforming to social hierarchies than in toppling them is social dominance theory. The classic statement of the theory (Sidanius & Pratto, 1999) opens with a counsel of despair:

> Despite tremendous effort and what appear to be our best efforts stretching over hundreds of years, discrimination, oppression, brutality, and tyranny

remain all too common features of the human condition. Far from having escaped the grip of human ugliness in the civil rights revolutions of the 1960s, we seem only to have increased the overall level of chaos, confusion, and intergroup truculence during the post-civil rights era and the resolution of the cold war. (p. 3)

The message couldn't be clearer: resistance is futile. At best it is an illusion and most likely it will make things worse. This is because it goes against the grain of human nature. Sidanius and Pratto spell out the three 'primary assumptions' on which social dominance theory is based: first, that all social systems have hierarchies based on age and gender and other categories besides; second, that "most forms of group conflict (e.g. racism, ethnocentrism, sexism, nationalism, classism, regionalism) can be regarded as different manifestations of the same basic human predisposition to form group-based social hierarchies" (p. 38); third, that there may be countervailing tendencies to attenuate hierarchies, but, still, these will always be weaker than the tendencies to enhance hierarchies and, at best, will moderate rather than eliminate inequality.

It would be unfair and misleading to leave our description at this. For social dominance theory is a rich and multi-dimensional account which addresses the role of ideologies (or 'legitimating myths') in promoting or challenging hierarchy and also the role of institutions in structuring the lived experience of inequality (see, for instance, Sidanius & Pratto, 1999, p. 40). Nonetheless, for all this sophistication, the theory still puts the universal urge for inequality and domination at the start of a one-way process; it still conceptualises this universal as driving the process, and while ideologies and structures may affect how the urge manifests itself, they are nonetheless fated to transmit it in one way or another. Once again, we are reminded of Sisyphus: we cannot roll away the burden of our hierarchical nature, and if we try it will come back to crush us. Sidanius and Pratto aim to spare us the pain and the disillusion involved. As they say at the end of the book: "we hope our work has helped reveal some of the consensually approved social practices and beliefs that prevent us all from realizing our collective democratic and inclusionary ideals" (p. 310)

This, then, takes the conservatism argument to a new level. If Milgram suggests that our psychology inclines us to obey authority figures and Zimbardo proposes that we do what is expected of us even without bidding, system justification theory and social dominance theory propose that, even if the local contingencies temporarily steer us towards social instability or even rebellion, our natures will inexorably lead us back towards recreating the *status quo ante*.

2.3   A Mass-Level Excuse?

In the previous chapter, we wondered whether bottom-up theories of collective violence—incidentally or deliberately—serve a function of exonerating elites. We now need to address the reverse question: Does framing collective violence in terms of simple obedience absolve the masses? Might it even be that, in part, that is precisely why these theories have become so popular?

Zimbardo is the most explicit about his motivation to seek "mitigating circumstances" for rank-and-file soldiers involved in grave human rights breaches. In the introduction to *The Lucifer Effect* he describes his feelings provoked by his participation as an expert witness for the defence of one US soldier, eventually condemned and sanctioned because of his role in torturing Iraqi prisoners in Abu Ghraib: "I was (…) frustrated and angry, first by the military's unwillingness to accept any of the many mitigating circumstances I had detailed that had directly contributed to his abusive behavior and should have reduced his harsh prison sentence" (Zimbardo p. X).

Not only does Zimbardo describe the Abu Ghraib trial as an unsettling and formative experience, he also uses his observations to sustain the conclusions from the Stanford Prison Experiment regarding the pre-eminence of situational forces over individual will, in a real-world context:

> One of the dominant conclusions of the Stanford Prison Experiment is that the pervasive yet subtle power of a host of situational variables can dominate an individual's will to resist. With this set of analytical tools at

our disposal, we turn to reflect upon the causes of the horrendous abuses and torture of prisoners at Iraq's Abu Ghraib Prison by the U.S. Military Police guarding them. The allegation that these immoral deeds were the sadistic work of a few rogue soldiers, so-called bad apples, is challenged by examining the parallels that exist in the situational forces and psychological processes that operated in that prison with those in our Stanford prison. (Zimbardo, p. XII–XIII)

In the context of the Abu Ghraib trial, the fact that only a very small number of soldiers were judged provoked a debate as to whether they were really exceptionally 'bad apples' or just chosen scapegoats—whether through their trial, all ordinary soldiers who had been similarly perverted by the system were symbolically tried. By contrast, there has been one recent judicial experiment where the masses were *literally* put on trial. Consistent with Rwanda's political option not to leave participation in the genocide unpunished, between 2002 and 2012 an estimated 700,000 suspects have been tried by 250,000 specially elected judges (McKnight, 2014) in local *Gacaca* proceedings, whose *ad hoc* procedures were created when the country had to face the unprecedented challenge of bringing to justice about a tenth of its entire population. In that context, Strauss (2006) collected his own testimonies among perpetrators. Among the reasons for taking part in the genocide, Strauss highlighted obedience:

> First, men participated in the killing because other men encouraged, intimidated, and coerced them to do so in the name of authority and 'the law'. Many respondent described situations where they believed that they faced a choice between being punished or committing violence and many choose the latter. (p. 141)

Finally, Strauss concluded that "intra-ethnic coercion and pressure appear to have been greater determinants of genocidal participation than inter-ethnic enmity". This conclusion was commented on in the following way by one of Strauss' colleagues, a direct observer at the *Gacaca* trials:

> This explanation is consistent with many of the testimonies I have heard in *gacaca* trials, but more systematic analyses of those testimonies and more micro-level studies are needed. A constant refrain that Straus hears from

confessed perpetrators is that they were following orders and that disobedience would have led to punishment or even death. This sounds like egregious self-absolution from admitted killers, but Straus makes us take it—and them—seriously. (Waldorf, 2007, p. 268)

Shall we take perpetrators seriously when they tell us that they only followed orders—knowing that this is their best chance to be granted mitigating circumstances? And how shall we judge the theories that do take seriously perpetrator's narratives of their own role in atrocities? These questions take on yet another dimension when the person claiming to have only followed orders is in effect a high-ranking official holding a key position in a genocidal chain of command.

2.4 The 'Banality of Evil'

Adolf Eichmann was in exactly such a position when the Nazi regime implemented its 'final solution'. He is widely regarded as the chief functionary of the Holocaust. He is the man who ensured that millions of Jews and others were delivered to the death camps. Not surprisingly, when he was captured in Argentina, smuggled to Israel and scheduled to stand trial for his immense crimes, there was a sense of fervent anticipation. Those sitting in the Jerusalem courtroom on the day the proceedings started—the German-Jewish political philosopher Hannah Arendt amongst them— were fascinated by the prospect of finally encountering the individual who bore responsibility for so many deaths. Surely a man who had done such monstrous things would have the aspect of a monster. He would display a "dangerous and perverted personality" (Arendt, 1963/1994, p. 21). He would be "a man obsessed with a dangerous and insatiable urge to kill" (ibid). The shock, then, was all the greater when Eichmann finally stepped into his glass booth, flanked by two security guards.

The man they saw appeared anything but monstrous. He seemed mild and inoffensive: small, thin and balding, slightly stooped, peering out from thick glasses, fastidiously taking notes on the proceedings. Far from being exceptional—a creature apart—he seemed typical. A typical bureaucrat. And this image, this paradox, the contradiction between what the man had done and how he seemed, lay at the core of Arendt's reports from the trial and her famous book *Eichmann in Jerusalem* first published in 1963. It generated what, for Arendt, was the key lesson of the trial and the key message of her analysis, that is, "the lesson of the fearsome, word-and thought defying *banality of evil*" (1963/1994, p. 252, emphasis in the original). It was the only time the phrase 'banality of evil' appeared in the text, but the phrase has come to dominate our understanding of human atrocities ever since.

Arendt does not only argue that ordinary people do have the capacity to do extraordinary harm, she also provides an account of the processes which can lead to such harmdoing. The problem, she argues, is cognitive rather than moral. Perpetrators do what they do through *thoughtlessness*. They become so fixated on the process of doing their jobs—on being trustworthy bureaucrats—that they lose sight of the consequences of their actions. Their focus is on how well they fulfil the demands put upon them as opposed to how they impact others. Their aim is to be good followers rather than good human beings. In Arendt's own words, Eichmann was someone who obeyed orders and who obeyed the law: he "had no motives at all. He merely, to put the matter colloquially, never realized what we was doing" (1963/1994, p. 287).

However, it was no accident that at his trial, Eichmann appeared as an insignificant, mild and fastidious bureaucrat. This was a deliberate strategy, agreed with his lawyer, to confound the expectations of the prosecution. As one analyst acerbically observes: "in suggesting that [Eichmann] was 'merely thoughtless' [Arendt] in fact adopts the very self-presentation he cultivated" (Vetlesen, 2005, p. 5; see also Cesarani, 2004). Moreover, Eichmann was not the first to adopt such a strategy. Neitzel (2007) has unearthed a fascinating archive containing secret recordings of German prisoners of war in British hands during World War II. In their unguarded conversations, senior officers are aware that they may be held culpable for their part in the Holocaust and they discuss ways of avoiding responsibility—including the argument that they were merely 'following orders'. Moreover, they realise that, for the argument to stick, all have to agree to the same line.

The interpretation of a text is not always in the hands of the author. In Arendt's case, the interpretation of *Eichmann in Jerusalem* and the meaning of 'the banality of evil' was irrevocably influenced by its conjunction with Milgram's investigation of the human capacity for harmdoing, which started exactly one week before Eichmann's trial finished. Milgram acknowledges his debt to Arendt in the early pages of the 1974 book, which at the same time foreshadows his account of the 'agentic state'. Referring first to the Holocaust, and then to his own studies, Milgram writes:

> After witnessing hundreds of ordinary people submit to the authority in our own experiments, I must conclude that Arendt's conception of the *banality of evil* comes closer to the truth than one might imagine. The ordinary person who shocked the victim did so out of a sense of obligation—a conception of his duties as a subject—and not from any peculiarly aggressive tendencies. (1974, p. 6, emphasis in the original)

It is arguable that Arendt's position has been much misunderstood (see, for instance, Newman, 2001). Certainly her notions of thoughtlessness and of responsibility (e.g., Arendt, 2005) are richer and more nuanced than what the Milgram–Arendt conjunction suggests. They are less to do with crude unawareness of one's acts than with a lack of reflection about what one does. They are to do with an uncritical acceptance of a tradition or an authority, more than a failure to heed them.

The publication of *Eichmann in Jerusalem* was met with a furious controversy, which had less to do with Arendt's comments regarding Eichmann himself than her critique of the role of the Jewish authorities during the Holocaust. At one point, Arendt was accused of being a self-hating Jew, one who was ashamed of her Jewishness and wished to disown it. She retorted that being Jewish is an indisputable fact, one which she cannot change and would not disclaim, but vigorously disputed that this means she must love the Jewish people or love what they do. If anything, her responsibility is to be critical of other Jews. She asserts that "there can be no patriotism without permanent opposition and criticism" and that "wrong done by my own people naturally grieves me more than wrong done by other people" (Arendt, 2007, p. 467).

Nonetheless, it is the synthetic reading of the 'banality of evil', in which Arendt is buttressed and read through the prism of Milgram, which has endured. It is a reading which sees obedience as almost natural, neurochemical and inevitable: people cannot help but obey orders, however extreme. This reading actually undermines Arendt's insistence on the choice and responsibility of those who commit 'crimes of obedience'. It is a reading which portrays the feelings, motives and beliefs of the masses as altogether irrelevant to the explanation of conflict and its excesses. Indeed, it renders the mass as a mere cipher of elite intentions. And (to repeat) it is a reading which has proved remarkably resilient and popular—for after all, if the historical and the psychological records concur, surely there must be something in it? To quote Novick (2000):

> 'From the sixties on, a kind of synergy developed between the symbol of Arendt's Eichmann and the symbol of Milgram's subjects, invoked in discussing everything from the Vietnam War to the tobacco industry, and, of course, reflecting back on discussions of the Holocaust'. (p. 137)

2.5 Beyond Obedience

There are several problems with the assumption that human beings are natural conformists, that they are destined to reproduce existing social relations of authority and inequality, and that this explains the human capacity to pursue the most vicious acts against others. This assumption radically *underplays the level of resistance* to authority, to the roles into which we are cast and to systems of inequality. What is striking is that, when one goes beyond the received accounts and looks closely at the primary materials, even those studies which have been used to entrench the 'conformity account' are replete with examples of people refusing to conform or to heed authority.

In the case of Milgram these examples are easy to find, because he was so systematic in documenting his findings, including a substantial archive which now resides in the Sterling Memorial Library at Yale University. As we have already outlined, Milgram conducted many variants of his basic paradigm—18 detailed in his 1974 book and several others, including some characterised as pilots, which are fully available in the archive (see, for instance, Rochat & Blass, 2014). This begs the question of why one condition, as described above, has been picked out and described as a 'baseline'. In fact, in the different conditions, the percentage of people who are fully compliant with the experimenter and who continue shocking to the end of the scale varies from 0 % to 100 % (Reicher & Haslam, 2012). There is no principled reason to pick out one of these studies and claim it is more foundational than the rest, and therefore to characterise the level of compliance in that study as more characteristic than the others. That is, the studies provide no basis for privileging conformity over resistance (or *vice versa*). Rather, seen in the round, they raise the question of when people comply in the face of authority and when they resist.

The same goes for the Stanford Prison Experiment—although here the argument is made more difficult by the fact that we only have a partial record of what exactly happened. Nonetheless, even from the materials that are available in the public domain (e.g., Zimbardo, 1989, 2007) it is clear that the received account is, once more, very partial. Far from being universally passive, the Prisoners at first acted together to challenge the authority of the Guards. Indeed, by the end of the first day they were dominant and until the end of the study some Prisoners continued to rebel, albeit now they were more isolated. Equally, far from accepting their role, many of the Guards were deeply uneasy about their authority. Some actively sided with the Prisoners, some sought to be scrupulously fair, and there is only one clear example of a Guard being systematically brutal (see Zimbardo, 1989; Reicher & Haslam, 2006).

Once again, this leads us to shift from asking 'why do people conform?' to 'when do people conform and when do they resist?' In order to address this latter question, Reicher and Haslam ran a study using a system of Guards and Prisoners in a simulated prison setting. The study was not a replication of Stanford, but rather introduced a number of interventions which were designed to inform the question of when people rebel. Even more than in Zimbardo's study, the Guards became divided over their use of authority and the Prisoners united in rejecting their subordination. This led to a reversal of the original power relations and ultimately to a collapse of the Prisoner-Guard system.

When the study was published, Zimbardo critically reacted, pointing out the artificiality of the setting: "what is the external validity of such events in any real prison anywhere in the known universe? In what kind of prisons are the prisoners in charge? How could such an eventuality become manifest?" (2006, p. 49). This is a fair challenge, but it is actually remarkable how easy it is to find evidence of resistance in prisons, even to the extent of prisoners effectively running the system (e.g., Carroll, 2006; McEvoy, McConnachie, & Jamison, 2007; Mariner, 2001). Even in the most repressive of settings (perhaps particularly in such settings) prisoners are able to be in control. Take, for example, the case of Robben Island where Nelson Mandela was for long imprisoned. Mandela writes: "ultimately we had to create our own lives in prison. In a way that even the authorities recognized, order in prison was preserved not by warders but by ourselves" (1994, p. 464). Moreover, Mandela provides some insights into how such control was achieved—insights which, as we shall see, will prove very helpful in our later discussions:

> Our survival depended on understanding what the authorities were attempting to do to us, and sharing that understanding with each other. It would be hard, if not impossible for one man alone to resist (…) The authorities' greatest mistake was to keep us together, for together our determination was reinforced. We supported each other and gained strength from each other. Whatever we knew, whatever we learned, we shared, and by sharing we multiplied whatever courage we had individually. (p. 463)

But, if we are talking of repressive settings and oppressive systems, we are necessarily led back to the context which generated our contemporary obsession with conformity and obedience. We are led back to the Nazi era and, in particular, to the carceral system of camps. The system was distinctive not only in its brutality but also in the way it was designed to keep people in a state where resistance would be impossible—divided from each other, set against each other, starved and humiliated (Sofsky, 1997). And yet, despite this, resistance did occur (Langbein, 1994; Unger, 1986). It took many forms, including open revolt. At the apex of the system were six 'death camps' designed for the systematic extermination of inmates: Auschwitz, Belzec, Chelmno, Majdanek, Sobibor and Treblinka. At three of these (Auschwitz, Sobibor and Treblinka) there were uprisings, and there are unconfirmed reports of another at Belzec.

The best documented uprising was at Sobibor where, on 14 October 1943, inmates seized arms, killed guards and broke free. Of 600 inmates, 300 escaped and 50 survived the war. Here, as elsewhere, most of those who resisted the Nazis died in the attempt. This was inevitable given the grossly unequal relations of power. As Mais reflects, summing up the current consensus on Jewish resistance during the Holocaust in general, "true, the Jews were slaughtered, but clearly not as sheep" (2007/2008, p. 19).

It is important not to swap from naturalising conformity to naturalising resistance. Resistance is not a universal phenomenon, and still less is resistance universally successful. However, even in the most oppressive settings that malignant human imagination has managed to devise, the potential for resistance remains present. There is nothing either in the world of psychological research or in the world beyond to sustain the view that people are natural conformists, inherently incapable of disobeying.

Obviously, by stressing resistance we stress the active nature of the subject: people do not just go along with a world made by others but also seek to shape their own social worlds. It is possible to take the argument further, and to address a second problem with the argument that humans are natural conformists: it radically *overplays the degree of passivity* of both elites and masses.

Actually, people are active when they conform as well as when they resist. To stay with the case of the Holocaust, let us now reconsider the biography of Adolf Eichmann. Unlike the way Eichmann presented himself during his trial, he and others were not just doing as they were told. Eichmann rose to prominence through the creative and innovative ways he found to deport the Jewish population in Vienna (Cesarani, 2004). The apogee of his impact came in 1944 when he was sent to Budapest to oversee the deportation of some half a million Jews to the death camps (and Eichmann, who had visited them, knew very well what went on beyond the barbed-wire). At that point, Himmler (Eichmann's superior) was well aware that Germany was losing the war. He tried to do a deal with the allies, asking for military materials in return for Jewish lives. Eichmann, however, was fiercely opposed and he challenged Himmler's proposals. Far from 'merely' following orders, Eichmann believed in the extermination of Jews, and he worked assiduously to achieve it—even against orders. The extent of this belief was revealed after the war when, speaking to a fellow Nazi, he insisted that:

> My innermost being refuses to say that we did something wrong. No—I must tell you in all honesty, that if of the 10.3 million Jews shown by [the statistician] Korherr, as we now know, we had killed 10.3 million, then I would be satisfied. I would say 'All right. We have exterminated an enemy'. (Cesarani, 2004, 219)

Nor is Eichmann distinctive in this regard. Kershaw (1993) makes the point that to argue that Nazis were blindly obedient is to misunderstand the nature of the Nazi State. Hitler certainly indicated broad objectives, but he rarely gave specific instructions. Hence, his underlings had to be creative in determining how to achieve these objectives and each competed to outdo the other in how far their achievements went. This, Kershaw describes as "working towards the Fuhrer". It is as true of the functionaries of the Holocaust as anyone else. As Lozowick puts it:

> Eichmann and his ilk did not come to murder Jews by accident or in a fit of absent-mindedness, nor by blindly obeying orders or by being small cogs in a big machine. They worked hard, thought hard, took the lead over many years. They were the alpinists of evil. (2002, p. 279)

There may be something very specific about the structure of the Hitler State—and the Fuhrer's aim to set his underlings to compete against each other rather than unite against him—which required Nazi functionaries to be such active conformists. Still, there are intriguing similarities with observations from psychological research made in completely different contexts. A conversation between two of the participants in the Stanford Prison Experiment, one the most brutal of the Guards, dubbed 'John Wayne' for his aggressive swagger, the other one of the Prisoners that he tormented, illustrates this point. The conversation occurred after the end of the study and 'John Wayne' (or rather, David Eshelman, to give him his real name) asked, "what would you have done if you were in my position?" The erstwhile Prisoner replied:

I don't know. But I don't think I would have been so *inventive*. I don't think I would have applied as much *imagination* to what I was doing. Do you understand? ... If I had been a guard I don't think it would have been such a masterpiece. (Zimbardo, 1989)

This tallies with Eshelman's own account where he claims that he was running his own 'experiment', trying out new forms of abuse and seeing how people would respond. In other words, he could be said to have been 'working towards the experimenter'—not mechanically doing the bidding of another but actively creating innovative ways of carrying out his task. Albeit on a totally different scale of brutality, this tallies with contemporary accounts of Nazi conformity. Yet, of course, it is based on a single anecdote and it would be rash to hang too much explanatory weight upon it. So it makes sense to turn again to Milgram's studies, both because of the systematic nature of the evidence and because of the significance of these studies in underpinning the 'banality of evil' account.

There are many indications from Milgram's own data which give the lie to his claim that "punishment of the learner shrinks to an insignificant part of the total experience". Perhaps the most dramatic evidence derives from Milgram's filmed record of the sessions.[1] In these one can see the participants agonise over what to do. They certainly show awareness of the learner's predicament. They alert the experimenter to his expressions of pain, his demands to be released, his silences. They argue and remonstrate with the experimenter and seek reasons to justify terminating the study (see Gibson, 2011, 2014 for a detailed analysis of their discursive strategies). They sigh and sweat and giggle nervously. And when, at the end, the learner emerges to reveal that he has not suffered, they show massive relief. It lacks all credibility to suggest that the learner is insignificant to them.

If such descriptive evidence is deemed insufficient, it is complemented by quantitative evidence that points to exactly the same conclusions. Thus, an analysis of the points at which participants are most likely to defy the experimenter points to the 150- and 315-volt points—respectively

---

[1] Many of these can be found online. See, for instance, Milgram's own film *Obedience* at http://veehd.com/video/4751627_Obedience-The-Original-Milgram-Experiment-1962-nYx64—especially the segment from 22 mins to 39 mins which shows a trial almost in its entirety.

the points at which the learner first asks to be let out of the study and first states categorically that he is "no longer part of the experiment" (see Milgram, 1974, pp. 56–7 for a full transcript of what the learner says at the various shock levels). Evidently, participants are paying attention to the learner.

But equally, the participants are listening carefully to what the experimenter says. They are not simply in thrall to anything he says. Thus, the different prods used to urge people on are differentially efficacious. Most obviously, three of the prods can be read as requests ("please go on") or as justifications ("the experiment requires that you continue"). Only one, the fourth and final prod, is unambiguously an order ("you have no other choice, you *must* go on") (see Milgram, 1974, p. 21, emphasis in the original). The evidence that is available suggests that the use of the fourth prod in particular led to heightened disobedience. Moreover, in a recent replication (Burger, 2009), every time that the fourth prod was used, disobedience ensued. Now, it is arguable that this has nothing to do with the content of the prod, but simply an order effect—that is, by the time it comes to the experimenter having to urge people on for a fourth time, nothing they say would be effective. So, in a recent study, Haslam, Birney and Reicher (2014) have untangled order from content, using different prods in different conditions of the study. Still we find that prod 4 incites greater disobedience. In the light of this evidence it seems that, whatever the Milgram studies do show, they certainly don't demonstrate that people always obey orders. Quite the contrary. People are making active choices between the experimenter and the learner based on precisely how each addresses them.

This argument has implications for the experimenters as well as the participants: once the former acknowledge that the latter are discerning and that they actively weigh what the experimenters do, then experimenters can no longer rest on their laurels. Once it is clear that just 'being there' is not enough, we need to attend to what authorities have to do and say in order to secure compliance. We have to attend to their activity as well as that of the participants. A number of recent studies have done precisely this. They unpick all the careful work that Milgram undertook—and had his experimenter undertake—in order to ensure that participants kept shocking. This includes the bureaucratic structure of the study (Russell,

2014), the design of the shock machine and the wording used to describe different shock levels (Russell, 2011), the careful choice of personnel to act as the experimenter and the learner, respectively (Russell, 2013), the various forms of contractual obligation that participants had to accept before they began the study, the careful scripting of the prods, the ways that, at times and seemingly with Milgram's consent, the experimenter would depart from the script during the study (Gibson, 2011, 2014), as well as the broad moral justification for the studies, couched within a discourse of scientific progress.[2]

In sum, whether we are dealing with conformity or resistance, with participants/masses or experimenters/authorities, everyone is actively involved in making sense of the situation and determining what should be done. Moreover, the activity of the mass and of the authorities is interdependent. It is because ordinary people actively weigh what is said to them that those who aim to influence them need to couch their words and actions so carefully. Equally, it is because different sources of influence address them with plausible and powerful arguments that ordinary people must work at choosing between them. So how do they decide? What determines which of the many voices that surround them people eventually heed?

A third and final problem with the natural conformist assumption is then that it does not allow these simple but fundamental questions to be addressed or answered. As we will now see, the reasons for this failure largely stem from the assumption's one-sidedness in relying solely on internal psychological mechanisms to explain why and when people do conform.

2.6 Conformity, Resistance and the Problem of Epistemic Isolation

When Milgram's experiment was moved from the prestigious Yale laboratories to an office building in downtown Bridgeport and the experimenter was introduced as working for an unknown private organisation

---

[2] The study was introduced as an important investigation into the topic of learning and of how much punishment is best to aid learning. When participants came to the laboratory it was stressed that: "we know very little about the effect of punishment on learning, because almost no truly scientific studies have been made of it in human beings" (Milgram, 1974, p. 18).

rather than for the University, the percentage of people who were fully obedient decreased from 65 % to 47.5 %. When the 'experimenter' was introduced as another 'ordinary person', obedience decreased further to 20 % and when there were two experimenters who disputed as to whether shocks should be given, no one fully obeyed. Indeed, no one went beyond point 11 (165 volts) of the 30-point scale (450 volts). That is, as the experimenter's scientific authority becomes less clear and more contested so people follow his instructions less. Or, in other words, people's willingness to obey depends in part on the epistemic capital of the authority.

But equally, obedience depends upon the epistemic capital of the participant. Consider the following interchange between the experimenter and Jan Rensaleer, an industrial engineer and a participant in one of the early studies:

MR. RENSALEER: The man, he seems to be getting hurt.
EXPERIMENTER: There is no permanent tissue damage.
MR. RENSALEER: Yes, but I know what shocks do to you. I'm an electrical engineer, and I have had shocks. (Milgram, 1974, p. 51)

Or again, read this interchange with Getchen Brandt, a medical technician and a participant in the only study involving women:

GRETCHEN: He has a heart condition, I'm sorry. He told you that before.
EXPERIMENTER: The shocks may be painful but they are not dangerous.
GRETCHEN: Well, I'm sorry, I think when shocks continue like this, they *are* dangerous. You ask him if he wants to get out. (Milgram, 1974, p. 85, emphasis in the original)

In both cases, the participants have technical expertise and technical knowledge which allows them to contest the claims of the experimenter and hence reject his authority to define the situation.

But it is important not to reduce epistemic certainty to attributes of the various parties involved in the study. Critically, it is important to consider also the relationships between them. Perhaps the best known subset of studies within Milgram's programme was the one where he varied the closeness of the participant to the learner. In the first study the participant is with the experimenter in a different room to the learner and gets no feedback apart from banging on the wall after 300 volts. All participants go up to this level, and 65 % are fully obedient to the end. In the second study, there is more voice feedback such that the participant hears the learner expressing complaints and making demands throughout the study. Here participants start breaking off earlier, from the 135-volt level, but much the same percentage (62.5 %) continue to the end. In a third study, the experimenter, participant and learner are in the same room so that the participant can see and hear all that goes on. Again people break off earlier and many less (40 %) continue up to 450 volts. Finally, in a fourth study, the participant is not only in the same room as the learner but also has to push his hand onto a metal plate in order (ostensibly) to deliver shocks. In this condition, full obedience reduces to 30 %.

The largest discontinuity, then, is less to do with precisely what the participant hears and does, but between a situation in which he is isolated with the experimenter in a separate room or not. Milgram himself, in one of his many early explanations that we have alluded to, suggests that these physical arrangements may be important in terms of group formation (see Milgram, 1965). Indeed, he briefly reprises the argument in his 1974 book:

> placing the victim in another room not only takes him father from the subject, it also draws the subject and the experimenter relatively closer. There is an incipient group formation between the experimenter and the subject, from which the victim is excluded. The wall between the victim and the others deprives him of an intimacy which the experimenter and the subject could feel. In the Remote condition, the victim is truly an outsider, who stands alone physically and psychologically. (1974, p. 39)

The quote is worth reproducing in full because it introduces a construct that will prove crucial as a thread that runs throughout our analysis. This is the notion that the extent to which people are in contact or else isolated from each other—and whose communications are privileged over others—is of central importance to how they understand who they are and what they should do. Alone with the experimenter, participants are subject overwhelmingly to their relationship with him. It is not simply that this has the cognitive effect of rendering their common inclusion within a scientific enterprise more salient. It is also that this has the pragmatic effect of shielding the participant from any alternative perspective which challenges the experimenter's account of scientific progress and what that justifies. In a phrase, epistemic isolation lends epistemic certainty to the perspective of authority.

When it comes to epistemic isolation, there is another relationship which is equally important, if not more so, as that between participants and learners. It is one that is largely hidden in Milgram's studies because the design generally involves just one participant at a time, whereas, outside the laboratory, there are often many of us together in the face of authority. That is, in these studies, participants are isolated from their fellow participants. They have no knowledge of what their peers think and do. They don't know if it is normal to privilege the interests of science or of the ordinary person. As Milgram acknowledges, they also don't know if shocking is bizarre behaviour or if *not* shocking would be bizarre. In this state, they are again confronted only with the position of the experimenter and the way they are positioned by him. They have no counterweight with which to challenge that positioning. Except in one condition.

In the so-called two peers rebel condition, the subject is in a room with the experimenter and (as the name suggests) two peers who co-operate in administering the task—these supposed peers being yet more confederates of Milgram. At the 150-volt point, one of these peers withdraws from the study. The others are told to continue without him. At the 210-volt point the other peer withdraws. Again, the remaining (authentic) participant is told to continue. In this condition only 10 % of these participants are fully obedient. Significantly, perhaps, only three pull out when the first peer rebels. Twelve pull out when the second peer rebels. One way of interpreting this is to say that in order to defy authority it is not enough to witness examples of defiance; it is necessary to establish a consensus that challenges the position of authority. Whether this precise interpretation is accepted or not, there is nonetheless clear support for the idea that the opinions of peers is critical to the way one sees one's own self, and that the impact of authority depends upon its ability to monopolise communication and interaction with members of the population.

Great harm is generally done in the name of a great cause. Those who we might condemn as doing ill tend to see themselves as doing good. However, critically, the underpinnings of identity and authority are always bound up with what others think and people's knowledge of what they think. Even if every single participant in Milgram's studies had doubts about the significance of the cause and the probity of administering shocks, these often came to nothing as long as they were isolated from each other and exposed only to the experimenter's narrative. The shift from conformity to resistance, then, may not be so much a matter of changing the minds of individuals as of *overcoming the isolation* between them. To draw on Foucault's famous use of Bentham's panopticon as a model of power in general—a structure in which the central authority is at the hub and gazes out at his subjects arranged as if on the rim of a wheel, each visible to the authority, each divided from and invisible to the other (see Foucault, Burchell, Gordon, & Miller, 1991)—change is a matter of overcoming the partitions between us more than the attributes within us.

There is much more that could be said here about the relationship between how we see ourselves and how others see us. But these are issues that we shall return to and elaborate throughout the book. For now, and before we conclude this chapter, let us briefly move for one last time between psychological studies and historical instances of conformity and resistance, and let us ask whether our overall argument is plausible in the latter as well as the former domain.

In a telling analysis, Einwohner (2014) makes a telling case that epistemic isolation was at the heart of Nazi extermination policies and was critical in determining levels of Jewish resistance. The Nazis did all they could to hide the fact that everyone was to be killed and that deportations meant death, and those ghettos that were more isolated from others and where rumours of the death camps were less likely to reach were also less likely to revolt (see also Gutman, 1971; Tiedens, 1997). The twisted charades at the death camps themselves—camp signs that read 'Arbeit Macht Frei' (Work Sets You Free), gas chambers disguised as showers—were designed to maintain the deceit to the very end and to allow the killings to be more orderly. And where people lived within the camps and the reality could no longer be hidden, other strategies were used to ensure that those who were concentrated physically remained isolated psychologically. That is, as Sofsky puts it, the aim was to ensure that "their orientation is not to each other but past one another" (1997, p. 154). One way of doing this was to set up a hierarchy so that some prisoners became accomplices of the Nazis. This blurred the boundaries between guards and inmates such that people did not know who were genuine peers and became reticent about saying what they thought for fear that an apparent ally could turn out to be the enemy. More crudely, the system was so brutal that few survived long enough to get to know each other, develop trust and thereby overcome their mutual isolation.

On rare occasions, however, inmates were able to overcome this isolation, often because groups who had prior links of solidarity were allowed to stay together in the camps (see Haslam & Reicher, 2012). This was the case in Sobibor where the roots of the revolt lay in the arrival of some 80 Jews who had served in the Red Army and who benefited from the leadership of a former lieutenant, Alexander Pechersky (see Arad, 1987; Pechersky, 1975). This tallies with the description we have provided of Robben Island where the authorities unwittingly empowered the inmates by facilitating communication and interaction between them. It is, perhaps, appropriate to draw our discussion to a close by reprising Mandela's words: "together our determination was reinforced. We supported each other and gained strength from each other. Whatever we knew, whatever we learned, we shared, and by sharing we multiplied whatever courage we had individually" (1994, p. 463).

2.7 Conclusion

In this chapter we have considered another simple but powerful explanation of intergroup conflict—and more particularly of the harm that people are capable of inflicting in such conflicts. As with the explanations considered in the previous chapter, these reduce conflict to the expression of something inherent in the human condition. But whereas in Chap. 1 this 'something' had to do with hostile urges within the actor, here in Chap. 2 it has to do with our supposed tendency to do as others urge. We need not hate our victims, we need have no motivations as concerns them. Our fatal flaw is that we are 'natural conformists'—in different variants, conformists to authority figures, conformists to roles or conformists to a hierarchical *status quo*.

We have examined how this view gained strength by weaving together historical and psychological strands of enquiry. And yet, we have sought to demonstrate that both the historical and the psychological evidence does not support the view that perpetrators have no will except to satisfy the will of others. In fact, it tells a very different story.

First, even in those seminal studies which are used to support accounts of our inherent conformity, resistance is rife. This is not to replace the notion that we are natural conformists with the idea that we are natural rebels. However, it does mean that we can't take conformity for granted—we must ask when it occurs and what produces conformity (or resistance) in particular contexts.

Second, once conformity can no longer be taken for granted, it becomes clear that people must make an active choice between as to whether they conform or not. Whether people decide to heed or to defy authority, they do not do so inattentively or by default. Rather, they make informed decisions, and whatever they choose, it is something that they consider to be the right thing to do. Equally, authorities must work hard to influence that choice and to produce conformity.

Third, the effectiveness of authorities depends upon their ability to shape the way in which people are in communication with or else isolated from various potential audiences. The more the authority can monopolise communication and isolate their target from others, the more they can control how people represent their world and hence choose to act within it.

This argument brings us back to three core concepts. First, to *identity*: people's decision to conform or to resist is a function of their sense of identity, and the extent to which authorities are able to speak for and to that identity. Second, to *violence*: the underlying concern of our whole discussion, the reason why conformity has been of such concern to those within social psychology and those beyond—indeed to all who live in the shadow of the Nazi Holocaust and succeeding genocides. Third, to *power*: the power to shape identities, in particular by creating settings in which people are led to meet each other as foes or friends, and the power that derives from shaping identities. Once again though, it is important to examine the reciprocal relationship between constructs: how violence derives from the ways that identity is defined and controlled, but also the way in which violence serves as a means of gaining power over identity and defining it in ways that establish particular people as authoritative.

In the following chapters, we will interrogate identity, violence and power, and the links between them, in much more detail. For now, we can conclude our discussion so far on a note of qualified optimism. There is no part of the human substance which impels us, either directly or indirectly, towards harming others. Rather, as Todorov has argued, "good and ill are of 'one substance' with human life because they are the fruits of our freedom, of our ability to choose at every point between several courses of action" (2004, p. 26). Nonetheless, we can examine the factors that constrain our choices. Even if these do not determine the outcome, they can make it easier or more difficult to conform or rebel; they can strengthen or weaken, reinforce or undermine different orientations. While these factors become consequential by the way that they work on our psychology, they themselves exist beyond us, between us, in the ways that we are dispersed and organised in the social world.

References

Adorno, T. W., Frenkel-Brunswik, E., Levinson, D. J., & Sanford, N. R. (1950). *The authoritarian personality*. Oxford: Harpers.
Arad, Y. (1987). *Belzec, Sobibor, Treblinka: The Operation Reinhard death camps*. Bloomington: Indiana University Press.
Arendt, H. (1963/1994). *Eichmann in Jerusalem*. New York: Penguin Books.
Arendt, H. (2005). *Responsibility and judgement*. New York: Shocken Books.
Arendt, H. (2007). *The jewish writings*. New York: Shocken Books.
Banyard, P., & Grayson, A. (2000). *Introducing psychological research: Seventy studies that shape psychology* (2nd ed.). Basingstoke: Palgrave Macmillan.

Blass, T. (2004). *The man who shocked the world: The life and legacy of stanley milgram*. New York: Basic Books.

Burger, J. M. (2009). Replicating milgram: Would people still obey today? *American Psychologist, 64*(1), 1–11. doi:10.1037/a0010932.

Carroll, R. (2006, September 30). Bars, brothels and a regime of terror: Inside the jail run by its inmates. *The Guardian*. Retrieved from https://www.theguardian.com/world/2006/sep/30/rorycarroll.mainsection

Cesarani, D. (2004). *Eichmann: His life and crimes*. London: Heinemann. Retrieved from http://gataxe.iblogger.org/w/the-left-and-the-jews-the-jews-and-the-left-by-david-cesarani.pdf

Einwohner, R. L. (2014). Authorities and uncertainties: Applying lessons from the study of jewish resistance during the holocaust to the milgram legacy. *Journal of Social Issues, 70*(3), 531–543. doi:10.1111/josi.12076.

Foucault, M., Burchell, G., Gordon, C., & Miller, P. (1991). *The foucault effect: Studies in governmentality*. Chicago: University of Chicago Press.

Gibson, S. (2011). Social psychology, war and peace: Towards a critical discursive peace psychology. *Social and Personality Psychology Compass, 5*(5), 239–250. doi:10.1111/j.1751-9004.2011.00348.x.

Gibson, S. (2014). Discourse, defiance, and rationality: "Knowledge work" in the "obedience" experiments. *Journal of Social Issues, 70*(3), 424–438. doi:10.1111/josi.12069.

Gutman, I. (1971). *Youth movements in the underground and the Ghetto revolts*. Jerusalem: Yad Vashem.

Haney, C., Banks, C., & Zimbardo, P. (1973). A study of prisoners and guards in a simulated prison. *Naval Research Review, 30*, 4–17.

Haslam, S. A., Birney, M. E., & Reicher, S. D. (2014). Nothing by mere authority: Evidence that in an experimental analogue of the Milgram paradigm participants are motivated not by orders but by appeals to science. *Journal of Social Issues, 70*, 473–488.

Haslam, S. A., & Reicher, S. (2012). When prisoners take over the prison: A social psychology of resistance. *Personality and Social Psychology Review, 16*, 154–179.

Jost, J. T., & Hunyady, O. (2002). The psychology of system justification and the palliative function of ideology. *European Review of Social Psychology, 13*, 111–153.

Kershaw, I. (1993). "Working towards the führer." Reflections on the nature of the Hitler dictatorship. *Contemporary European History, 2*(02), 103–118. doi:10.1017/S0960777300000382.

Langbein, H. (1994). *Against all hope: Resistance in Nazi concentration camps 1938–45*. London: Constable.

Mariner, J. (2001). *No escape: Male rape in U.S. prisons*. New York: Human Rights Watch.

McEvoy, K., McConnachie, K., & Jamieson, R. (2007). Political imprisonment and the 'war on terror'. In Y. Jewkes (Ed.), *Handbook of prisons* (pp. 293–323). Cullompton: Willan.

McKnight, J. (2014). The anatomy of mass accountability: Confronting ideology and legitimacy in Rwanda's *Gacaca* courts. *Conflict Trends, 1*, 35–42.

Milgram, S. (1965). Some conditions of obedience and disobedience to authority. *Human Relations, 18*(1), 57–76.

Milgram, S. (1974). *Obedience to authority: An experimental view*. New York: Harper & Row.

Neitzel, S. (2007). *Tapping Hitler's generals: Transcripts of secret conversations, 1942–45*. Barnsley, South Yorkshire: Pen & Sword Books.

Newman, L. S. (2001). *The banality of secondary sources: Why social psychologists have misinterpreted Arendt's thesis*. Unpublished manuscript, Syracuse University, Syracuse, NY.

Novick, P. (2000). *The Holocaust in American life (First Mariner Books.)*. New York: Houghton Mifflin Company.

Pechersky, A. (1975). Revolt in Sobibor. In Y. Suhl (Ed.), *They fought back: The story of Jewish resistance in Nazi Europe* (pp. 7–50). New York: Shocken Books.

Reicher, S. D., & Haslam, S. A. (2006). Rethinking the psychology of tyranny: The BBC prison study. *British Journal of Social Psychology, 45*, 1–40.

Reicher, S. D., & Haslam, S. A. (2012). Obedience: Revisiting Milgram's obedience studies. In J. R. Smith & S. A. Haslam (Eds.), *Social Psychology: Revisiting the classic studies* (pp. 106–125). London and Thousand Oaks, CA: Sage.

Rochat, F., & Blass, T. (2014). Milgram's unpublished obedience variation and its historical relevance. *Journal of Social Issues, 70*(3), 456–472. doi:10.1111/josi.12071.

Russell, N. J. C. (2011). Milgram's obedience to authority experiments: Origins and early evolution. *British Journal of Social Psychology, 50*(1), 140–162. doi:10.1348/014466610X492205.

Russell, N. J. C. (2013). Gina Perry. Behind the shock machine: The untold story of the notorious milgram psychology experiments. *Journal of the History of the Behavioral Sciences, 49*(2), 221–223. doi:10.1002/jhbs.21599.

Russell, N. J. C. (2014). The emergence of Milgram's bureaucratic machine. *Journal of Social Issues, 70*(3), 409–423. doi:10.1111/josi.12068.

Sidanius, J., & Pratto, F. (1999). *Social dominance: An intergroup theory of social hierarchy and oppression*. Cambridge: Cambridge University Press.

Sofsky, W. ([1993]1997). *The order of terror: The concentration camp* (trans: William Templer). Princeton, NJ: Princeton University Press.

Stoessinger, J. (2007). *Why nations go to war* (10th ed.). Cengage Learning (first published in 1978).

Strauss, S. (2006). *The order of genocide*. New York: Cornell University Press.

Tiedens, L. Z. (1997). Optimism and revolt of the oppressed: A comparison of two polish Jewish Ghettos of World War II. *Political Psychology, 18*(1), 45–69. doi:10.1111/0162-895X.00044.

Unger, M. (1986). The prisoner's first encounter with Auschwitz. *Holocaust and Genocide Studies, 1*(2), 279–295. doi:10.1093/hgs/1.2.279.

Vetlesen, A. J. (2005). *Evil and human agency: Understanding collective evildoing*. Cambridge: Cambridge University Press.

Waldorf, L. (2007). Ordinariness and orders: Explaining popular participation in the Rwandan genocide. *Genocide Studies and Prevention: An International Journal, 2*(3), 267–270.

Zimbardo, P. (1989). *Quiet rage: The Stanford prison study (video)*. Stanford, CA: Stanford University.

Zimbardo, P. (2007). *The Lucifer effect*. New York: Random House. Retrieved from http://www.goodreads.com/work/best_book/964959-the-lucifer-effect-understanding-how-good-people-turn-evil

Part II

Model

3

Identity: The Group as a Collective Performance

In the previous chapters, our argument was developed in two steps. First, we discussed the challenges arising when public discourse or scientific analysis of political violence takes an ethnic or 'civilisational' turn. We added our voice to those who plead for vigilance such that we avoid taking descriptions of events in terms of (say) 'ethnic conflict', 'ethnic violence' or inferred 'ethnic hatred', as an explanation of these events. We concluded that a non-circular analysis needs to take a step back and, instead of taking ethnic or cultural categories for granted as the primary units of analyses, we need first of all to explain how these categories came into being. Or rather, we need to show what makes people accept such categories as 'real' in the pragmatic sense that they provide a grid for interpreting social experience and for giving a direction to social behaviour.

In the second chapter, we then criticised a pervasive model of why people accept and act on particular versions of category and category relations—that is, the notion that human beings are somehow programmed to obey authority, no matter how cruel those authorities might be and how brutal their instructions.

The main problem with both approaches is that they transform specific instances into general rules. Certainly, ethnic hostility occurs at some times and in some places. But it doesn't always happen and it takes specific political forces and social processes to make it occur. Equally, toxic obedience occurs, but it is far from ubiquitous and one can find ample evidence of dissent events in the classic studies used to highlight obedience phenomena.

In Chap. 2, we introduced the notion of epistemic isolation as a key pre-requirement for toxic obedience: people conform unconditionally to a particular authority when the understandings of that authority stand uncontested and they are sealed off from any opportunity to act jointly on the basis of alternative understandings. In this chapter, we will develop a similar argument about hostility between groups: before a set of people will act together as a coherent 'us' against a hostile 'them', the range of interpretations of social reality must be radically curtailed so as to exclude anything which questions who 'we' are, who 'they' are, and how the two interrelate.

In the next chapter, we will go on to discuss the specific role of violence in bringing about situations of extreme epistemic isolation where alternatives to ingroup conformity and outgroup hostility are difficult to conceive and impractical to act upon. For now, let us examine more closely how epistemic isolation or else epistemic co-ordination affect the terms in which conflicts are experienced, and why the balance between the two is at the heart of the matter.

3.1 Defining Conflict, Defining Identity

So what, concretely, is involved in incidents of violence? What, in particular, has to happen for an incident to become critical and feed into a spiral of violence—say ethnic violence?

First, both the victims and the wider community must be defined in ethnic terms. Thus, an attack on a neighbour is less of an attack on an individual than an attack on a 'Serb', a 'Croat', and so on. And, to the extent that I also define myself as a 'Serb' or a 'Croat', the attack becomes an attack on 'me'. Indeed, once people are defined as interchangeable members of a common category, it is a matter of mere chance and hence of diagnostic irrelevance as to which individuals happened to be attacked. It might just as well have been me.

Second, the perpetrators also have to be defined in ethnic terms, and, more specifically, as members of the ethnic outgroup. They cannot be 'the poor', 'the desperate' or 'the criminal'. They must be the Serb to my Croat, or the Croat to my Serb. This then means not just that we are under attack, but that we are under attack *by them*. And just as every member of the ingroup is potentially under attack, so every member of the outgroup is potentially an attacker.

Third, it is necessary to attribute violence to an enduring hatred that members of the ethnic outgroup have for the ethnic ingroup. If the violence were to be explained in terms of other causes—say people were provoked by agitators or they were goaded by specific frustrations—then one might be able to deal with the violence by removing these specific causes. If the hatred were to be temporary, then one might not have to fear for the future. But if the cause is ingrained hatred, and hence the hatred is continuous, then they will always be a threat to us. Any of them living amongst us are fifth columnists, and we can only be safe by getting rid of them.

As we can see, then, the spiral of violence depends upon a complex set of representations, explanations and attributions. Violence will only breed violence if it is interpreted in a very particular way. So where do these interpretations come from and how, at some point, do they trump others? Those who subscribe to fatalistic models of conflict eschew these questions. They assume that such interpretations just arise naturally (e.g., we have evolved to see things in ethnic terms, to be mistrustful of ethnic others and, presumably, to see them as mistrustful of us). This is problematic because it describes the phenomena in ways that presuppose precisely what is at issue. It involves imposing the ethnic lens of the analyst on the participant, and projects ethnic categories forged by violent conflict into the past, thereby providing anachronistic explanations of the onset of conflict and violence.

To avoid a similar pitfall, we proceed in a different way and rather than portraying enduring ethnic conflict as something so familiar as to barely require comment, we seek to render it as something strange and rare. We see it as an anomaly to the normal pattern of social relations which are characteristically fluid and, from moment to moment and site to site, are based on many different social categories. We then discuss how this anomaly can arise—how, more precisely, epistemic isolation freezes the definition of categories into a rigid (ethnic) pattern under specific and extreme circumstances.

To fully grasp what is at stake, let us consider a related issue, which fatalistic models of conflict and fatalistic models of obedience both struggle to account for, that is, variability across space and time. If our psychic apparatus makes us naturally defiant or even hostile towards ethnic outgroups, why are there then about as many types of reactions to 'diversity' as there are culturally diverse societies? How can the same territory accommodate the highly integrated multi-cultural society that was pre-war Bosnia-Herzegovina, and equally the ethnically genocidal society of the war years? Similarly, if our psychic apparatus renders us chronically inclined to obey authority, how can we possibly account for the fact that the seemingly quiescent societies of Eastern Europe and the Arab world surprised everyone with the rise of mass revolutionary movements in 1989–1990 and 2011–2012, respectively?

When so many people almost simultaneously engage in actions they have never endorsed before, it seems obvious that these behavioural changes cannot be caused by previous changes in everyone's core personality—that is, in the intimate beliefs and values forged by a singular life history. The rapid diffusion of very specific social behaviours, which leads to riots, revolutions or collective violence, must have something to do with changes in the way people *relate* to one another, more than with changes in their personalities. When certain behaviours spread like wildfire, where initially moderate actions and modest demands give rise to an escalating series of ever more radical actions and demands, where historic turning points are reached, we have to concentrate on the mechanisms that enable or disable a set of people from communicating, interacting and co-ordinating their practices. The conceptual framework that we want to develop needs to address these mechanisms. It should show both how a sense of shared identity emerges through such mechanisms and how it facilitates them in turn. Given that large-scale collective action presupposes that many individuals who do not know each other personally are still able to imagine and recognise each other as members of one group, their capacity to reach a shared interpretation of palpable *markers of identity*—defining who is 'in' and who is 'out'—becomes critical in the process.

A few years ago, together with Willem Doise, we tackled the theoretical problem of epistemic co-ordination, focusing on how separate individual representations of the world become integrated into social representations (Elcheroth, Doise & Reicher, 2011). We argued then, and still argue today, that the general mechanisms governing how people co-ordinate to understand and transform their social worlds can be conceptualised adequately by articulating the two traditions of thought that have developed under the banners of social representation theory, originating in the works of Serge Moscovici (1961, 2008), and of social identity theory, originating in the work of Henri Tajfel (1975, 1981) and developed by John Turner, Hogg, Oakes, Reicher & Wetherell (1987).

We identified four defining characteristics of social representations: shared knowledge, meta-knowledge, enacted communication and world-making assumptions. In the following passages, we now propose a revised version of the critical passages in the 2011 article, elaborated for present purposes to make more explicit the indivisible relationship between social representations and social identities. We show how these same four characteristics relate to the way identities are made, un-made and re-made, through co-ordinated knowledge, experience and behaviour. That is, we explain identity processes by reference to social practices—practices that speak to each other, become possible by communication and constitute acts of communication themselves.

3.2 Shared Knowledge: Identity as Epistemic Co-ordination

The first premise of our approach is that what shapes social behaviour is shared social knowledge. This is true in two connected senses. On the one hand, what counts is not our idiosyncratic experience but our knowledge of things that are experienced at a collective level. There is evidence, for instance, that belief and action are less a function of whether 'I am unemployed' or else 'I have suffered from discrimination', but more of whether 'we suffer high levels of unemployment' or 'we are the subjects of discrimination' (Elcheroth, 2006; Kinder, 1998; Mutz, 1998).

On the other hand, experience impacts our knowledge through the way we make sense of it in terms of shared bodies of knowledge. These exist not only in our own minds but are offered to us by peers, pundits and politicians. Critically, they are also instantiated in material culture: books, films, newspapers, statues, museums and so on. Moreover, there is an 'intertextuality' to these representations such that, when new phenomena come along, we achieve knowledge by anchoring them in already existing stocks of knowledge (see Moscovici, 2008). For instance, when Saddam Hussein first came to the world's attention after the invasion of Kuwait, he and his acts were interpreted by rooting them in widely shared understandings of Hitler and Nazism. Indeed, on one notorious *Time* magazine cover, Saddam's moustache was manipulated to look more like Hitler's (see Herrera & Reicher, 1998).

Critically, the importance of shared knowledge is not just that it is broader, but also that it is deeper. That is, understanding undergoes a *qualitative epistemic transformation* by being shared. An individual viewpoint is always contingent. If, say, I am refused a job, it might have been because I performed badly or the individual interviewer took against me personally. But if *we* are consistently denied jobs, then that constitutes discrimination. In other words, opinion is transformed into *social fact* through the accomplishment of common interpretations of shared experiences. And, if opinions are an insecure basis for undertaking potentially costly actions, social facts are a firm foundation from which one can act in the world. Take, for instance, a study conducted by Wright (1997) in which participants faced strong discrimination. When they faced the situation alone, without any clue as to how others interpreted the situation, they reacted with resignation. However, as soon as there was a minimal breach in their epistemic isolation—that is, if they heard what they supposed to be a fellow participant expressing anger at what he named as 'discrimination'—they began to mobilise and enlist others in a collective boycott of the experiment. As the study demonstrates, a sense of meaning, of justice and injustice, of mastery and agency, along with all their consequences, derives from participation in collective meaning-making practices.

This focus on knowledge as shared logically leads us to ask *how* it comes to be shared. The obvious answer is through communication. But the critical qualification is that much of this communication is implicit. We therefore need to look at what a set of people have, jointly, to take for granted in order to be able to communicate at all. Often, to state one thing explicitly, dozens of other things need to be implied at the same time.

To take an example, all the more powerful for being banal, a discussion of whether the weather will be good tomorrow presupposes, first, an agreed definition of 'good' which privileges particular communities and particular practices (good normally means calm, hot and sunny, which is pleasant for the leisure of those who work mainly indoors but may be less desirable for farmers needing rain for their crops or sailors becalmed without wind). Second, it presupposes an agreed spatial frame of reference—where do we want the weather to be good: in the local town, the region or the country? (as Billig, 1995, points out, often terms like 'the weather' assume a national frame of reference.) What is true of 'will the weather be good?' would be all the more true were we to discuss more explicitly social and political issues: 'is the economy doing well?', 'is the President a good leader?' and so on.

For the most part, we don't have the opportunity to discuss or even to think consciously about all these assumptions and all their consequences. The sum of these never-fully-spelt-out ideas continuously spins an invisible web of meanings and associations, which shape what we do, think and say. In this way, implicit communication creates the conditions through which different practices of sharing knowledge become possible.

The invisible web allows us to interact seamlessly with others who subscribe to the same assumptions, and it functions as the discrete context within which all new claims will be interpreted. That also implies that communication feels much more like hard work between individuals whose semantic associations overlap more weakly. As de Toqueville described in his *Democracy in America*, this is one of the burdens of being a stranger in a new country. As a corollary, we are often able to intuit similarities or differences of identity through the daily experience of ease or effort in communicating with others.

Hence, people's ability to articulate their own understanding with that of others will be constrained by the ways they are able to relate to others in the world, and by the unspoken assumptions they share or don't share with others. This is all the more important as people need to make their social environments intelligible if actions are to be organised into meaningful sequences. Where the world cannot be rendered intelligible, the psychological consequences are generally severe: stress, strain, a sense of estrangement, a feeling of helplessness.

But even with these various practical, discursive and ontological limits to the types of representations we produce together, there is still considerable room for manoeuvre. The primary task is then to investigate the complex and slippery processes by which people jointly produce specific meanings.

3.3 Meta-Representations: Identity as Collective Awareness

To grasp these processes, we first need to clarify the statement that people act on the basis of shared knowledge. As this statement stands, it could be misinterpreted. Take, for instance, Wright's study on discrimination that we invoked earlier. In the 'isolation' condition, it may be that every single participant believes that they are experiencing discrimination. In this sense, they already share the same knowledge. However, as we saw, this was not enough to invoke resistance. What is important, as shown in the 'communication' condition, is that they become *aware* of the thoughts that they share with others. It is only in this condition that people gain the certainty and the confidence to resist. The message, then, is that what counts in social representations is not only what we think, but what we think that other people think: what we will refer to as their meta-knowledge.

But as we have already suggested, not all such meta-knowledge is equivalent. We respond very differently to what different others think and do. If, for instance, I am on the left and I see people at a political rally laugh and applaud, I am likely to react very differently as a function of whether I have categorised them as on the left or on the right. In both cases, what they do is likely to influence how I interpret the message to which they are responding. But in the former case (where they are part of my political ingroup) it is likely to make me more supportive, whereas in the latter case (where they are outgroup) it is likely to make me more critical. It is here that the representation of social categories becomes critical in organising whether we embrace the beliefs of others or eschew them (cf. Platow, et al. 2005).

The psychological underpinning of identity therefore resides in the human capacity to simultaneously process information from two perspectives. On the one hand, we analyse information from an egocentric perspective—in terms of what it means to us and for us. On the other, we analyse it from an allocentric perspective—in terms of what it might mean for relevant others, for our relation to them, and for how they might react to our own different reactions to that information. In other words, we are inherently reflexive beings who operate on our knowledge of our own minds, our knowledge of other minds, and even our knowledge of other mind's knowledge of our minds.

This approach also suggests that those who wish to change how people interpret the world (i.e., who wish to achieve influence), might best do so by working on the assumptions people hold about the interpretations that are shared by others. After all, on the whole we have greater epistemic certainty about what we think than about what others think. Hence, it is generally easier to shift the latter than the former.

The power of the mass media is particularly pertinent here. Their influence derives, not least, from the fact that as people surf the net, listen to the radio, read the paper or watch TV, they are aware that many others are accessing the same website, listening to the same radio programme, reading the same paper or watching the same television programme as them. So, even if every single consumer remains sceptical about the information they are exposed to (and will readily express such scepticism when asked), they can still be influenced by virtue of their inferences about the impact of the media on others. This in turn can lead individuals to incorporate media messages into their own personal communication strategies, thus resulting in a multiplicity of interpersonal conversations which sustain the impression that the message is relevant and hence reinforce its impact. Conversely, the impression that certain interpretations of the world are not shared can generate a self-fulfilling prophecy by generating multiple acts of individual self-censorship.

This long-standing intuition is supported by Paluck's (2009) work in post-genocidal Rwanda. She examined the impact of a radio soap opera specially designed to promote reconciliation on relations between ethnic groups. The results were highly encouraging. Those who listened together in small local communities did indeed bond more with others across ethnic boundaries and did speak out against sectarianism. But when it came to just how these beneficial effects were produced, the findings were far more nuanced. Contrary to the expectations of those who created the soap (Staub & Pearlman, 2009), listening had no effect on people's own opinions and beliefs about the conflict. What did change, however, was what they thought others exposed to the programme now believed—the expectation was that there would be a shift towards greater support for reconciliation. And, as we are suggesting as a more general mechanism, it was beliefs about the beliefs of others in their communities which produced the changes in their own actions.

3.4 Enacted Communication: Identity as Joint Performance

While Paluck's study was about the impact of *discourse* diffused through the mass media on consciously shared representations, words are not always required to change beliefs about how relevant others experience the world, and position themselves in the world. There are indeed a number of illuminating examples of how we will misunderstand the nature of representations if we look at what people say to the exclusion of what they do. A case in point is Jodelet's (1991) classic work on representations of madness. As she showed, people may not say that they think mental illness is contagious, but the ways in which they separate their own crockery from that of sufferers suggests otherwise.

But it is not just that practices are important in terms of communicating the perspective of others; it is arguable that they are more powerful than explicit discourses to the extent that they are more silent. To hear someone state things overtly ('this is what people think') always opens up at least the possibility of disagreement ('oh no they don't'). To see someone act requires us to infer their position without inviting a challenge. It draws on implicit assumptions which we have already seen to be so important to social representations and social identities.

Take, for instance, Falasca-Zamponi's (1997) analysis of how the fascist salute operated in Mussolini's Italy. Her point is precisely that the impact of this practice did not primarily occur through the act of changing individual beliefs. Anyone who gave the salute could retain a sense that he or she was doing it reluctantly, pragmatically, without being a 'true believer'. However, each person, seeing everyone else give the salute, could not take the risk of believing (or acting on the belief) that they were insincere. They had to infer belief from the silent act. The salute was therefore a particularly powerful means of changing perceptions of shared beliefs; it created the illusion of a consensus and it thereby discouraged dissent.

The relevance and importance of practices goes further. We previously mentioned that the creation of shared knowledge operates through the dynamics of intertextuality—prior representations supporting subsequent representations. However, invoking prior understanding is something *active*. It is a matter of practices of remembering, of celebrating and of commemorating together in ways which enact particular understandings of the world. National days, anniversaries of famous victories, birthdays of past and present leaders are all ways of bringing us together and getting us to act together on the basis of selective beliefs about who we are.

But, powerful as such spectacular practices might be, they tend to be more powerful to the extent that they are more mundane and inscribed into the textures of everyday life. It might be a matter of different treatment of different groups at airport security checkpoints, the maintenance of traditional practices or else the establishment of different schools for different ethnic and religious minorities; it might be checks on certain groups to ensure that they are entitled to social benefits, to the use of public services and so on. Such practices don't only point to these groups as 'other', but also to the nature of their otherness—'they' are dangerous, culturally alien, un-trustworthy and so on. That is, they tend to transform people into *threatening* others.

All in all, our understanding of social reality, of other people and of the ways they relate to us, is not only constructed through social communication (at both interpersonal and mass media levels) but equally derives from the accumulation of concrete experiences that fill an ordinary life. These experiences provide us with a sense of interdependence with other people. All of us have concretely experienced the fact that others can confirm or challenge our viewpoint, can support or impede us, can sustain or harm us. Correspondingly, we have all developed interpretative strategies for distinguishing between who might do the one and who might do the other. Obviously, those interpretative activities draw upon shared narratives that render our idiosyncratic experiences meaningful. But, equally, these narratives are rendered relevant and plausible through recurrent patterns in the concrete organisation of social interactions. That is, the social narratives which are offered to people as frames of interpretation need to make sense of mundane experiences. They need to help us to act appropriately in various social situations. In Gramsci's formulation, they need to have practical adequacy (see Sayer, 1979).

The key point here is that narratives and practices are not in opposition. Each is powerful to the extent that it is complemented by the other: what is said highlights what is done, and what is done makes sense in terms of what is said. And what binds narratives and practices together are *social institutions*. These both tell stories about how the world needs to be organised and also organise the social world. They structure social interactions in particular ways and they create regularities in collective experience which leads people to gain a common feeling that particular forms of social interdependency are authentic realities. They thereby give credibility to accounts of social relations which presuppose such forms of interdependency. In other words, institutionalised social structures allow narratives about collective identities to sound plausible and become relevant in the light of concretely experienced patterns of interdependence.

To be somewhat more concrete and to continue with the themes introduced above, the Nazi ideology of Adolf Hitler as the supreme leader of a homogenous ethnic German nation from which Jews (among others) were totally excluded was both the subject of a relentless ideological assault (Kershaw, 1987) and also inscribed in a series of institutionalised practices, from the mundane realities of the 'Heil Hitler' salute (which all 'ethnic' Germans were required to give, but which Jewish people were explicitly prohibited from giving—see Allert, 2009) to the exclusion of Jewish people from trades and professions, and to the expulsion of Jewish people from their homes and homelands—ultimately to the death camps.

There is one final point we wish to make about narratives, practices and the nature of/relations between social groups. That is, these exist in a dynamic and developing relationship which depends not only upon differences of understanding but also upon commonalities of understanding between these groups. Take, for instance, the Hindu who deliberately provokes a riot by throwing a dead pig on the steps of a mosque in India. This act is performed on the basis of understanding the narrative lens through which it will be viewed by the Muslim community (a fundamental act of desecration), the consequent practices to which it will give rise in this community (collective anger and violence), and how this in turn will be viewed by the Hindu community (the barbarity and threat of the Muslim 'other') and feed into their practices (retaliatory violence and communal retrenchment).

On the one hand, then, we see how practices feed into narratives which generate new practices, which in turn affect narratives … and so on. On the other hand, we see (ironically) that the ability to create violence in this way occurs not despite but because of a shared heritage and accurate presumptions about interpretative activities across religious groups. In this sense, common understandings and collective awareness are organised as sets of *dialogues* enveloped in practices (see Marková, 2003; Gillespie, Cornish, Aveling and Zittoun, 2008), where opposite positions and antithetical 'themes' are enacted all the more effectively when both sides are able to understand the core of *both* lines of argument.

3.5 World-Making Assumptions: Identity as Collective Agency

Common understandings of the world and collective awareness hence not only arise from social practices, they also often make possible those social practices (and only those social practices) that then sustain them. Effective nationalism creates the national categories that it assumes (see Reicher & Hopkins, 2001). Seeing someone as an enemy can lead us to treat them in ways that make them behave as an enemy. Therefore, we need to be precise about the meaning of 'social context'. Any reading of the problem solely in terms of the question 'how do people give meaning to what is already out there?' misses the most interesting point. Social and historical contexts are not just sets of external background factors that impact shared representations, but are themselves realities brought into existence through such representations.

This ontological stance is easily misunderstood or else misrepresented. Hence, we must be clear about what is meant by this and what it implies. The starting point is to appreciate that the day-to-day reality in which we live is largely constituted by what Searle (1995) labelled *institutional facts*. All aspects of our everyday lives—from the time we get up in order to get to work, the traffic regulations which govern our drive to the office, the rules which govern what we do once there, to the value of the money that we earn—are part of a human-made world. Such institutional facts can be defined by two properties. On the one hand, they exist only as a consequence of human agreement; on the other, from an individual perspective, they appear as objective facts: (at least part of) their consequences are independent of subjective cognition.

Things like money, citizenship, degrees, classes, mortgages and crimes would not exist if no one *believed* that they existed. Or, to be more precise, they would not exist if there were no storekeepers, border guards, students, bankers or police officers *acting on the basis of the belief* that they do exist. But then, it becomes important to make a key distinction. What we are *not* implying is that, were an individual to deny these institutions, they would go away. Changes in *individual* representations do *not* alter the existence or essence of specific institutional facts. Were you to drive on the wrong side of the road, try to use conch shells as currency or else claim to live in your own independent republic with its own laws, you would soon discover this. We are, therefore, not proposing an extreme form of philosophical solipsism which is easily caricatured. What we do assert, however, is that changes in shared representations can and frequently do lead to changes in the institutional world.

The relationship between shared representations and institutional realities is therefore bi-directional. On the one hand, formalised regulations, especially when they are perceived as legitimate by a critical mass of people, are generally powerful tools for clarifying and thus stabilising mutual expectations. Moreover, fostering the creative nature of normative expectations by formalising them is not limited to the scope of classical legislators operating within classical nation-states. As Doise (2002) claimed, the international diffusion of human rights has genuinely transformed social relations across manifold spheres of lives and places (see also Elcheroth, 2006; Gély & Sanchez-Mazas, 2006; Spini & Doise, 2005). On the other hand, giving institutional support to a particular position by making it a law does not inoculate that position against change. One pertinent example, in some countries and states at least, concerns the privileging of heterosexual marriage through various forms of legislation. As alternative forms of relationship have gained greater legitimacy, the law has fallen out of step. In the end, *the law* has had to change in order to accommodate actual social practices.

Our argument so far, then, is that social realities are created, maintained and transformed by collective practices that generate and uphold shared systems of meaning and shared expectations. There is a corollary to this: although individual dissent is insufficient to change institutional realities, once an individual's discontent is articulated with his or her belief that it is shared with others, action for social change becomes a viable option. Similarly, once a person's unease with the way in which a valued group identity is defined becomes articulated with his or her belief that others share this unease, a re-definition of the identity becomes possible.

Such *mobilising beliefs* draw on the invisible web of meanings we referred to earlier on, composed, for example, of common sense truisms, widely diffused political slogans or basic legal prescriptions. The awareness that a significant proportion of community members have access to this background knowledge can create a dynamic of *escalation* whereby individuals presuppose the support of others and, hence, act in ways that elicit support from others—such as when one or two members of an audience start clapping after a speech, driven by the confidence that others will follow, and then others infer that clapping is an appropriate response, and, soon, individual acts are transformed into the collective practice of ovation. Or else, and perhaps more consequentially, when a few people turn up to a protest, believing that they will not be alone, which leads yet others to turn up to subsequent events and culminates in mass demonstrations with genuinely revolutionary potential. Such a process was critical to the Arab Spring (Ghonim, 2012).

To take our argument a little further, we can see that the effectiveness of an individual actor in shaping the world lies not so much in his or her own actions *per se*, but more in the way in which he or she is able, through those actions, to shape the expectations and, hence, the actions of others. Understood in this way, agency comes down to the *capacity to shape mutual expectations* within a group, in such a manner as to enable or impede co-ordinated actions directed towards a given purpose.

3.6 Demystifying Identity

The theoretical approach to identity that we have introduced in this chapter changes our way of looking at its role in producing 'hatred' as well as 'conformity'. Let us now try to summarise the insights gained, proceeding in two steps: first, by showing how some of the most powerful and intriguing aspects of collective identity become conceivable with no need to assume immutable binding forces related to common descent, destiny or other essential factors; and second, by inferring why we need to look more closely at the mobilisation of collective identity to advance in our understanding of both intergroup conflict and ingroup conformity.

To put it briefly, many approaches to identity lay their emphasis on an examination of people's intimate sense of self and other. We wish to complement that with an equal emphasis on an examination of visible, sometimes ostentatious, expressions of identity. We focus on the way in which certain markers of identity become shared, highlighted as important, and hence become pragmatically relevant.

In practice, the question of whether individuals consider their own or another person's language, accent, religion, skin colour or place of birth as a relevant piece of information or not will often depend on whether they anticipate that such markers of identity will make a difference in the way other people will act towards them or a third person. In Germany under the Nuremberg race laws, as in South Africa under the Apartheid regime, the question whether anyone truly believed that 'race' matters—that

Jewish descent or skin colour was an appropriate criterion to judge a person—was of limited pragmatic value. By contrast, what mattered was the knowledge that these markers were publically defined as foundational, and hence anyone who ignored them when engaging in romance, friendship or work relationships would be in deep trouble. So too in less extreme contexts, identity markers matter because of what we understand others to make of them. Employers treat class and racial markers seriously because of the way they believe customers will react. Adults might worry about the political identity of their acquaintances for fear of alienating their friends, while adolescents might be more concerned by cultural markers (what music someone likes, for instance) for similar reasons.

To be clear, our argument here is not to deny the importance of our intimate sense of self—we know that to be important and that both our mundane sense of self and our passionate sense of self drive many key behaviours. What we are denying is the idea that identity is solely or even primarily about such a sense of self. Only when we complement this with the insight that identity is equally to be understood as a set of concrete markers of identity that are perceived as being shareable in a given social context can a number of seemingly mysterious attributes of identity become intelligible. And the first of these is precisely *why people do invest so much in their identities*—why we spend so much energy in categorising ourselves and others (even in the cultural context of Western-capitalist-post-modernist societies that so highly valorise individual distinctiveness); why we are so attached to our identities and why we agonise so much about the loss of identity.

The explanation is that identity connects us to other people—something that can only happen because of public agreement about the markers of identity such that I can be confident that the way I define myself will be accepted by others and will be the way they define me. This connection is not only something sentimental or perceptual but also highly concrete and pragmatic. A common understanding of identity leads people to assume a common understanding of the world and a common set of goals. It thereby allows people to co-ordinate their behaviour, to take joint action, and to achieve such social power as makes them more able to actually achieve their goals.

The second question which can be better addressed by combining the intimate and public dimensions of identity is *why policymakers talk so much about identity*. In contrast to a common view in political science, we propose that 'identity' in political rhetoric is more than an attempt to circumvent more weighty political issues like economic management, social policy or foreign affairs. The capacity of policymakers (or those who challenge them) to create results in any or all of these fields is critically contingent upon the enlistment of public support. In a democracy (and even in autocracies), you can't mobilise troops to go to war unless you can also mobilise the population in favour of war. Now, insofar as the creation of shared identities brings masses of people together with a shared understanding of the world and a shared understanding of what is in their interests—in other words, identities create constituencies—then successful mobilisation will be dependent upon the ability to define identities in ways that make the politician's project mesh with the population's interest. That is, the effectiveness of a politician in *any* area—economic, social, military, cultural—will depend upon their capacity to act as an authoritative "entrepreneur of identity" (Reicher & Hopkins, 2001).

It is all very well to explain why politicians will talk about identity and will seek to entrench particular definitions of identity. But, of course, this would be of little consequence if these definitions were without consequence. So our second question leads irresistibly to a third—one to which we devote most attention in this book: *Why is identity so vulnerable to manipulation?* If it were true that an identity (say national identity) were entirely an internal and intimate matter—the sum of millions of citizens' answer to a lifelong quest to discover who they truly are—then it is most unlikely that something as ephemeral as a few mass-mediated speeches could have any impact on it at all. How could a few words re-define the content or meaning of that identity? How could passing rhetoric trigger shifts in public opinion leading a national majority to see their nationhood as impelling them towards building a welfare state or else cutting social benefits, embracing those displaced by war or else policing migrants, going to war or else suing for peace? Once again, malleability and change is the best possible argument against taking identity as an essence within the person. It is the best argument possible for relating what we think and feel on the inside to what happens between us on the outside. It is at this latter level that political rhetoric largely exerts its effect, altering what we believe about what others believe and specifically believe about us; consequently, altering how we act towards those others and hence how they act towards us; ultimately re-framing the organisation of the social world and hence the social categories which are able to make sense of it.

3.7   A Mobilisation Perspective

Underpinning our arguments about identity is an assumption about the nature of understanding which is at odds with much (but certainly not all) of psychological theorising. That is, we eschew a perceptual approach which assumes that people come to comprehend their world through a silent neutral process of contemplation: we individually look at what is out there, we process the information through a combination of generic processes and personal biases, and we thereby generate a picture of the way things are. Rather, when it comes to any issue of significance—how do we deal with immigrants, what do we think of people of a different religion or 'race' or ethnicity, what do we think of those who are jobless and on welfare—we are subject to a cacophony of different voices providing us with different definitions, explanations and solutions. We are enjoined to see the world in different ways. Our understandings are actively mobilised.

Drawing on our analysis of identity, there are multiple reasons why it is important to look at the ways that identities are mobilised, crafted and used. The first is that the definition of identities is not the background to intergroup conflicts but always *part of these conflicts*. Different parties to the conflict will advance different definitions. Much of the struggle is actually over the representation of the conflict itself—what categories are involved (who are 'we' and who are 'they'?), what is the category content (what does it mean to be 'us'?), what are the category boundaries (who belongs to 'us' and who to 'them'?), what are the category relations (what do 'they' portend for 'us'?). It is also about the way these definitions have moral consequences (what sort of actions are right or wrong, and what is the legitimacy of different actors?) and practical consequences (what sorts of courses of action are possible?). Once these representations are determined, most of the work is done, and many other things follow.

Take, for instance, the Arab–Israeli conflict—or is it the Palestinian–Israeli conflict, or even a conflict between Palestinians and Western imperialism? This problem of description is emblematic of the issues. The Israeli state tells a story in which they are a small, vulnerable and historically oppressed people threatened with annihilation by the might of the combined Arab countries. In this context, the moral responsibility of outsiders in the international community is to protect them against the shadow of another Holocaust (see Gamson & Herzog, 1999). The Palestinian leaders tell a story where the small, vulnerable and historically oppressed Palestinian people are threatened with annihilation by the might of the Israeli Defence Force, which is backed by the even greater imperial might of the United States. So here, the moral responsibility of the rest of the world stands against Israel. How much credit is given to each of these narratives by various actors, both locally and in the global arena, is highly consequential for the dynamics of the conflict, the balance of forces and the way things are likely to play out.

The next reason for looking at mobilisation is that it is critical to understanding the relationship between identity definition and context. On the one hand, context shapes rhetoric. More specifically, the ways that categories are defined depends upon the nature of the audience one seeks to mobilise. Thus, Klein & Licata (2003) show that the nationalist leader Patrice Lumumba altered his representation of Belgians and Congolese as a function of whether he was addressing the former or the latter. In front of the colonialists, and in order to demobilise their opposition to independence, he would describe Belgians as benevolent and the Congolese as pacific. In front of the colonised, and in order to mobilise them for independence, he would describe the Belgians as oppressors and the Congolese as victims.

On the other hand, rhetoric shapes context. More specifically, context is invoked in order to sustain particular versions of category relations. So, as Stevenson, Condor and Abell (2007) showed, the answer to the question of whether Irish Catholics or Irish Protestants are the minority group depends on the framing of the relevant context as either 'Northern Ireland', 'Ireland' or the 'United Kingdom'. Different political leaders invoke these different contexts in order to render plausible their own version of who is the minority and who the majority. Sometimes even the *same* leaders refer to different contexts at different moments, when political opportunities and strategies change.

Once again, we can see how these matters are the very stuff of the relevant conflicts. They should therefore be the focus of analysis, not only its backdrop. Furthermore, while sometimes the goal of expressing a given version of identity is to mobilise the collective toward a form of action, at other times it can be 'just' to consolidate the identity. That is, rather than being aimed at promoting a specific and immediate instrumental purpose, identity is invoked to achieve, maintain or deepen a shared understanding that the group exists and that it has a specific culture (see Klein, Spears and Reicher, 2007).

Finally, we need to look at the mobilisation of identity in order to appreciate *the critical role of mass communication*, and hence of mass media, in shaping collectivities and collective action. In political affairs in general, and in large-scale conflicts in particular, the collective experience of events is necessarily mediated, since no one can have a complete picture of the conflict by drawing only on his or her immediate perceptions, or even those of his or her personal contacts. The media circulate explicit narratives and discourse about conflicts, but also images and perspectives that sustain (or contradict) these narratives. For example, Lipson (2009) provides a systematic analysis of camera shots broadcast by the BBC and by CBS during one week in the early stage of the invasion of Iraq in 2003. He shows how 'embedded journalism' meant that British and American troops were pictured up close. We see their facial features and their emotions, making it all the easier to identify with them, with their hopes and their fears. By contrast, shots of Iraqis tended to be rare and at a distance. Only 20 % of pictures coming from Iraq displayed locals and even then they were generally only of people in the mass, of crowds, of soldiers running and shouting.

At this point, the critic might respond that people are media-savvy. They are well aware of these devices and biases and are not swayed by them. But that is of little comfort if the media work by affecting what we think others think and, hence, what positions can reasonably be expected to be shared. The fact that mass communication does not so much affect what each of us feels and thinks in private does not imply that its impact on what we are capable of doing collectively is not critical.

Therefore, if you want to escape from the influence of the mass media, it is not enough to switch your TV off. You also need to let your neighbours know that you are doing so. This is precisely what inhabitants of the small Polish city of Swidnik did in February 1982 (Crawshaw & Jackson, 2010), during the early years of the 'Solidarnosc' protest movement. Exhausted by the pro-regime news coverage of the state-controlled television, which either entirely ignored or unilaterally delegitimised the protest movement, an increasing number of Poles decided not to watch the daily news broadcasts any more. In Swidnik though, people started to realise that their private boycott would have much more impact if they found a way to express it publicly. At that point, an increasing number of residents started to go for a walk at exactly the time when the news was transmitted. Some went so far as to take their televisions with them on a pushchair or other improvised vehicle. This made it very clear to any observer that 'I am going for a walk at 19:30' actually meant 'I am not watching the news'. The movement soon spread to other cities and the regime eventually became so nervous about it as to impose a daily curfew from seven o'clock, thereby obliging people to stay at home during the news. At this point, the ruling elite was obviously not in a position to make people *watch* the state-controlled news, let alone to make them *trust* the news, but at least they could make it as difficult as possible for each individual to be confident that other individuals had also switched their TV off.

3.8 Conclusion

Our analysis of identity in this chapter has four key elements.

First, we argue against the notion that identities are fixed, set, immutable either for all time or at any particular point in time. Across time, identities are always fluid and always contingent on what they enable a set of people to do together. As social practices change, old categories become obsolete and new categories are formed. If, for a period of time, identities do become frozen in a particular configuration, that is the exception to the rule. That is what requires explanation. In short, identities are always performed and our task is to elucidate the processes of their performance.

Second, when it comes to this task, it is important to appreciate that our sense of self is not down to us alone. Who we are is also a matter of how we think others will see and treat us, how we act in consequence and how in turn that impacts the perceptions of others. It follows that performing identity in new ways is as much, if not more, a function of change in people's awareness of how others see them as of change in how they see themselves.

Third, important as it is to investigate how identities come into being, it is equally important to investigate what particular identities make possible or impossible. We have seen how identities don't just reflect the ways that people are organised in the world but that they also organise people in the social world. Identities mobilise people into collective actors. They thereby create the social power to change the world: identities are world-making resources (Reicher & Hopkins, 2001).

Fourth, precisely because identities do produce social power, those who wish to wield such power (politicians, leaders and other activists) will actively seek to construct versions of identity that sustain their practical projects. On the one hand, then, identities will always be contested. On the other, identities will always be actively mobilised. Understanding identity is therefore a matter of asking how particular versions of identity gain traction and ultimately come to be seen as self-evident.

In the next chapter, we examine the role of violence in this process. We examine how the threat, the actuality and the memory of violence serve to reconfigure our relations to others, what we can know of others (and what they know of us), and thereby serve to reconfigure identity and power in society.

References

Allert, T. (2009). *The Hitler salute*. New York: Metropolitan Books.
Billig, M. (1995). *Banal nationalism*. London: Sage Publications Ltd.
Crawshaw, S., & Jackson, J. (2010). *Small acts of resistance: How courage, tenacity, and ingenuity can change the world*. New York: Union Square Press.
Doise, W. (2002). Les représentations sociales : leçons du passé et défis d'aujourd'hui : Social representations (Vol. 41, pp. 101–110). Presented at the Conférence internationale sur les Représentations Sociales, Sage Publications.

Elcheroth, G. (2006). Individual-level and community-level effects of war trauma on social representations related to humanitarian law. *European Journal of Social Psychology, 36*(6), 907–930.

Elcheroth, G., Doise, W., & Reicher, S. (2011). On the knowledge of politics and the politics of knowledge: How a social representations approach help us rethink the subject of political psychology. *Political Psychology, 32*(5), 729–758.

Falasca-Zamponi, S. (1997). *Fascist spectacle: The aesthetics of power in Mussolini's Italy*. Berkeley: University of California Press.

Gamson, W. A., & Herzog, H. (1999). Living with Contradictions: The taken-for-granted in Israeli political discourse. *Political Psychology, 20*(2), 247–266.

Gély, R., & Sanchez-Mazas, M. (2006). The philosophical implications of research on the social representations of human rights. *Social Science Information, 45*(3), 387–410.

Ghonim, W. (2012). *Revolution 2.0*. London: Fourth Estate.

Gillespie, A., Cornish, F., Aveling, E. L., & Zittoun, T. (2008). Conflicting community commitments: A dialogical analysis of a British woman's World War II diaries. *Journal of Community Psychology, 36*(1), 35–52.

Herrera, M., & Reicher, S. (1998). Making sides and taking sides: An analysis of salient images and category constructions for pro- and anti-Gulf War respondents. *European Journal of Social Psychology, 28*(6), 981–993.

Jodelet, D. (1991). *Madness and social representations: Living with the mad in one french community*. Berkeley: University of California Press.

Kershaw, I. (1987). *The 'Hitler Myth': Image and reality in the Third Reich*. Oxford: Oxford University Press.

Kinder, D. R. (1998). Opinion and action in the realm of politics. In D. T. Gilbert, S. T. Fiske, & G. Lindzey (Eds.), *The handbook of social psychology, Vols. 1 and 2* (4th ed., pp. 778–867). New York: McGraw-Hill.

Klein, O., & Licata, L. (2003). When group representations serve social change: The speeches of Patrice Lumumba during the Congolese decolonization. *British Journal of Social Psychology, 42*(4), 571–593.

Klein, O., Spears, R., & Reicher, S. (2007). Social identity performance: Extending the strategic side of SIDE. *Personality and Social Psychology Review, 11*(1), 28–45.

Lipson, M. (2009). "If it wasn't rolling, it never happened": The role or visual elements in television news. In L. Harman & L. Lombardo (Eds.), *Evaluation and stance in war news: A linguistic analysis of American, British and Italian television news reporting of the 2003 Iraqi War* (pp. 140–169). London: Continuum.

Marková, I. (2003). *Dialogicality and social representations: The dynamics of mind*. Cambridge: Cambridge University Press.

Moscovici, S. (1961/2008). *Psychoanalysis: Its image and its public*. Cambridge: Polity Press.

Mutz, D. C. (1998). *Impersonal influence: How perceptions of mass collectives affect political attitudes*. Cambridge: Cambridge University Press.

Paluck, E. L. (2009). Reducing intergroup prejudice and conflict using the media: A field experiment in Rwanda. *Journal of Personality and Social Psychology, 96*(3), 574–587.

Platow, M. J., Haslam, S. A., Both, A., Chew, I., Cuddon, M., Goharpey, N., et al. (2005). 'It's not funny if they're laughing': Self-categorization, social influence, and responses to canned laughter. *Journal of Experimental Social Psychology, 41*, 542–550.

Reicher, S., & Hopkins, N. (2001). Psychology and the end of history: A critique and a proposal for the psychology of social categorization. *Political Psychology, 22*(2), 383–407.

Sayer, D. (1979). *Marx's method*. Brighton: Harvester Press.

Searle, J. R. (1995). *The construction of social reality*. New York: Simon and Schuster.

Spini, D., & Doise, W. (2005). Universal rights and duties as normative social representations. In J. Finkel & F. Moghaddam (Eds.), *The psychology of human rights and duties: Empirical contributions and normative commentaries* (pp. 21–48). Washington, DC: American Psychological Association.

Staub, E., & Pearlman, L. A. (2009). Reducing intergroup prejudice and conflict: A commentary. *Journal of Personality and Social Psychology, 96*(3), 588–593.

Stevenson, C., Condor, S., & Abell, J. (2007). The minority-majority conundrum in Northern Ireland: An orange order perspective. *Political Psychology, 28*(1), 105–125.

Tajfel, H. (1975). The exit of social mobility and the voice of social change : Notes on the social psychology of intergroup relations. *Social Science Information, 14*(2), 101–118.

Tajfel, H. (1981). *Human groups and social categories: Studies in social psychology*. Cambridge: Cambridge University Press.

Wright, S. (1997). Ambiguity, social influence, and collective action: Generating collective protest in response to tokenism. *Personality and Social Psychology Bulletin, 23*(12), 1277–1290.

4

Violence: How Collective Shocks Transform Social Practices

We now come to the heart of our concerns: the matter of violence. Where prior research has tended to focus on the question 'how is violence produced' we argue that this needs to be complemented by asking 'what is produced by violence?' Correspondingly, the core question in this chapter is how violence serves to transform identity.

The performative model of collective identity, outlined in the previous chapter, proposes that a set of people will only perceive themselves as being bound together by a common identity if they can concretely act together in the terms defined by that identity. That is, identity is fundamentally about *doing*, not just about *thinking*. It follows that anything which alters what people can do together will likewise alter their sense of identity. Violence is just such a thing—in fact, it is a dreadfully effective way of reshaping shared action.

To be slightly more formal, violence affects identity to the extent that it re-patterns the social practices through which a group of people perform and uphold their common identities. In part, such transformation might be achieved through the creation of new practices, or else by making previously rare practices more common. For instance, Angus Calder (1992) shows how, due to processes like the evacuation of children and the use of public shelters during the Blitz, Britons in World War II were able to come together across previously impenetrable boundaries of class. Nonetheless, above all, violence operates in a negative way. By making it more difficult for people to do certain things, or impossible to interact with certain others, it contributes to the obsolescence and oblivion of the identities sustained by these activities and interactions.

Collective identities in the aftermath of violence therefore represent the bonds of solidarity and sociality that are left over once many, if not most of, people's ordinary social connections have been broken. They are *radical reductions of identity*. As a consequence, one typical feature of identities re-shaped by violence is their rigidity: by giving up alternative ways to define themselves, people also lose—sometimes temporarily, sometimes chronically—their capacity to navigate flexibly between a variety of relevant identities. Therefore, violent turning points do not simply provoke shifts from one prevalent form of identity to another; they also transform the nature of identity, from something fluid into something frozen.

This point about the loss of fluidity and the freezing of identities through violence is sufficiently foundational for us to spend a considerable portion of this chapter in illustrating and explicating it through a concrete example. This concerns the siege of Sarajevo, to which we already alluded in our first chapter. We choose this example because, if identities came to be reduced to one single overarching (ethnic) dimension in the previously vibrant and cosmopolitan Sarajevo of the early 1990s, there is no fundamental reason why war could not produce the same sombre outcome anywhere else.

Having worked through the Sarajevan case, we will then develop our argument in two different ways. First, we will argue that the re-patterning of practices and identities does not depend upon the actuality of war. Things don't have to be as bloody as they were in Bosnia for violence to make a difference. Indeed they don't have to be bloody at all. The mere anticipation of violence can be sufficient to generate processes of transformation. That is, believing that we might plausibly come under attack from others can be enough to corrode our everyday practices—where we go, who we talk to, who we interact with. We will show how our social world and social identities begin to close down as soon as people behave collectively *as if* war is real, *as if* previous practices are now dangerous, *as if* erstwhile friends are now enemies. The collective imagination of conflict can be every bit as toxic and produce just as powerful a collective shock to the system as the collective experience of conflict.

Second, we will consider a critical implication of the realisation that violence induces profound qualitative alterations in collective identity: by transforming the identity of the groups involved, it transforms the very meaning and purpose of collective conflict. As a consequence, what set conflict in motion in the first place (its so-called root causes) tends to become increasingly irrelevant for understanding the conflict—what drives it, what is at stake, and what can be done to contain it—as it unfolds.

4.1 Performing Ethnic War

Sarajevo might be an overused symbol. History textbooks tell us that World War I started here and with it the first act of the short twentieth century, which Hobsbawm (1994) dubbed the 'age of catastrophe'. Much later, between 1992 and 1995, as the city's siege unfolded in front of the eyes of the world's press (unlike the mass killings committed in Bosnia's hinterland), it became the dramatic epilogue to the selfsame century. The sinister images of senseless sniper-fire terrorising a starving civilian population appeared to epitomise the end to an illusion of socialist 'brotherhood and unity'.

When French President François Mitterrand landed at Sarajevo airport on 28 June 1992—the same date on which Archduke Ferdinand of Austro-Hungary was assassinated in 1914—he made a dramatic connection between the first and the last great European tragedies of the twentieth century. Hobsbawm (1994) would later comment on the event as revealing the historic amnesia of his contemporaries. The significance of the date—and hence of Mitterrand's gesture—went largely unnoticed by younger citizens. But one might also wonder whether those who did perceive the relationship read the gesture as intended. Instead of seeing a plea for solidarity with the Bosnian people, could Mitterrand's linking of conflicts across time ironically have fed into the narrative of 'Balkan ghosts'? Could he have reinforced the idea, so insistently spun by Robert Kaplan, that Sarajevo was simply the latest in a long line of conflicts that derive from the primordial and tribal nature of the region. As Kaplan formulated it, with his unerring capacity for dramatising and for using simplistic clichés, "Twentieth-century history came from the Balkans. Here men have been isolated by poverty and ethnic rivalry, dooming them to hate. The politics have been reduced to the level of near anarchy that from time to time in history has flowed up the Danube into central Europe" (Kaplan, 1993, p. XXVII).

The problem with this claim, of course, is that it involves an arbitrary selection of conflictual moments from across history in order to sustain the claim of a conflictual essence. But, moving beyond the clichés and the bloody drama, what was life really like in pre-war Sarajevo and how did it change? What did the siege actually mean for ordinary Sarajevans in their daily struggle for survival? And what can we learn from their experiences about the way collective violence transforms collective identity? Thankfully, we have the work of anthropologist Ivana Maček (2009), whose meticulous ethno-graphic observations of Sarajevan life behind the headlines allow us to address these questions.

The first surprise that awaits readers of Maček's book *Sarajevo Under Siege*, especially those who were exposed to the relentless ethnic framing of the world's media, concerns the composition of the city's improvised defence forces. In the first stages of the war, Sarajevans from families of different religious or cultural backgrounds—'Muslims', 'Croats' and 'Serbs' as others might label them but not how, initially at least, they labelled themselves—fought *together* on the frontlines. At that stage, the dominant interpretation of the war was not in terms of conflict between ethnic groups, but more in terms of an urban/rural divide. Sarajevo was defending its sophisticated and cosmopolitan way of life against brutal attacks bred in the backward and parochial countryside.

As a consequence, the large numbers of mainly Muslim refugees who came to the city in order to flee fighting in the neighbouring villages and towns were viewed with suspicion by city-dwellers—even Muslim city-dwellers. Indeed, if the ethnicity of the refugees had any significance to Sarajevans, it lay in the contrast between their mono-ethnicity and the sophisticated multi-ethnic identity of the city.

We can go further: it wasn't just that many people eschewed simple ethnic categories, but that they actively subordinated these categories to what they considered to be more fundamental lines of divide. Thus, rather than employ a category such as 'Serb', Serbs were divided according to whether they stood for or against the city: 'good Serbs' or 'orthodox people' were friends; 'Chetniks' (a reference to World War II Serbian paramilitaries with a decidedly chequered history) were the enemy.

Yet, for all that the city inhabitants were uneasy with the ethnic framing of the conflict and found it to be in contradiction with their own experiences, they were well aware that others did see events through an ethnic lens and that in some situations their own religious affiliation might become critical. Maček reports a joke that circulated in Sarajevo during the siege, as a reflection of the opportunistic approach to religion which spread through a largely secular population:

> How do people manage to leave Sarajevo? When they pass Croatian snipers they raise two fingers (which is the Catholic way to cross oneself), when they pass Serbian snipers they raise three fingers (the Orthodox way to cross oneself), when they pass Muslim snipers they raise five fingers, the whole hand (the Muslim way of praying), and when they finally get out they raise one finger, the middle one (an expletive gesture). (Quoted by Maček, 2009, p. 168)

It wasn't only in the world of jokes that people re-discovered religion as a means of leaving the city. Croatia offered citizenship and a road out of the Bosnian war zone to inhabitants who could document that they were baptised Catholics—an opportunity many were happy to seize. Equally, religion wasn't only relevant to getting out of Sarajevo; it was also a means of surviving in Sarajevo. Life became increasingly hard. Shortages became endemic. Access to humanitarian aid became vital. However, distribution of food supplies was in the hands of religious associations who delivered aid only to their co-religionists, assuming that other associations would take care of 'their' communities. Caritas, for example, provided food to those who accepted having their houses blessed by a Catholic priest. Since Caritas was the most efficient food supplier in the city, objective inequalities arose between those who could claim some link to Catholicism and those who could not.

The worst off in town were those people who were not linked to any of the main religious communities. They had to face the shortages, dangers and uncertainties of life during the siege without being able to count on the solidarity of an organised community—a critical resource in the chaos of war. Against this backdrop, it is not surprising that, during the war years, an increasing number of Sarajevans attended religious services, learnt how to pray in public as Catholics, as Orthodox, as Muslims or as Jews, and started to celebrate religious holidays together with their families, friends and neighbours. In this context, acts of devotion that might initially seem foolish and irrational (such as gathering in front of the Catholic cathedral after mass even though the space was openly exposed to sniper fire) can be seen to make sense.

In short, the contingencies of survival under siege increasingly made Sarajevans behave as if religion was a central part of their identity—and exposed them to others acting as if religion mattered (possibly more than life itself). They thereby became increasingly aware of their friends', neighbours', colleagues' and comrades' religious identity. They also became more expert about the relevant markers of identity, allowing them rapidly to tell an Orthodox Serb apart from a Catholic Croat, or a Muslim.

More critically, perhaps, these developments in town had their repercussions amongst those in the trenches defending the town. As the ethnic/religious polarisation proceeded apace, and as Sarajevan Muslims learnt of the ethnic massacres in Eastern Bosnia, they began to consider that they too might be at risk—again, not because of what it meant to themselves to be 'Muslim', but because of what it might have meant to others who categorised them as 'Muslims'. Moreover, without knowing exactly who might see them as such and attack them as such, it began to make sense to view others as 'Serbs'. Solidarity in the trenches began to give way to distrust.

For the Serbs such distrust, and its implications, was equally corrosive. Rather than remain under constant suspicion, many young Serbs chose to quit the city's defence forces and to move to the other side of the frontline, to the 'Serb-held' neighbourhoods of the town, where they expected to find a more accepting environment. But this only made the situation worse, especially for those Serbs who remained behind.

4 Violence: How Collective Shocks Transform Social Practices

To flit overnight across the line was seen by Muslims as an act of betrayal. How could you trust people who might desert in the midst of a war and who, still worse, might then shoot at you from enemy trenches? Rather than suffer a potential fifth column in one's midst, was it not better to exclude such potentially disloyal elements? The distrust of Serbs grew; the screw was tightened. More Serbs left and so the spiral grew more vicious.

A second wave of ethnic homogenisation among the city's defence forces was initiated in Spring 1993 when a new front opened in the Lašva Valley, northwest of Sarajevo, which pitted Croat against Muslim fighters. This led Muslim commanders to conclude that it was too risky to leave the defence of Sarajevo in Croat hands. So they decided to disarm Croat combatants. One of them recorded his own sense of betrayal at this policy: "They woke you in the dormitory with the gun aimed at your head, the comrades who were in the trench with you" (quoted by Maček, 2009, p. 196).

Eventually, despite (and not because of) the will of those involved, an ethnic grid was superimposed on the war and the Sarajevan defence forces mutated *de facto* into a Muslim army. As that happened, non-Muslims in Sarajevo began to fear for their own safety from erstwhile neighbours.

As this chronicle shows, the siege of Sarajevo represents a textbook case of a violent turning point in the trajectory of collective identities. Ethnic identity was not a pre-eminent frame to Sarajevans before violence broke out—it was largely irrelevant to most aspects of their lives. But it became an inescapable dimension in their lives through the social practices that developed under conditions of the siege. Sarajevans then had to live with this new social fact. It became all but impossible to ignore their own and their neighbours' ethnic identities during the siege, and difficult to simply go back and forget these identities after the siege. But if the Sarajevo case lends itself particularly well as a starting point to a discussion of how violence impacts upon identity—as violence was so obviously present in daily life and its consequences so clearly discernable—it should not lead us to think of the impact of violence as necessarily conditional upon such dramatic conditions, where an entire civilian population live in a war zone and could, at almost any point, be the target of snipers or shells.

To get a sense of the actual boundary conditions of the psychosocial processes at play, we rather need to consider the diversity of the circumstances under which violence can be *real in its consequences*, and these circumstances go far beyond the frontlines of war zones. This diversity is what we will explore next, using a deliberately broad set of examples. Indeed, to illustrate just how broad the applicability of the analysis might be, we will start our analysis in Switzerland, a country renowned for peace not war; for neutrality not partisanship; for the mundane not the dramatic.

4.2 The Second World War *Did* happen in Switzerland

In 2011, viewers of a French-language Swiss TV show elected General Henri Guisan, who led the Swiss army during World War II, 'Romand of the century'. At one level, this might seem an entirely unsurprising choice. Similar TV shows in other places had asked audiences to elect their greatest figure of all time. De Gaulle was chosen as the greatest Frenchman of all time. Churchill was elected as the greatest Briton of all time. Being a World War II leader seems to convey a distinct advantage.

But, on reflection, the choice of Guisan is rather different to that of De Gaulle or Churchill and might give us pause for thought. The first difference is anecdotal and concerns the use of categories. Whereas De Gaulle was a proud Frenchman who achieved for France and Churchill was an emblematic Briton who achieved for Britain, Guisan was selected as a great *Romand* (the western francophone region of Switzerland that corresponds to the boundaries of the TV station's audience). But his fame is entirely due to the fact that he commanded the federal army, as a Swiss general.

Once again, we see here the contingency and flexibility of social identities at work: how the same person or people can be defined in terms of different categories (national, regional, etc.), how different definitions of social categories are used as a function of different ways of organising social practices (since Switzerland has no national TV channel, but rather different language channels for the different linguistic regions of

4 Violence: How Collective Shocks Transform Social Practices 107

the country, the category 'Romand' makes sense insofar as it corresponds to the boundaries of this particular channel's audience); and how the ways others define us may differ from the ways we define ourselves (we don't know what it meant to Guisan himself to be a Romand even if he was defined as such in this exercise). Further, it hints at the conditions under which an individual may be categorised in different ways. Would there have been such eagerness to claim Guisan as a Romand if he had been less successful in his career? We are reminded of Einstein's wry comment that "if my theory of relativity is proven successful, Germany will claim me as a German and France will declare me a citizen of the world. Should my theory prove untrue, France will say that I am a German, and Germany will declare that I am a Jew".

The second difference between the choice of Guisan and De Gaulle/Churchill is more central to the argument in this chapter. An outsider might reflect that the choice of a World War II leader makes sense in France and Britain because of the huge impact of the war in those two countries. France was under occupation. Britain was all but invaded. Moreover, the war made fundamental changes to British society: it transformed social relations in the country and it transformed Britain's place in the world. In addition, it is arguable that Britons continue to obsess about the war and continue to cherish it as 'our finest hour'. But Switzerland? World War II self-evidently did not take place in Switzerland. Apart from a few bombs that allied countries accidentally dropped on the wrong side of the Swiss–German border, the country was not exposed to combat. So why would a war exert such a hold in a country where it didn't happen? How could a commander of an army that did not actually fight become a collective hero, and be recognised as such even among a generation that, in its overwhelming majority, was born well after the war in question?

To the outsider, the more one reflects on the choice of Guisan, the more surprising it becomes. But for the insider, things are rather different. The premise that generates such surprise—the observation that World War II did not take place in Switzerland—doesn't seem quite so self-evident. It may well be true that the Swiss army didn't engage in combat with enemy troops but that didn't mean that it was inactive. The army may not have fought in a conventional sense, but under General Guisan's leadership it was prepared and daily preparing for combat:

it was 'mobilised', according to the terminology used by Swiss officials and people.

Nor was the general public unaffected by the war. The fact that a German invasion was deemed possible at any moment produced a great deal of sympathy and solidarity with the soldiers who were ready to fight (and die) for their country. To some, the fact that Nazi Germany never attempted to invade Switzerland was evidence of *how well* they prepared and how effective they were. The lack of combat, then, did not indicate a lack of Swiss military involvement. To the contrary, it was evidence of their involvement, their prowess and the brilliance of their leader. From this perspective, Guisan won the battle (and the war) by not having to fight it.

Just like the French, the British and others, the Swiss therefore feel entirely justified in remembering World War II as the most dramatic chapter in their own national history. So when, in more recent years, critical historians argued that Hitler's decision not to invade Switzerland had more to do with his appreciation that a neutral Switzerland better served Nazi Germany's financial and economic interests than an occupied Switzerland, and less with his anticipation of strong military resistance (see Bergier, 2002), they provoked a highly emotional public debate. Many accused these historians of betraying the bravery and devotion of the Swiss troops during World War II.

Even in Switzerland, that quintessential land of peace, war can be experienced as real, violence can be seen as imminent, and this can lead to both new forms of mobilisation in the moment and powerful memories which dictate what can and can't be said long after. More generally, in arguing that violence re-defines social identities through re-patterning social practices, we need to be clear that the boundaries of violence do not equate to the boundaries of the combat zone. Rather, we need to look at the ways violence is imagined—where it could occur, when it could occur—and how this imaginary of violence impacts what people do. In other words, we must explore the spatial and temporal boundaries to the ways that communities live with violence rather supposing we know them in advance.

The temporal boundaries to imagined violence are particularly important: the impact on practices and identities does not necessarily come to an end with the end of violence. Kusturica's film masterpiece *Underground* provides a metaphorical illustration of this insight: after the end of World War II, an isolated community lives on in an underground bunker, as if the war was still in progress. For more than a generation, they entirely subordinate their individual lives to a collective cause—the liberation of Yugoslavia by partisan fighters. They continue to believe that the weapons that they manufacture in the bunker are being used by these partisans in their fight.

But we don't need to look to fiction to see how past violence continues to shape societies in the present. Similarly, we don't need to infer that people are deluded, that they don't realise that the old war is formally over and that the shooting and killing has stopped. In contemporary South Africa, no one lives in a shelter believing that the structures of apartheid are still in place. But despite the dismantling of segregation laws, an end to forcible removals and the formal opening of public spaces to all, those previously designated as 'Blacks' and 'Whites' still tend to avoid proximal interaction, whether on the beaches, in residential neighbourhoods or even in University cafeterias (Clack, Dixon, & Tredoux, 2005; Dixon & Durrheim, 2003; Durrheim & Dixon, 2001).

In the South African case, this enduring segregation is not explicitly justified by reference to apartheid and apartheid-era conflicts. After all, apartheid is a spoilt ideology and the official discourse has been structured around truth and reconciliation as means of moving beyond the past (O'Brien, 2001). Where segregation is argued for, it is in terms of different, seemingly more liberal discourses such as environmentalism. That is, poor black squatter camps in lush white neighbourhoods are criticised as a 'blot on the landscape' (Dixon, Reicher & Foster, 1997). However, in many other cases, past conflicts are explicitly invoked to maintain contemporary social practices. Enemies and threats are not invented from scratch at the point when violence begins to escalate. That is, there is generally a long-term context to short-term crises—one which makes representations intelligible, practices familiar and hence facilitates the production of violence. If, as we have seen in Sarajevo, a siege has profound effects on social relations, the same is true of a siege mentality.

Israel is a case in point. Present-day relations with Palestinians are incomprehensible without considering the way that Jewish history is represented. In his great *Social and Religious History of the Jews*, Salo Baron (1969) delineates (and challenges) what he terms the 'lachrymose' version of Jewish history. According to this viewpoint, from biblical times onwards, Jewish experience equates with suffering and this is linked to the view that Jews are always surrounded by enemies who seek to destroy them—an ongoing experience of which the Holocaust is only the latest and most virulent manifestation, but certainly the most salient. In a 2009 survey, an astounding 98 % of Jewish-Israeli adult respondents stated that remembering the Holocaust is a guiding principle in their life, even more important than having a family (Arian, 2012, cited in Klar, Schori-Eyal, & Klar, 2013).

Such a view of history feeds into psychological orientation which Klar and colleagues dub a 'perpetual ingroup victimhood orientation', which in turn frames the way current conflicts are viewed. For instance, amongst those who subscribe to this victimhood orientation, outgroup members are perceived as having more hostile intentions and there is less guilt at extreme actions taken against them—especially when they are actively reminded of past catastrophes. The argument has been eloquently formulated by Bar-Tal and Antebi (1992) who referred to the Jewish siege mentality as a set of collective beliefs that "come and go, riding the crests of associations incessantly flowing through the individual's mind, especially primed by contextual objects and events" (p. 635).

This notion of 'come and go' is crucial, for it implies that such beliefs are not self-evident, that they do not automatically stay alive (as 'ancient hatreds' arguments imply) and that they have to be kept alive—or at least invoked at particular points in time. So how does this happen?

The Israeli case provides us with some insights. To start with it is important to stress that the 'lachrymose' version of history is a very selective account. As Baron memorably observed, "suffering is part of the destiny" of the Jewish people; "so is repeated joy as well as ultimate redemption" (cited in Eckhardt, 1992, p. 135). Moreover, even if one subscribes to this version, one can draw different lessons from it—not only "never be a passive victim again" but also (albeit less prominently) "never be a perpetrator" (Klar et al., 2013). So the notion of Jews as victims who must strike first to ensure that they survive is one of many narratives of Jewishness and it has to be actively invoked—as, for instance, by Prime Minister Benjamin Netanyahu when addressing the nation on Holocaust Memorial Day, 2010:

4 Violence: How Collective Shocks Transform Social Practices   111

in every generation there are those who stand against us. And in this generation we must fortify our strength and independence so that we will be able to prevent the current enemy from carrying out its plan. (Cited in Klar et al., 2013, p. 135)

The important thing about this example is not just what is said, but the context in which it is said: Holocaust Memorial Day. The Holocaust is woven into Israeli society in a plethora of different ways: memorial days, memorial sites, museums, statues, textbooks, films, trips. To take just two telling statistics (both from Klar et al., 2013), in just one (relatively liberal) newspaper, the term *Holocaust* (Shoah in Hebrew) appeared as often as Israeli–Arab conflict. Every year, 16 % of the entire high school cohort go on trips to the death camps, mainly in Poland. As Liebman and Don-Yihya noted in 1983, the memory of the Holocaust is still omnipresent in Israel, cutting across age, education and country of origin.

Another way of putting this—invoking the work of Billig, 1995—is to say that memories of the Holocaust have become banal in Israel—not in the sense of trivialising the event of course, but rather in the sense of being so pervasive as to become embedded in all areas of life, as part and parcel of what it means to belong to the Israeli nation. Billig gives many powerful examples of the banality of nationhood—how it is presupposed in terms of the way we talk about the weather, sporting results, what is newsworthy (because it matters for the nation) and whether the news is good or bad (because it does or does not serve the national interest). When this occurs insidiously and continuously, and particularly when the national interest is seen to be threatened, it can be used to far less banal effect. To cite Billig himself:

> As the Gulf and Falkland Wars indicated, forces can be mobilized without lengthy campaigns of political preparation. The armaments are primed, ready for use in the battle. And the national populations appear also to be primed, ready to support the use of those armaments. (Billig, 1995, p. 7)

As in Israel, though, it is not enough to expose people to banal nationalism. One doesn't become a banal nationalist simply by sitting in an armchair and absorbing banal nationalist rhetoric. One has to be actively involved. One has to be involved in *rehearsing* nationhood. While in many US schools children literally rehearse around the flag every morning (singing their national anthem together), there are many other ways that people can practise their banal nationalism in daily routines: by expressing their joy when a fellow national wins a sports competition, by commenting on the national weather forecast or by passing on news that is important for the nation.

While it is perfectly possible (although potentially self-isolating) to choose not to rehearse nationhood when it comes to sporting events, to the weather or to the news, there are other areas of life where people will find it much harder not to play their active part. Billig gives the example of national currencies: Who could afford the luxury of not using them (and why exactly would anyone do that)? When Croatia became a sovereign nation-state in 1991, its government chose to label the new national currency the 'kuna'. As this was the name given to the currency during World War II, when the ruling fascist regime perpetrated massacres against the Serb minority, many saw the new currency as a fascist and anti-Serb symbol. Yet, inhabitants of the new Croatian state quickly became used to enacting the reality of their (soon to be war-ridden) national state several times a day by the small act of taking the kuna out of their wallet. By the same token, they quickly became accustomed to the ambiguities surrounding the definition of their national identity that were materialised in the coins and banknotes they used.

This example, like the Israeli example, shows that the way in which people rehearse their national identity not only serves to make the nation real but also gives substance to that reality. It helps define the values and the ideology of the nation, who is included and who is excluded, how the nation relates to others and how others relate to it, who is seen as an ally and who a threat. The same is true the other way round. The way a nation prepares for potential threats from an outgroup serves to define the nation itself. To act as if our country could come under existential threat at any time is a powerful means of constraining social relations. That is, if the recollection and re-enactment of past violence can reconfigure identities as much as actual violence, the same is true of rehearsing for future violence. Cold War experiences are emblematic of this. They show how communities can be profoundly transformed by a credible threat of mass destruction—even when that threat never materialises.

4 Violence: How Collective Shocks Transform Social Practices   113

Extensive archival research conducted across the USA, Canada and the UK by Davis (2007) shows how the nuclear threat by the Soviet Union became a tangible reality for the Western public during the 1950s and 1960s through recurrent large-scale emergency civil exercises. Across the USA, Canada and the UK, casualties of nuclear radiation, burning or physical injury were made up with great attention for detail, in order to increase the realism of these exercises.

In the USA, systematic civil defence training found its way into an overwhelming majority of classrooms between 1950 and 1952. A generation of school pupils learnt and practised how to 'duck and cover' as soon as a nuclear flash appeared, and thereby to protect themselves from shockwaves in school, at home or outdoors. Most states implemented curricular reform in the early 1950s to make sure that pupils acquired the necessary knowledge to cope with the challenges of nuclear age, from the chemistry of heat to international relations. But education was not limited to children. In the early 1970s, American test families dug themselves into their own home-made shelters, thus demonstrating that it was possible to protect yourself under your own steam in less than a day.

Apart from behaviour increasing the chances of physical survival following a nuclear strike, particular emphasis was laid on practising skills that were deemed essential to prevent a breakdown of social order: obedience to orders, not starting rumours and dispelling myths that could cause panic. In the UK, Anna Freud advised families to "make quite a confident ritual of air-raid precautions" (quoted by Davis, 2007, p. 109), where everyone has a clearly assigned role—for example, children were to take their teddy bears to the shelter—in order to foster everyone's sense of orderliness and security.

Overall, then, the goal of such mass dramas was not only to instruct people how to survive individually in the aftermath of a nuclear explosion, but also to instil in them a sense of civic responsibility. By rehearsing for nuclear war, people were not only taught what an attack would concretely mean to them in terms of physical survival, they were also given an education in how they must be pro-active if they were to survive *as a community*, to avoid group collapse and social paralysis. There was a clear moral imperative not to let a social catastrophe—the breakdown of the social fabric—add to the nuclear catastrophe and the destruction of the physical environment. The discipline enacted during the mass rehearsals sent out a clear message: no defeatism or dissent was tolerated on the social front. In that sense, rehearsals for nuclear war must have been a paradoxical experience for those who took part in them, making salient their moral duty to be prepared to cope with the announced apocalypse. To cite Davis:

> Role-play and acting in repeated rehearsals during peacetime was integral to governments' recommended preparations for their citizen's survival in wartime. Thus, acting was not only the method but also the ontology of the populace to preserve life, the ethos of their nation, and the fabric of their culture. It was the bulwark against nihilism, the motivation for belief, and the insurance of survival. Acting was the way to buy into the idea that civil defence could be efficacious; it was also, at the same time, the means to see how it did not work. (p. 219)

The key moral lesson, then, was that conformity is the key to survival because individual fate depends upon the fate of the nation as a whole and on state policies. This is exemplified in a script prepared by British contingency planners for the BBC in November 1964, as part of a simulated emergency programme. The script has never been broadcast; its main purpose was to raise awareness within the media on their role in case of a nuclear attack. In the imagined scenario, the following text was to be read immediately following the announcement that several regions across Britain had come under attack by nuclear weapons:

> Serious fires are raging in these places and there are very many casualties. Civil Defence and other rescue services are doing everything they can to rescue survivors. Immediate retaliatory measures were taken by our own forces and there have been no further attacks since 3 o'clock. (Quoted by Davis, 2007, p. 191)

Through imagined broadcasts such as this, the journalists could project themselves into a concrete nuclear war scenario. While the impact is depicted as very severe ('serious fires' and 'very many casualties' are mentioned), state services are still functioning: they are rescuing survivors and retaliating against the aggressor. The fact that the latter piece of

4 Violence: How Collective Shocks Transform Social Practices

information is immediately followed by the announcement that 'there have been no further attacks' suggests that the state's retaliatory actions have been effective in stopping further destruction. So the authorities are seen to apply effective retributional justice as well as effective protection for the national community. Whether all this is plausible does not need to be explained. Emergency rehearsals leave no time for critical reflection or political argument. They need to focus on the—imagined (!)—facts.

Taken together, the highly diverse examples discussed in this section—from Switzerland to Israel, and from the Cold War to the wars in the former Yugoslavia—both clarify the argument that violence transforms collective identity and also broaden it. They show that there are very different ways in which people can 'experience violence': on the frontline or far away from it; as something that has already happened, that is currently happening or as something that might plausibly happen in the future; as something directly experienced, or as something heard about from others who were directly involved, or reported by the media, and made real through communication, imagination and empathy. Whatever is the exact nature of people's experience of violence, the critical factor determining whether and how the experience will affect their collective identity is the active part they all play in it and which they see each other as playing. By performing their identities differently, people transform these identities. By adapting to violence as a shared social reality, people create new social facts that make it increasingly difficult to return to old ways and eventually impossible to live as if violence had never happened. Ironically, this pertains even if violence never did happen but is merely imagined in the past or in the future.

The fact that violence changes the very terrain on which it was built makes life tremendously difficult both for the academic and the activist, as we shall now see. On the one hand, it becomes more difficult, if not impossible, to make confident predictions about the way violence will unfold. On the other hand, it becomes impractical to assume that the best way out of conflict is back through the way in. Drawing these various points together, we cast doubt on the optimism of those who believe that we can both explain and resolve violence by uncovering its root causes.

4.3 The Elusive Hunt for Root Causes

In 1962, the American sociologist James C. Davies published an article in which he made an ambitious promise: to pave the way "toward a theory of revolution". In concluding his seminal reflections, Davies readily acknowledged that social scientists "are *still* not at the point of being able to predict revolution" (p. 19, our emphasis). But he was no less confident that they "should eventually be able to escape the embarrassment that may have come to Lenin" (p. 19) who, six weeks before the upheavals of February 1917, expressed doubts as to whether he would ever witness revolution in his own lifetime.

How did Davies hope to accomplish such an ambitious intellectual endeavour? At the core of his predictive approach was an attempt to identify structural patterns that would systematically precede the outbreak of revolution. According to Davies, it was "*the dissatisfied state of mind* rather than the tangible provision of 'adequate' or 'inadequate' supplies of food, equality, or liberty which produces the revolution" (p. 6, our emphasis). However, this did not mean that his model was primarily psychological, for Davies aimed to specify the objective conditions which gave rise to such dissatisfaction. His core thesis was that when deprivation is constant, we find it hard to imagine any other state of being and hence learn to live with the burden. But when levels of deprivation change—and more particularly, when we experience a rapid downturn after a period of steady improvement—then we find the burden unbearable. So people will fight against their regimes when a gap opens between rising expectations and declining fulfilment of these expectations, when restrictions are imposed on them at a time when previous progress led them to see deprivation as no longer inevitable.

Since Davies developed his ideas, the social sciences might have become less interested in economic class-based clashes and more in conflicts across ethnic or cultural cleavages. However, it is less certain that they have become more humble about their ability to predict the future. After the Cold War ended, Fukuyama (1992) promptly proclaimed the end of history, before (as discussed in Chap. 1) Huntington (1996) announced the coming clash of civilisations. The ensuing years, culminating in the post-nine-eleven wars, gave impetus to Huntingdon's thesis. In this context, political scientist Roger Petersen (2002) seemed to offer the academic book market exactly what it has been waiting for: a treatise on ethnic violence, proposing a predictive theory about when one ethnic group will violently target another.

In his book, Petersen argues that ethnic violence follows changes in the objective relationships between ethnic groups brought along by new state boundaries and/or shifts in the balance of resources available to the respective groups. People will fight against ethnic outgroups when structural changes create new threats or frustrations incarnated by the outgroup target, or else when new opportunities to attack a specific target group arise.

For Petersen, as for Davies, changing structural circumstances ultimately drive collective behaviour, while collective emotions mediate the process. To engage in joint aggressive action, all those involved need to be driven by similar emotions, which in turn are provoked by similar circumstances. These circumstances can take different forms. Sometimes it is a matter of breeding antagonisms. Petersen argues that loss of relative status breeds resentment. So, for instance, it was the fact that Bosnian Croats and Bosnian Serbs became minorities in the new Bosnian nation-state following the dissolution of the former Yugoslavia which would have led to their attacks on the Bosnian Muslims. Sometimes it is a matter of removing the constraints upon the expression of pre-existing resentments (as in the 'ancient hatreds' narrative we have discussed in a number of places). Thus, Petersen suggests that the reason why Serbs aggressed against Kosovo Albanians in the wake of the dissolution of the former Yugoslavia was basically because they (now) could.

Despite all the differences between Davies' theory of revolution and Petersen's theory of ethnic violence, both seek to provide a predictive framework for violent unrest which is concretised through the analysis of structural factors, seen as the ultimate determinants of collective behaviour. Both theories build upon the assertion that similarly changing circumstances provoke similar motives among large enough groups of people to account for mass mobilisation, be it against state authorities or ethnic outgroups. In both cases, the structural circumstances are seen to gain effect by the way that, in predictable terms, they unleash a kind of convergent collective will. In this line of thinking, revolution or ethnic violence is conceptualised as a sequence of events that only occur when a large mass of people want them to occur—when a collective is driven forward by some intrinsic "existential motivational force", to borrow Petersen's own terminology.

There are various problems with such thinking, some of which we have already discussed in some detail. So, for instance, much of what we do stems less from what we ourselves think, intend or desire, and more what we believe others think, intend or desire. So, I may aggress against you not because I want to hurt you but because I think you want to hurt me and so need to deter you from the start. This raises the very obvious point that violence is a product of interaction between two parties. Once one invokes this interactive context, the inadequacies of an approach which reduces violence to the will of any single party become even more obvious. Thus, the consequences of my actions depend upon the way they are apprehended by you and how you choose to respond. This may often be in ways that I hadn't intended or anticipated. So, by acting on the basis of one understanding of reality, I provoke you to create a new reality, which then provides a different context for my subsequent actions. I may therefore end up doing things I never dreamt of at the start.

Rather than being atypical, that is the way that things work in general. Therborn (1982), for instance, argues that no revolutionary movement sets out to create a revolution, but only in the way that the state responds to reformist demands does a more radical dynamic develop. Revolutions, and other forms of violent clashes, arise as chains of events that generate new realities in successive waves, chains in which conflict dynamics shift from one fragile equilibrium into the next, without a clearly discernable linear direction or overarching 'motivational force' that would span over the entire chain to link its starting point and its end point in a consistent way.

The most dramatic historic example of such a chain of events without a clear direction or collective motivation can be found in the few months in summer 1914 during which the European continent descended from an era of prosperity, progress and stability into Hobsbawm's 'age of catastrophe'.

In his autobiography, the Austrian novelist Stefan Zweig describes his stay at the Belgian seaside, in the short period between the assassination of Franz Ferdinand in Sarajevo and the outbreak of World War I. His account provides a vivid illustration of the climate in which Europeans drifted to war, without feeling concerned about what was happening or anticipating what was about to happen:

> All imaginable nations gathered peacefully, one heard particularly many German voices as, as every year, nearby Rhineland sent his people for summer vacation preferably to the Belgian beaches. The only interruption came from the newspaper boys who, to boost their sales, shouted the threatening headlines: "Austria provokes Russia", "Germany prepares for mobilisation". One could see how the faces of the people, when they bought a newspaper, became more sombre, but always just for a few minutes. After all we knew these diplomatic conflicts for years already; they have always been settled at the last moment, before things would have become serious. Why not this time again? Half an hour later one could see the same people again cheerfully snorting and splashing in the water, the kites rose, the gulls fluttered, and the sun was shining bright and warm through peaceful land. (Zweig, 1944/1997, pp. 251–252, our translation)

Arguably, this lack of awareness amongst ordinary people mirrored a similar lack of alertness amongst the European political elite who were actually dealing with the crisis. At least this is the impression that arises from historian Christopher Clark's (2012) analysis of the pre-war diplomacy. *Sleepwalkers*—the evocative title of Clark's book—alludes to his perception of these elites on the eve of war. It is a perception repeated and elaborated in the very final words of a 562-page chronicle of the various twists and turns which culminated in Armageddon: "the protagonists of 1914 were sleepwalkers, watchful but unseeing, haunted by dreams, yet blind to the reality of the horror they were about to bring into the world".

There are three key arguments which lead Clark to this conclusion and which are highly relevant to our argument in this book. The first is an explicit rejection of any notion that the war expressed a firm will, and that therefore it was inevitable. So, Clark asserts firmly: "the myth that European men leapt at the opportunity to defeat a hated enemy has been comprehensively dispelled" (p. 553). Instead, "for most places and for most people, the news of mobilization came as a profound shock, a 'peal of thunder out of a cloudless sky'" (p. 553).

Second, and as a corollary, Clark takes contingency seriously. He studiously avoids the danger of, retrospectively, converting the actual into the probable. On the contrary, he asserts:

> Some of the most interesting recent writing on the subject has argued that, far from being inevitable, this war was in fact 'improbable'—at least until it actually happened. From this it would follow that the conflict was not the consequence of a long-run deterioration, but of short-term shocks to the international system. Whether one accepts this view or not, it has the merit of opening the story to an element of contingency. And it is certainly true that while some of the developments I examine in this book seem to point unequivocally in the direction of what actually transpired in 1914, there are other vectors of pre-war change that suggest different, unrealized outcomes. (Clark, 2012, p. XXIX)

Third, what lay behind such lack of inevitability and contingency was the fact that, repeatedly, actors were driven by their assumptions concerning the intentions of others, that they acted in order to send a signal to others, and that both intentions and signals were repeatedly misread. So, for instance, when Russia finally decided to mobilise its troops it was because it over-estimated the extent and aggressiveness of Austrian mobilisation. This led Germany to perceive Russia as aggressive and mobilise in turn. Thus, Clark refers to "the tendency we can discern in the reasoning of so many of the actors in this crisis, to perceive oneself as operating under irresistible external constraints while placing the responsibility for deciding between peace and war firmly on the shoulder of the opponent" (p. 519). Cumulatively, this produced a situation where everyone may have been willing to fight, not because anyone wanted a war to happen but rather due to what Clark terms "a defensive patriotism":

> the aetiology of this conflict was so complex and so strange that it allowed soldiers and civilians in all the belligerent countries to be confident that theirs was a war of defence, that their countries had been provoked or attacked by a determined enemy, that their respective governments had made every effort to preserve the peace. (Clark, 2012, p. 553)

World War I, then, constitutes a powerful argument against any attempt to explain violence as a predictable outcome of the collective will.

4 Violence: How Collective Shocks Transform Social Practices 121

But, however important the case, one might object that it is unique, incomparable, unsuitable as the basis for a general argument. One might further object that World War I is the quintessential case of a war fought between national armies, led by a tiny elite through highly disciplined chains of command, and in that respect very different from cases of civil unrest, rebellion or communal violence, which rely much less on pre-existing forms of institutionalised hierarchy and order. It is therefore important to look more systematically at multiple cases, and to look at intrastate violence in particular, before drawing any conclusions about the respective roles of structural factors or root causes, on the one hand, and chains of events that develop a dynamic on their own, on the other.

In the early 1990s, Ted Gurr undertook just such a study in a quest to identify structural factors that can predict minority group collective action in its generality. The *Minorities at Risk* project involved expert coding of the behaviour of 227 "politicised communal groups" across 90 nations, during the entire period from 1945 to 1989. This huge and comprehensive data set allowed Gurr to ask questions such as: Are people more likely to join a collective struggle for rights when these rights are disrespected? Are groups that face greater disadvantage more likely to take violent action? The conclusion can briefly be summed up as 'yes and no'.

Yes, minority groups that face higher economic or political disadvantage are more likely to mobilise politically. They will raise grievances more often and initiate various forms of social protest. But no, there is no direct relationship between the magnitude of a group's disadvantage or experiences of discrimination, and the likelihood that this group will ever be involved in *violent* rebellion:

> Objective conditions (poverty, discriminatory treatment, loss of autonomy) determine the issues around which leaders are able to mobilize collective action. The greater the differentials between groups, the easier it is for leaders to recruit members of disadvantaged or threatened groups. During the mobilization process communal leaders give stronger voice to grievance (…) and commit their followers to strategies of protest or rebellion. But once a group is committed to a particular strategy, self-sustaining conflict dynamics tend to develop: fighting groups and their opponents get locked into action-reaction sequences from which it is difficult to escape. (Ted Gurr, 1993, p. 189)

Actually, Gurr found that a group's degree of organisation—cohesion and leadership—not its degree of disadvantage, predicted its likelihood of future rebellion. However, empirically, the most important predictor of violence had nothing to do with the disadvantaged group itself, but with its state environment: minorities facing more autocratic state structures and/or repressive state reactions to their grievances were more likely to take arms than minorities acting in circumstances offering more space to the non-violent voicing of grievances. Furthermore, the transnational environment in which groups act also appeared to play a role: other things being equal, minorities were more likely to rebel after 'twin groups' in other states had previously taken up arms or where rebellion among similar groups occurred more frequently in the larger region.

In other words, Gurr's monumental analysis shows that objective factors can tell us whether people are likely to set off down the path of protest (though even here, the process is not deterministic since such factors don't directly drive people to take to the streets, but rather constitute evidence that leaders can interpret in order to mobilise people for action). However, objective factors cannot say where people will end up once they have set off. And, as we have argued in general and as we also saw from Clark's analysis of the lead-up to World War I (which now we can see as exceptional by the magnitude of violence involved, but not by the process of escalation that led to this outcome), that is because of the interactive dynamics of collective action. Context impacts on the actions of one party, party A. But then the actions of party A are interpreted by party B, whose responses alter the context in which party A takes its subsequent actions—and so on (for a similar analysis of the escalation of violence within single events of collective action, see Drury & Reicher, 2009; Reicher & Hopkins, 1996).

Gurr's analysis therefore compels us to look at groups, states and their international environment as *systems* of collective actors whose respective course of action is dependent upon the strategies of each other actor in the system. It also highlights the fact that, when a certain point is reached in the dynamics of escalation, violent struggle tends to become *self-sustaining*: violence is driven by violence, not by the circumstances that initially led to the conflict.

When laying out a revised and more comprehensive version of his theory in *People versus States*, Gurr (2000) referred to the so-called chicken and egg issue in explaining the causes of ethno-political conflict (p. 74): on the one hand, group identities become 'salient' in part as a consequence of systematic disadvantage or state repression; on the other hand, the salience of group identities is a condition for group mobilisation and, possible, minority–majority conflict. The identification of 'root causes' to ethno-political conflicts is hence necessarily problematic. What appears as an independent causal factor in one specific analysis might become a dependent outcome, for example when the temporal scope of the analysis is broadened or shifted.

A similar argument can be made with regard to spatial context. An analysis focusing on a minority–majority dyad within a specific nation-state might conclude that the minority's radicalisation preceded a majority reaction. However, a broader trans-national focus might reveal that the radicalisation itself followed repression of a kindred group in a neighbouring state. More generally, Gurr (2000) re-asserted the importance of state, international and global contexts to explain minority group collective action. Interestingly, explanatory factors identified at each of these levels of analysis often have different effects on the empirical likelihood of non-violent protest on the one hand and on violent rebellion on the other. Democratic state regimes are more likely to face minority protest, but autocratic structures are more likely to face rebellion (p. 85). Spillover effects across trans-national communal groups increase the likely of rebellion, but not of protest (p. 91). Core nations in the world system, or nations that are closely connected to international governmental associations, are more likely to face protest, but peripheral or more isolated nations are more likely to face rebellion. All of these comparative findings speak against explanatory models that treat any specific form of collective action—notably collective violence—as explicable in similar terms to the occurrence of group mobilisation or intergroup conflict *per se*. As Ted Gurr put it:

> Understanding of ethnopolitical conflict that emphasize the supposedly crucial role of a single factor, such as historical animosities or cultural differences between groups, should be avoided. Such explanations usually become significant because they are invoked by contemporary ethnopolitical leaders seeking to mobilize public support, not because cultural or historical differences generate a primordial urge to conflict. (Gurr, 2000, p. 95)

4.4 Conclusion

In this chapter and the previous one, we have sought to disrupt the standard narrative according to which identities and violence (and also power—but we shall come to that in a moment) exist in a simple linear relationship. To put it at its simplest, identities (somehow) produce violence. Identity is productive and violence is produced. Our argument is that the relationship is much more nuanced, flexible and bi-directional. Accordingly, in the last chapter we concentrated on how identity is produced (as well as being productive) and in this chapter we have focused on how violence is productive (as well as being produced).

There have been three elements to our argument. The first has been to show how violence re-configures identities by re-configuring the social practices through which identities can be performed. The reason for this is to do with the way that violence so radically alters the contingencies of action. If I am aware that people defined in terms of membership of another ethnic group (say a Serb) have attacked someone because they were seen as a member of my ethnic group (say Muslim), can I take the risk that any other Serb may not also see me as a Muslim and attack me as such? Even if the probability is (at least initially) fairly low, for safety's sake, don't I have to ignore the fact that this Serb is also a worker, a father, a punk rocker and many other things besides, and act as if the ethnic identity is what counts? Because the costs of not taking them as a Serb and myself as a Muslim and getting it wrong (death) are incomparably more severe than taking them as a Serb and myself as a Muslim and getting that wrong (embarrassment).

What this example also tells us is that violence doesn't just change the identities we use; it closes down the possibilities of social practice and thereby limits the identities we can enact. Violence is therefore something that limits us, which takes particular identities that correspond to one mode of being and freezes them into our only possible ways of being.

The second element of the argument is that one doesn't need actual violence to freeze identities. The awareness of violence elsewhere, the memory of violence past and the anticipation of violence in future can become almost equally effective. It is important to clarify that this is not a reversion to the ancient hatreds argument. Rather, the representation of violence as something imminent always has to be actively mobilised by invoking certain versions of the past and something that is sustained by ongoing social practices.

Third, because of the way that violence transforms how people see themselves and others—and hence changes the way they value things and interpret events in the world—it is impossible to impose a simple narrative on events such that what the involved actors believed and desired at the start explains where they got to at the end. More simply, hunting for the root causes of violence is a futile exercise. The notion that an analysis of how violence came about provides us with an understanding of how to end violence is based on a misconception of the phenomenon. It ignores the fact that violence changes the social terrain. *The path in no longer exists as a path out.*

So, if the notion of a settled collective will to cause violence is so wrong and so unhelpful in explaining actual events, we must ask, like Gurr, why those involved in such conflicts so often invoke such a will? And, like Gurr, our answer is that invoking a popular will and claiming to act as representative of the popular will is a particularly potent means by which leaders can achieve influence. Moreover, by asserting a will to violence and by producing violence, leaders further solidify the identities they purport to represent. Violent conflict, as we have seen, is a particularly dreadful vehicle through which to make masses of people behave *as if* they accept the identities that are implied by the fighting. It is also a particularly effective vehicle through which to get people to stick together, venerate their leaders and stifle dissent.

In short, having previously challenged the argument that people are naturally inclined or programmed to always obey authority, we are now in a position to offer at least a partial answer to the question of when and why people sometimes obey authority. Consent has to be manufactured, and violence is a potent instrument for manufacturing consent.

One can only understand violence by bringing the role of activists and leaders in its manufacture out into the open. Where there is violence, we need to make political effort visible just as it seeks to make itself invisible. We need to bring the problem of power—how power is used to produce violence and how violence is used to produce power—to the forefront of our analysis. That is what the next chapter is about.

References

Arian, A. (2012). *A portrait of Israeli Jews: Beliefs, observance, and values of Israeli Jews, 2009.* Jerusalem: The Israel Democracy Institute and the AVI CHAI—Israel Foundation.

Baron, S. W. (1969). *A social and religious history of the Jews.* New York: Columbia University Press.

Bar-Tal, D., & Antebi, D. (1992). Beliefs about negative intentions of the world: A study of the Israeli siege mentality. *Political Psychology, 13*(4), 633–645.

Bergier, R. (2002). *La Suisse, le national-socialisme et la Seconde Guerre mondiale.* Zurich: Pendo.

Billig, M. (1995). *Banal nationalism.* London: Sage Publications Ltd.

Calder, A. (1992). *The People's War.* London: Pimlico.

Clack, B., Dixon, J. A., & Tredoux, C. (2005). Eating together apart: Patterns of segregation in a multiethnic cafeteria. *Journal of Community and Applied Social Psychology, 14*, 1–16.

Clark, C. (2012). *The sleepwalkers: How Europe went to war in 1914.* London: Penguin.

Davis, T. (2007). *Stages of emergency. Cold war nuclear civil defence.* London: Duke University Press.

Dixon, J., Reicher, S. D., & Foster, D. (1997). Ideology, geography, racial exclusion: The squatter camp as 'blot on the landscape'. *Text: An Interdisciplinary Journal for the Study of Discourse, 17*(3), 317–348.

Dixon, J., & Durrheim, K. (2003). Contact and the ecology of racial division: Some varieties of informal segregation. *British Journal of Social Psychology, 42*(1), 1–23.

Drury, J., & Reicher, S. D. (2009). Collective psychological empowerment as a model of social change: Researching crowds and power. *Journal of Social Issues, 65*, 707–726.

Durrheim, K., & Dixon, J. A. (2001). The role of place and metaphor in racial exclusion: South Africa's beaches as sites of shifting racialisation. *Ethnic and Racial Studies, 24*, 433–450.

Eckhardt, A. R. (1992). *Sitting in the earth and laughing.* London: Transaction Publishers.

Fukuyama, F. (1992). *The end of history and the last man.* London: Penguin Books.

Gurr, T. R. (1993). Why minorities rebel: A global analysis of communal mobilization and conflict since 1945. *International Political Science Review, 14*(2), 161–201.

Gurr, T. R. (2000). *Peoples versus states: Minorities at risk in the new century.* Washington, DC: US Institute of Peace Press.

Hobsbawm, E. J. (1994). *The age of extremes: A history of the world, 1914–1991.* New York: Pantheon Books.

Huntington, S. P. (1996). *The class of civilizations and the remaking of World order.* New Dehli: Penguin Books India.

Kaplan, R. D. (1993). *Balkan ghosts: A journey through history.* New York: Picador.

Klar, Y., Schori-Eyal, N., & Klar, Y. (2013). The "Never Again" state of Israel: The emergence of the Holocaust as a core feature of Israeli identity and its four incongruent voices. *Journal of Social Issues, 69,* 125–143.

Maček, I. (2009). *Sarajevo under siege: Anthropology in wartime.* Pennsylvania: University of Pennsylvania Press.

O'Brien, A. (2001). *Against normalization: Writing radical democracy in South Africa.* London: Duke University Press.

Petersen, R. D. (2002). *Understanding ethnic violence: Fear, hatred, and resentment in twentieth-century Eastern Europe.* Cambridge: Cambridge University Press.

Reicher, S., & Hopkins, N. (1996). Self-category constructions in political rhetoric; An analysis of Thatcher's and Kinnock's speeches concerning the British miners' strike (1984–5). *European Journal of Social Psychology, 26*(3), 353–371.

Therborn, G. (1982). *The ideology of power and the power of ideology.* London: Verso.

Zweig, S. (1944/1997). *Die Welt von Gestern. Erinnerungen eines Europäers.* Frankfurt am Main: Fischer.

5

Power: The Role of Leadership at Critical Junctures

In one way or another we have addressed the issue of power repeatedly throughout the last two chapters. For while we may make analytic distinctions between identity, violence and power in order to help lay out our argument, and while our method of exposition so far has been to put the focus on each term in turn, the core point is that the three are systemically interlinked such that to address any one of them is necessarily to invoke the other two. In the present chapter, then, power moves from the background to centre stage. In so doing, the chapter ties the various elements of our argument together, until we effectively end up back at our point of departure—looking at the production of identities.

In Chap. 3, we challenged those approaches which take identity as a given, as fixed and as invariant, and instead developed an understanding of identity as rooted in social practice. This then allows us to understand how our sense of self shifts as the options and organisation of social practice differ from place to place, and from time to time. But equally, changing definitions of identity impact the nature and organisation of social practice. When people define themselves as members of

© The Author(s) 2017
G. Elcheroth, S. Reicher, *Identity, Violence and Power*,
DOI 10.1057/978-1-137-31728-5_5

a common social category, they are brought to act together on the basis of common values, interests and goals. They are able to coordinate and to support each other in reaching those goals. Identities, then, produce social power.

Therein lies the reason why elites in particular spend so much time in seeking to shape identities. Those who are in a position to define who we are, what we value, what we desire and aspire to, and what we must do in order to realise our aspirations, thereby create a world-making force and put themselves in a position to wield it (see Reicher & Hopkins, 2001). This makes the question of how one can make one version of categories and identities stick, and marginalise all alternatives, a central one for both theorists and practitioners.

In Chap. 4, our argument was that violence is one such means—and a dreadfully efficient one. When violence divides people on the basis of particular social identities, it becomes risky to act on the basis of any other categories, sometimes even long after the violence has stopped. It makes alternatives difficult in practice. Therefore, when the group is under threat, it becomes easier for elites to eliminate dissent and demand that the entire group rallies around them. Perhaps the most baleful example of this is the decision of the 10th Congress of the Russian Communist Party in 1921—in the midst of the civil war—to ban all factions and suppress any opposition to the leadership. It is worth quoting from Lenin's opening speech to the Congress on 8th March:

> discussion means disputes; disputes mean discord; discord means that the Communists have become weak; press hard, seize the opportunity, take advantage of their weakening. This has become the slogan of the hostile world. We must not forget this for a moment … Our efforts should be more united and harmonious than ever before; there should not be the slightest trace of factionalism—whatever its manifestations in the past. That we must not have on any account. That is the only condition on which we shall accomplish the immense tasks that confront us.[1]

---

[1] Retrieved on 28th June 2016 from https://www.marxists.org/archive/lenin/works/1921/10thcong/ch01.htm.

5 Power: The Role of Leadership at Critical Junctures

So, if it is true that identities are mobilised because they are the basis of power, it might equally be true that the importance of violence in producing and freezing identities is tied to the consequences in terms of consolidating power.

In both of the previous two chapters, our argument has been premised on the ways in which power—and particularly the power of elites—is produced through violence and identity. Having shown this, in this chapter we now look at the ways in which elites use their existing power in order to organise, enable or incite violence, and thereby consolidate their power for the future. Specifically, we discuss three ways in which leaders can affect the occurrence of violence and use it for their own political ends: by directly ordering violence, by avoiding measures to stop violence or by creating a climate where violence appears unavoidable. While the first two paths refer to the explicit power of leaders in an institutional command structure, allowing them to create violent facts by commission or by omission, the third path is special insofar as it refers to leaders' symbolic power. That is, it has to do with their capacity to invoke violence as a plausible scenario and to do so in ways that make the actual occurrence of violence more likely.

Before starting this discussion, it is important to identify two potential traps. The first is the replacement of one form of fatalism with another: to swap the claim that groups can't help harming each other because it is in their nature with the claim that leaders can't help abusing their power because that is in the nature of power. The second is to go to the opposite extreme and to assume that, rather than being completely predetermined, the exercise of power is completely undetermined, as if leaders respond to each new set of events from scratch, with no preconceptions or prior constraints. To avoid both traps, we will follow our discussion of how leaders can promote violence with a consideration of the ways in which long-term legacies both facilitate and constrain the ways in which leaders can act. These histories provide a cumulative and large stock of cards which leaders can choose to play (or not to play) when dealing with events in the present. These choices are important, and leaders can take different paths. But the stock of cards is still limited and so are the paths down which leaders can take us.

5.1 Repressive Power: Making Violence Happen

When NATO started its bombing campaign against Serbia in March 1999, it led to the longest suspension of public protest against President Milosevic for years. Far from turning a demoralised public against its leader—as Western strategists (at least officially) expected—the bombs actually brought the Serbian people "unity from heaven", as the *New York Times* ironically commented (quoted by Mandić, 2008, p. 25). This unity did not simply express itself by a suspension of regime-critical collective action in Serbia. On the contrary, Mandić identified an impressive 313 events (rallies, marches, riots, concerts …) during the 11 weeks of the bombing campaign. Overwhelmingly, these were public expressions of *support* for the domestic regime. Most importantly, these supportive demonstrations were as frequent in municipalities where oppositional parties prevailed as elsewhere. As Mandić (2008, p. 36) puts it: "The war, it seems, suspended internal divisions and encouraged unified support for the state, at least provisionally". After this episode, which was the only time during the 1990s when the war was actually fought on the territory of Serbia proper, it took months before the opposition could again organise effective mobilisations against the regime. Milosevic remained in power until October 2000, benefiting from the one last moratorium on challenges to his weakened regime which had been brought about by the NATO intervention.

The Serbian public's reaction to NATO bombings is far from an exception. As early as 1964, Nelson Polsby gathered anecdotal evidence for so-called rally effects in the USA. He concluded that, in times of war, conflict and crisis, popular responses to the president are invariably favourable, "regardless of the wisdom of the policies he pursued" (p. 25). Soon, this claim was to be backed up by more systematic data (e.g., Mueller, 1970). In 1978, Kernell showed how temporal fluctuations in US presidential popularity from Truman to Nixon were systematically structured, among other factors, by the wars the nation had fought. War entry typically provoked substantive short-term increases in the president's popularity—but then this support progressively declined due to the negative effects of mounting war fatalities on public support.

For decades, these findings set the benchmark for the way social scientists looked at rally effects. However, in 2001, the field was shaken by the work of Baker and Oneal (2001). Using a broader set of variables and more flexible techniques of data analyses, they dismissed the popular notion of invariable, spontaneous and almost mechanical rally effects when a nation goes to war. Instead, they pointed to the critical importance of political communication. Rally effects are likely when the US government actively prosecuted a foreign military campaign and when presidential statements and/or prominent media coverage drew attention to and supported the conflict.

Analyses of rally effects in the UK, conducted by Lai and Reiter (2005), similarly suggested that the variability of public reactions to international crises may have been strongly under-estimated. While these authors did find substantial rally effects for both the Falkland and Gulf wars, they failed to do so for the Korean, Suez and Kosovo wars, as well as for the generality of non-violent crises in which Britain was involved. These findings led Lai and Reiter to conclude that "rallies seem most likely and largest after the nation has been clearly attacked or challenged and when vital national values are at stake, although admittedly it is difficult to delineate uncontroversially what is and is not the national interest" (p. 266). Their conclusion therefore leaves open the key question of when 'the national interest' is perceived to be under threat (and why support for the nation's leadership is perceived as an appropriate means of containing the threat).

In sum, the political pay-offs of conflict are not as reliable or as durable as once thought. But nor are they negligible. With astute communication, the outbreak of war can boost internal political support for two to three months (e.g., Lai & Reiter, 2005). Whether that pay-off is sufficient is a highly political question. A year after NATO bombed Serbia, Milosevic was out of power, ending his days in a prison cell in The Hague. Did the few months breathing space he was accorded in 2000 make any difference to his regime? Equally, did the few months after the invasion of Iraq in 2003, in which the British public rallied around Tony Blair (as we shall discuss in more detail in Chap. 8), count for anything compared to the years of public outcry which eventually forced him to resign in 2007?

A tentative answer is that these periods, as fleeting as they might be, are of particular importance because they provide leaders with formidable windows of opportunity to create new and irreversible facts, and that these windows are of particular importance at times of social and political flux. In a stable period, then, three months support for a lifetime of political exile might seem a poor bargain. But as old regimes are disintegrating and new entities are coming into being, a short time may be sufficient to alter the course of history. Then, the rally effects of war may prove critical in allowing political elites to create new social facts that pursue their own agenda. In the Serbian case, Gagnon (2004) has argued that the different wars it had been involved in during the 1990s bought the elite the time that they needed in order to convert their privileged party position in a collapsing socialist state to a privileged economic position in an emergent capitalist state. In such a period of rapid transition, by the time the rally effects had begun to fade, the old apparatchiks had emerged as the new entrepreneurs.

Just as short-term rally effects can prove valuable in times of transition, it is arguable that they are equally valuable in times of trouble. That is, weakened leaders might be especially tempted to deliberately use armed conflict to divert attention from their bad handling of state affairs, increase their popularity, marginalise their opponents and generally restore their chances of remaining in power. This *diversionary war hypothesis* has received considerable attention among analysts of international relations. Attempts to test the hypothesis have produced mixed findings, however. While single cases can be found in which domestic political motives seem to explain a rush to war, systematic comparative studies suggest either that the magnitude of internal problems is unrelated to the likelihood that a state will go to war (Levy, 1989, 1998), or that there is a relationship, but it has little to do with a motivation to divert public attention (Gleditsch, Salehyan, & Schultz, 2008).

However, there is one notable exception to this general (lack of) pattern: time-series analyses focusing on the USA have shown that the country did go to war significantly more often in periods where the incumbent administration was economically unsuccessful or when the president was losing popular support in public opinion polls (James & Oneal, 1991; Ostrom & Job, 1986).

As disappointing as the lack of more consistent findings might be, there are a series of rather simple reasons why seeking domestic support through foreign war is an implausible phenomenon within the current interstate system. Given that positive rally effects are generally short-lived and that they are generally overtaken by the negative impact of mounting casualties, going to war against another state is only likely to bring very short-lived political rewards to the elite, except when a rapid and successful campaign can be expected. But very few states have the means to attack another and count on a quick military victory, or have the political and diplomatic resources to ensure that an attack will not provoke international sanctions or even military intervention against them.

If one adds to this the fact that even short-term rally effects are unlikely in regimes whose leaders either have not been legitimated by general elections (Gelpi, 1997) or which are facing strong separatist tendencies (due to the fact that much of the population may not see the conflict as their own—see Chap. 8), then the range of state governments that are in a position to expect rewards from diversionary interstate warfare becomes remarkably small. The USA might be democratic, united and, above all, militarily strong enough to be in that position, but few others are.

At this point it is worth emphasising that the arguments do not apply to the diversionary war hypothesis in general, but specifically to diversionary *foreign* wars. It is ironic, then, that most investigations of the hypothesis are limited to such cases. One exception to this is the work of Tir and Jasinski (2008). They have pointed out a number of good reasons why weakened leaders might be much more tempted to direct diversionary violence against minority groups *within* a country, rather than against other countries. First, there is generally no shortage of potential targets. Virtually every country in the world has minorities and can invoke history to constitute that group as a current threat of some sort. Ethnic primordialists would probably agree with the statement that ethnic diversity and past ethnic conflict are ubiquitous realities across all nations. Constructivists might go even further and claim that the national 'stock' has no absolutely defined boundaries, which implies that the range of groups in a nation is theoretically infinite. All one has to do is invoke some arbitrary but shareable marker (dress, accent, appearance …) in order to identify a group as such. Even the dullest of governments should have the wit to single out some minority within the nation (in our current globalised world, immigrants always provide a handy candidate) and to associate them with some kind of negatively laden collective experience within the nation.

Second, the balance of power is almost inevitably in favour of the state. In our contemporary world of nations, the default condition (and normative assumption) is that nation-states, not non-state groups, control the material resources that are necessary to manage armed conflict.

Third, even if a minority finds a way to fight back, the imbalance in political, diplomatic and symbolic resources generally gives the advantage to states when it comes to the interpretation of the violent conflict, domestically as well as internationally. Foreign powers are generally more reluctant to intervene in a state's 'internal affairs' than in interstate conflict. To the extent that armed resistance or rebellion can be branded as 'terrorism', a state engaged in internal armed struggle might even be able to mobilise international support in its own favour.

Fourth, potential resistance to rally effects can be anticipated and countered by deliberately targeting dissenters as traitors or as 'enemies within'.

Overall, then, a range of considerations support the contention that war on internal enemies is more effective than war on external enemies as a means of suppressing dissent and enforcing conformity. To those already listed we can add one more, drawing on our theoretical discussion in Chap. 4: intrastate violence doesn't just create boundaries between people who might otherwise join forces against state authorities, it also creates a bunch of pretexts which require every citizen to behave *as if* the threat from the minority group were real, and the need for state protection was pressing.

So much for the conceptual arguments. What about the evidence? To test the domestic diversionary violence hypothesis, Tir and Jasinski (2008) combined Gurr's (1993, 2000) *Minorities at Risk* data set with the *Cross-National Time-Series Data Archive*, for the years from 1996 to 2002—the only period for which *Minorities at Risk* comprised complete enough data about the use of state force (defined in a wide sense from limited repression to fully fledged military attacks) against internal minorities. During this short period, the Israeli government used force against Palestinians, the Turkish government against Kurds, the Russian government against Chechens, the Spanish government against Basques and the Thai government against Muslims, all in periods of economic downturn and/or growing government unpopularity.

In an average year, across the entire world, more than one state in three used force at least once against one of the minority groups inventoried by Gurr. The frequency of this phenomenon alone can be taken as an indication of how easily state powers exploit their monopoly on the exercise of violence within the boundaries of their jurisdiction. But this still leaves the question of whether governments were more likely to use force against minorities when they faced domestic difficulties.

They clearly were. Even when other factors known to impact the likelihood of domestic violence were kept constant (the country's overall level of economic development, the government's military resources, the timing of elections, the involvement in ongoing armed conflict, the demographic strength of minority groups), governments were still more likely to use force against minorities in years during which their country was experiencing either an economic downturn or political unrest, in the form of protests, strikes or riots. Both factors had significant independent net effects. That is, either economic downturn *or* political unrest alone was sufficient to increase the risk of violence against minorities. It is also noteworthy that the statistical effects are considerable but not extreme in size: the risk of violence against minorities increased by more than 50 % between the lowest and the highest observed values of either economic downturn or political unrest. The effect is therefore too big to occur by chance, but too small to allow for a deterministic interpretation of the phenomenon. Governments facing economic downturns or political unrest will *not inevitably* target ethnic minorities to divert public attention. Such violence is only one out of many possible strategies to counter the erosion of political support and among those states that were in such a situation between 1995 and 2002, many did opt for a different course of action.

5.2 Structural Power: Letting Violence Happen

The use of overt state force against minority groups is the most direct but not the only way in which calculations and decisions by state officials impact the occurrence of violence against minorities. Sometimes the decision *not* to act can be just as consequential as the decision to act. The critical question is not only to know when those who control repressive forces will actively intervene to create violence, but also when they will let violence develop by choosing not to intervene in order to stop it. Studies of so-called ethnic riots illustrate this point.

These riots are generally thought of as spontaneous outbursts of violence, fuelled by popular anger. When violent mobs appear to spontaneously attack, injure and kill members of different ethnic groups, this is often used as unarguable evidence for deeply ingrained ethnic resentments which lie at the base of collective violence. Certainly, it is largely because ethnic riots are *interpreted* in this way that they create and freeze ethnic oppositions for the long term. How could people continue to engage with neighbours of different ethnicity once these people have shown their 'true colours' by participating in bloody riots?

However, such a perspective overlooks three important aspects of rioting. The first is simply that bloody riots are very rarely spontaneous, even if described as such. Rioting, like any collective action that requires a tight synchronisation of the behaviours of many individuals, presupposes some degree of coordination and common background knowledge (e.g., 'they have committed an outrage against us', 'they have attacked us')—which begs the question of where that knowledge comes from and provides space for it to be manipulated.

Second, the application of an ethnic frame to a riot often occurs after the event, and not during it. As Ramanathapillai (2006) has shown with anti-Tamil riots in Sri Lanka, complex and chaotic events are retrospectively simplified and structured throughout politicised memories: "Particular memories are selected, kept alive, and retold as a collective way of understanding and relating the experience (…) For example, at the time of the riots the stories of Sinhalese atrocities were widely told, yet the stories of Sinhalese protecting Tamils were not retold in Tamil political narratives" (p. 4).

Third, and perhaps most critically, the assumed relationship between the intensity of popular anger and degree of violence in ethnic riots is largely unfounded. Whether people are harmed in such riots—and, if so, how many—rarely depends on the size or determination of the crowd itself. It is generally much more a function of how state forces manage the situation. Such is the conclusion reached by Wilkinson (2007) after extensive research into ethnic riots in many historic and contemporary

5 Power: The Role of Leadership at Critical Junctures 139

sites, stretching from mid-nineteenth century anti-Catholic riots in the North of Ireland to riots against minorities across post-communist States in the late twentieth century:

> In virtually all the empirical cases I have examined, whether violence is bloody or ends quickly depends not on the local factors that caused violence to break out but primarily on the will and capacity of the government that controls the forces of law and order. Abundant comparative evidence shows that large-scale ethnic rioting does not take place where a state's army or police force is ordered to stop it using all means necessary. (Wilkinson, 2007, p. 5)

The bulk of Wilkinson's analytic effort then goes into disentangling the relative contributions of 'will' and 'capacity' in the governments that control repressive forces, with a focus on the states of twentieth-century India. A first set of analyses led the author to rule out 'capacity' as a critical variable in this context:

> Independent inquiries and newspaper investigations into the worst outbreaks of Hindu-Muslim violence have found that in almost all cases local police officers and magistrates had the forces available to prevent violence (or could have quickly called them in) but that they failed to take preventive action, either because of direct orders from their political masters or because they feared retribution if they acted without first seeking political approval. (Wilkinson, 2007, pp. 94–95)

That leaves 'will'. Wilkinson's analyses combine a variety of factors in order to predict the number of Hindu–Muslim riots in each state of India, for each month from 1961 to 1995. While controlling for a series of factors—demographics, economics and also the occurrence of past violence—ethnic riots were much more likely when state elections were to take place in the ensuing six months compared to when there was no ongoing electoral campaign. The risk of riots was reduced by a factor of four when the Communist party—which draws on electoral support *across* ethnic communities—was in power. The risk increased when the Congress party, whose political support is concentrated within the Hindu electorate, was in power. Furthermore, the risk of riots was only half as high in contexts split into multiple groups than in those split more cleanly into two groups. Together, these various findings suggest politicians were much more easily tempted to let ethnic violence occur when the resulting ethnic divisions could bring them victory in upcoming elections. Conversely, they were more motivated to suppress potential violence when electoral success was contingent upon building cross-ethnic coalitions with smaller minority parties.

5.3 Symbolic Power: Inciting Others to Make Violence Happen

There is a third way in which those who have (or contend for) political power can influence the occurrence of collective violence. In addition to deciding whether or not to order violence, or whether or not to let it happen, in their daily business they also face a seemingly much more trivial, but sometimes just as consequential, choice: whether to *invoke* violence or not. On 28 June 1989, Slobodan Milosevic chose 'invoke':

> The lack of unity and betrayal in Kosovo will continue to follow the Serbian people like an evil fate through the whole of its history (…) Six centuries later, now, we are being again engaged in battles and are facing battles. They are not armed battles, although such things cannot be excluded yet. However, regardless of what kind of battles they are, they cannot be won without resolve, bravery, and sacrifice, without the noble qualities that were present here in the field of Kosovo in the days past. (Slobodan Milosevic, 28 June 1989)

As always, the context of the speech is as important as its content. On the 600th anniversary of the mythicised 'battle of Kosovo', Milosevic's party had bussed no fewer than a million Serbs to the historic battlefield so as to commemorate the event. This unprecedented mass gathering was probably meant to signify to each single participant how important the event was to them as a whole. Whether or not the defeat previously had any significance to those present, it now came to function as a common background knowledge that no one could ignore. According to the speech that they all heard together, the reason why their people had suffered defeat 600 years ago was that there had been traitors in their midst. The reason why they had to stand together now—literally and metaphorically—was that the 'lack of unity and betrayal' that once brought an 'evil fate' to them could under no circumstances be tolerated again.

United to face whom? Milosevic did not name current enemies, but in the fourteenth century these had been foreign invaders of Muslim faith. The medieval battle provides the context and pretext to refer to current battles—and to specify that *armed* battles "cannot be excluded yet". The statement that "regardless of what kind of battles they are, they cannot be won without resolve, bravery, and sacrifice" clearly signifies that Serbs are expected to be prepared for *all kinds* of battles. Two years after the speech, Serbs were fighting in Croatia against Croatian Catholics, the following year they were fighting in Bosnia against Bosnian Muslims and by the end of the decade in Kosovo against Albanian Muslims. Milosevic's sinister prophecy had materialised more fully than the deepest pessimists could have imagined in 1989. Would that have come to pass had there not been a million Serbs—and beyond them, millions of people across Yugoslavia and further afield—to hear the prophecy?

What we are saying here is that Milosevic was in the game of generating a 'self-fulfilling prophecy'—a term initially coined by Merton (1948), which he himself labelled the 'Thomas theorem', in homage to early twentieth-century sociologist William I. Thomas: "If men define situations as real, they are real in their consequences". The first example given by Merton to illustrate the theorem remains as timely in the early twenty-first century as it was in the mid-twentieth century: a bank becomes insolvent when its customers believe it is insolvent. Or, to be more precise, insolvency results when a critical mass of customers does what would be rational if the belief were to be true: they withdraw their money from the bank. This behaviour will then lead others to believe that the bank faces liquidity problems—or that it might be led to face them if other people continue to behave this way—and hence to withdraw their own money. At a certain point the assumption that the bank faces some problems *becomes* true (no matter how false it might have been before).

Rumours can thereby create the realities they invoke, provided they reach a critical mass of people and that there is a clear rationale for each of them to act *as if* the belief was true. Whenever rumours do not arise by chance or accident, but because they serve the prophet's interests, self-fulfilling prophecies can be seen as a process of effective mass manipulation. In part, this effectiveness is due to the fact that it is hard to denounce claims which seem to be proven true by the course of events:

> The self-fulfilling prophecy is, in the beginning, a false definition of the situation evoking a new behaviour which makes the originally false conception come true. The specious validity of the self-fulfilling prophecy perpetuates a reign of error. For the prophet will cite the actual course of events as proof that he was right from the very beginning. (Merton, 1948, p. 193)

When it comes to collective violence, however, there are two ways in which the metaphor of the prophet can be misleading. A first problem derives from the singular form. War-mongering policymakers are not isolated prophets. Their prophecies become social facts only by being repeated by those who share their interests or obey their orders. A second problem is that policymakers do not just sit back, contemplate the world and comment on it. Precisely because they act collectively, there can be a division of labour between those who spread the word and those who go further in making the prophecy become true. While one part of the elite might refer to violence only in words, others might invoke it in more practical ways—for example, by provoking alleged enemies into a violent response.

Events preceding the start of the so-called second *intifada* vividly illustrate both points. Bar-Tal (2004) has documented how domestic public opinion evolved among Israeli Jews in the period from the Camp David peace talks in summer 2000 to the resurgence of armed conflict with Palestinians by the end of the same year. In Israeli public discourse, the failure of the peace talks was immediately portrayed as hard evidence for lack of genuine will on the Palestinian side to reach an agreement with Israel. But in summer 2000, the prophets of war had not yet achieved a consensus around their version of reality. In public opinion polls, one participant out of two still expressed support for the peace process. Despite all that their elites said, 49 % of respondents still held firm and supported the Oslo agreement on 26–27 September. This figure would go into free fall over the following days.

On 2nd October it had dropped already to 41 %. What had happened during the five days in between? On 28 September, Ariel Sharon, then leader of the conservative opposition, visited the Temple Mount in Jerusalem—a sacred site in both Muslim and Jewish traditions—and provoked fury among Palestinian onlookers. Demonstrators started throwing stones. The Israeli security forces responded forcefully. In the following four days, riots took the lives of 45 people. Now the political narrative of aggressive Palestinians could be supplemented and seemingly confirmed by images of violent crowds. The notion that Palestinians want to make war on Israel rather than make peace appeared to be validated by the events. By 2002, after two years of violence, the proportion of Israeli Jews who still supported the Oslo peace process had fallen to a mere 25 %.

5.4 Past Legacies and Present Crises

In this last example, we can see how a previous discourse (Palestinians are dangerous) gains traction in the context of a new crisis (the outbreak of the second *intifada*)—or, to put things the other way round, how the existing discourse provides a frame for interpreting and responding to the newer event. Here, the older and the newer refer to a short timescale of months. But the same processes operate over much more extended timescales, and indeed—thinking back to our discussion of past violence in the previous chapter—the notion of Palestinians as dangerous after Oslo fits into the much longer tradition whereby the Jewish people are invited to see themselves as continuously under threat of destruction from their foes.

In effect, the priming of public opinion rarely starts from a blank slate. The architects of violence never invent the fears that they invoke from scratch. They work with building blocks that are already available, and have, in many cases, been available for a very long time. Let us therefore complete this chapter with three examples that show how the exercise of power is embedded into multiple layers of history that span the years, the decades and even the centuries.

Our first example concerns the political climate surrounding the policy that, arguably, has had the most far-reaching implications for the current world order: the 'war on terror' led by successive US presidents. The obvious turning point, which generated public support for this war, was the attack on New York's twin towers on 9/11/2001. For many, the events of that day were quite sufficient to generate martial policies over the ensuing years. But would these events have had quite so quick and so clear an impact on US society and US policy had they not served to confirm anxious expectations nourished well before?

In a public opinion poll conducted in 1986, 80 % of US citizens considered the danger of terrorism as 'extreme', and terrorism came out as people's prime concern (Zulaika, 2003). This was not only well before 9/11 but also before the major terrorist incidents that preceded it—the bombing of the World Trade Centre in 1993 and the Oklahoma bombing of 1995. Indeed, only 17 people had been killed in terrorist attacks across the entire USA over the previous five years compared to the approximately 150,000 people who had been killed through non-terrorist violence over the same period. To feed this concern, no less than 1322 books on terrorism were published in the USA between 1989 and 1992 according to Zulaika (2003)—again, before any major terrorist incident had taken place.

These figures illustrate that a 'terrorist frame' was highly available to the US public long before mass terrorism actually struck the country. The 2001 attacks did not create this frame, but they validated it in the most dramatic way. The subsequent funerals, remembrance ceremonies and collective mourning then provided numerous opportunities to rehearse the new patriotic script.

The rest of the story is well known: during the last months of 2001, George Bush benefited from an outstanding rally effect, and his administration seized the opportunity to frame subsequent military campaigns overseas, and restrictions of civil rights at home, as part of the 'war on terror'. When Bush announced the start of the war against Iraq to the US public on 18 March 2003, he was able to refer to terrorism and so-called terror states as inescapable realities: "The cause of peace requires all free nations to recognize new and undeniable realities (…) a policy of appeasement could bring destruction of a kind never before seen on this earth".

Our second example concerns the single most horrific outburst of violence in recent history: the Rwandan genocide of 1994, and its long-term roots in colonial policies of divide and rule. In a remarkable historic analysis, Mamdani (2001) traces back the long path from colonialism to genocide. While acknowledging the fact that the genocide was orchestrated by a small elite, as an extreme means of achieving their political ends in the present, Mamdani argues that looking backwards is necessary to understand the responses of ordinary people which were critical to its implementation: "If the violence from below could not have spread without cultivation and direction from above, it is equally true that the conspiracy of the tiny fragment of génocidaires could not have succeeded had it not found resonance from below" (p. 7).

In Rwanda, as elsewhere, European colonisers had granted a series of privileges to a minority, as a tactic to divide the colonised and to stabilise the power of the colonisers. In doing so, they not only relied on existing ethnic groups, but also creatively constituted groups that echoed their own racist ideology and which they used to legitimise social hierarchy under colonial order. It was in this context that a myth concerning the foreign ancestry of Tutsi people was created and associated with their role in the colonial administration and society. The construction of an ethnic minority group, and the combination of privilege and alien status conferred upon it, encouraged the Hutu majority to re-direct the grievances and the hostility created by colonial cruelty towards the local Tutsi minority. This then laid the ground for future calamities, once power relations shifted in favour of the Hutu, in the wake of decolonisation. Mamdani explains:

> To understand the logic of genocide (…) it is necessary to think through the political world that colonialism set into motion. This was the world of the settler and the native, a world organized around a binary preoccupation that was as compelling as it was confining. It is in this context that Tutsi, a group with a privileged relationship to power before colonialism, got constructed as a privileged alien settler presence, first by the

great nativist revolution of 1959, and then by Hutu Power propaganda after 1990. (Mamdani, 2001, p. 14)

The third example takes us much further back into the past, to the European medieval societies of the twelfth and thirteenth centuries. Moore (2007) has identified this as a time when sporadic acts of persecution were transformed into mechanisms that were a matter of policy, were made systematic and became universally available. It was also a time when a set of ideological justifications for persecution were developed. In the process, the practice of persecution became largely independent from the specific characteristics of any given targeted group, or from the particular danger they were supposed to represent. The *persecuting society* was born, with the "creation (…) of a single account of the victim as enemy of God and society, which might be transferred at will to any object, either as a class of persons already existing, such as Jews, whom might seem desirable or convenient to persecute, or a new one, such as sodomites or witches, which by an act of classification might be invented for the purpose" (p. 160).

If it is independent of the characteristics of the victims, the phenomenon has to be related rather to the motives of the persecutors and/or to the functioning of society at large. The core of Moore's argument is precisely that the persecuting society came into being at the same point in time as new elite groups arose, and sought to strengthen their power. It emerged in a historic transition period, during which the relationships between states and subjects were being redefined, and emerging bureaucracies controlled ever more domains of people's lives ever more closely. These societal changes generated the need to justify more intrusive centralised powers, at the same time as they generated a new class of people ready to do the job:

> a new class of functionaries—clerics and courtiers, for whom persecution might serve the twin purposes of providing the means to extend the power and advance the interests of their masters, while consolidating their own positions and undermining potential rivals. The systematic persecution of minorities in European history had its origin in the interests and concerns of this body of people, and not in the unregulated passions or prejudices of the populations at large. (pp. 144–45)

5 Power: The Role of Leadership at Critical Junctures 147

Obviously, it is not enough to refer to a tradition of persecution invented in medieval times, or to the legacy of colonial brutality during the past two centuries, to explain violent clashes in the twenty-first century. But neither is it enough to refer to contextual changes in the present, deriving from the end of the Cold War and the growth of violent non-state actors. The question is, when we face new times and new crises, how do we make sense of them? Here, this historically stratified stock of explanations constitutes a set of tools which facilitate sense-making and which provide resources to elites in providing accounts that are instrumental in expanding or protecting their influence.

To be more concrete, in the first chapter we referred to Brubaker and Laitin's (1998) argument that in the post-Cold War area, incentives for ideological conflict frames have vanished and incentives for ethnic conflict frames have increased: trans-national diasporic communities have replaced ideological blocs as reservoirs of support, and the institutionalisation of a new generation of human rights makes it more likely that a plea for the respect of community rights will be heard and legitimised in the international arena. In the process, ethnic frames have become highly available. We have grown used to viewing the world through an ethnic prism and, moreover, we expect others to do likewise. So ethnic histories can be invoked as a resource by powerful elite groups as they seek to unite the population around their leadership, claiming a common destiny and interest with the majority (even if these do not share their interests) in opposing a dangerous minority (who are not essential to their political capital).

The key terms in this argument have to do with words like 'invoked', 'tools' and 'resource'. History has to be brought into the present, and this is done selectively as a means of advancing political projects. Moreover, it is not entirely necessary to use accounts of the present rooted in the existing historical repertoire. Human ingenuity and imagination always allows us to come up with new ways of seeing. However, as with building a house, if you have to create your own building blocks, it will necessarily require more effort and take longer than using blocks that are already available. So it will be a harder task, and in fast-moving periods of crisis, time in particular may be of the essence. Those who use accounts that are more immediately intelligible and familiar will always start with an advantage.

In sum, past legacies should be seen as part and parcel of the active exercise of power. History does not entomb us, it does not condemn us to repeating past mistakes, it does not substitute for agency. Rather, invoking history is one of the principal ways in which people exercise their agency.

5.5 Conclusion

In much analysis, antagonisms, hatreds and violence between people are treated as errors, the result of inherent biases over which we have no control, something we do not actively intend. Sometimes those biases are attributed to the personalities of particular individuals, sometimes to aspects of the psyche which we all have in common, sometimes to histories we cannot escape. There is a plethora of such approaches for which the worst of our actions derive from a fatal flaw in the human condition—something we may all regret but for which no one can be held accountable.

This chapter has challenged that viewpoint. We have started from the premise that violence doesn't 'just happen'. It is made to happen. And we look at the various ways in which elites can deliberately, knowingly and systematically act to produce violence. Most directly, those who control the state apparatus can use state forces to instigate violence, particularly against internal minorities. Less directly, they can prevent state forces from intervening when members of the majority take it upon themselves to attack the minority—thus both sending a signal that violence is deemed permissible and making the expression of violence practically possible. Least directly, leaders can incite the population to violence both by words and acts—and most effectively by combining the two. That is, certain groups can be portrayed as a threat and then provoked to anger so as to create a consonance between discourse and reality. In laying out these three paths to violence, we don't suggest any priority between them or indeed that in practice they can be clearly separated out. For instance (as we will see in the case of India which forms the focus of the next chapter), one may both instigate violence in the population and then ensure that the police stand by and let pogroms proceed.

This chapter has also addressed the tricky and nuanced issue of the relevance of the past to the present—seeking to navigate the narrow channel between historical determinism (past events are recapitulated in the present) and historical amnesia (past events are irrelevant to the present). Our argument has been that the past is important insofar as it is *made relevant* to the present. This isn't automatic: which past events are made relevant and how they are interpreted is an active choice.

So now, we have arrived full circle. Going backwards from the end we return to the start of our argument: leaders use their power to create violence because violence is a particularly effective way of freezing people into identities, and because the construction of identity is the source of political authority and power. We have chosen to outline our argument in a particular order, starting with identity, then looking at violence and finishing with power. But that is an analytic choice. In fact there is no starting point or end point to the process. One could enter or leave at any point, and each term is both input and output to the others. Or at least that is true in principle. In different societies at different times, identities will be more or less set or fluid, violence will be more or less endemic, the power of elites will be more or less established. Equally, then, the concrete political opportunities, pay-offs and risks associated with mobilising along ethnic or cultural lines—and their perception by elite groups—vary across time and place. This means that, if we want to study them, we need to take context seriously and to examine the relevant processes by reference to specific contexts.

Our conclusions, then, are not just theoretical but methodological as well. We have got just about as far as we can by taking a general comparative approach to the analysis. To progress further we need to look at particular cases and to develop new methods for the analysis of case histories, which concentrate on critical junctures where the world is in flux and can develop along several radically opposed paths. We need to examine the role of violence in determining which path is taken. We also need to examine the role of leadership in these processes. The third part of the book will now be devoted to three such case studies, and to the development of a methodological approach suitable to their analysis.

References

Baker, W. D., & Oneal, J. R. (2001). Patriotism or opinion leadership? The nature and origins of the "rally "round the flag" effect". *Journal of Conflict Resolution, 45*(5), 661–687.

Bar-Tal, D. (2004). The necessity of observing real life situations: Palestinian-Israeli violence as a laboratory for learning about social behaviour. *European Journal of Social Psychology, 34*(6), 677–701.

Brubaker, R., & Laitin, D. D. (1998). Ethnic and nationalist violence. *Annual Review of Sociology, 24*, 423–452.

Gagnon, V. (2004). *The myth of ethnic war: Serbia and Croatia in the 1990's*. Ithaca, NY: Cornell University Press.

Gelpi, C. (1997). Democratic diversions governmental structure and the externalization of domestic conflict. *Journal of Conflict Resolution, 41*(2), 255–282.

Gleditsch, K. S., Salehyan, I., & Schultz, K. (2008). Fighting at home, fighting abroad: How civil wars lead to international disputes. *Journal of Conflict Resolution, 52*(4), 479–506.

Gurr, T. R. (1993). Why minorities rebel: A global analysis of communal mobilization and conflict since 1945. *International Political Science Review, 14*(2), 161–201.

Gurr, T. R. (2000). *Peoples versus states: Minorities at risk in the new century*. Washington, DC: US Institute of Peace Press.

James, P., & Oneal, J. R. (1991). The influence of domestic and international politics on the President's use of force. *Journal of Conflict Resolution, 35*(2), 307–332.

Lai, B., & Reiter, D. (2005). Rally 'round the union jack? Public opinion and the use of force in the United Kingdom, 1948–2001. *International Studies Quarterly, 49*(2), 255–272.

Levy, J. S. (1989). *The diversionary theory of war: A critique* (pp. 259–288, Chap. 2). Boston: University of Minnesota.

Levy, J. S. (1998). The causes of war and the conditions of peace. *Annual Review of Political Science, 1*(1), 139–165.

Mamdani, M. (2001). *When victims become killers: Colonialism, nativism, and the genocide in Rwanda*. Princeton: Princeton University Press.

Mandić, D. (2008). Myths and bombs: War, state popularity and the collapse of national mythology. *Nationalities Papers, 36*(1), 25–54.

Merton, R. K. (1948). The self-fulfilling prophecy. *The Antioch Review, 8*(2), 193–210.

Moore, R. I. (2007). *The formation of a persecuting society: Authority and deviance in Western Europe 950–1250* (2nd ed.). Oxford: Wiley-Blackwell.

Mueller, J. E. (1970). Presidential popularity from Truman to Johnson. *The American Political Science Review, 64*(1), 18.

Ostrom, C. W., & Job, B. L. (1986). The president and the political use of force. *The American Political Science Review, 80*(2), 541.

Ramanathapillai, R. (2006). The politicizing of trauma: A case study of Sri Lanka. *Peace and Conflict: Journal of Peace Psychology, 12*(1), 1–18.

Reicher, S., & Hopkins, N. (2001). *Self and nation*. London: Sage.

Slobodan, M. (1989, June 28). *Milosevic's Speech*. Kosovo Field. Retrieved from http://emperors-clothes.com/articles/jared/milosaid.html

Tir, J., & Jasinski, M. (2008a). Domestic-level diversionary theory of war: Targeting ethnic minorities. *Journal of Conflict Resolution, 52*(5), 641–664.

Wilkinson, S. I. (2007). Explaining changing patterns of party-voter linkages in India. In H. Kitschelt & S. Wilkinson (Eds.), *Patrons, clients and policies* (pp. 110–140). Cambridge: Cambridge University Press.

Zulaika, J. (2003). The self-fulfilling prophecies of counterterrorism. *Radical History Review, 85*(1), 191–199.

Part III

Case Studies

6

Riots, Religion and the Mobilisation of Communal Hatred in India (with-Rakshi Rath)

For a number of years, two of us (Reicher and Rath), have, as part of a larger research team, been studying one of the largest collective gatherings in the world—the Magh Mela at Allahabad in Northern India. This gathering is an immense annual Hindu fair that lasts throughout the lunar month of Magh (generally January–February). Large numbers of pilgrims—mostly North Indians, predominantly elderly and from the higher castes—come to the junction of the Ganges and Yamuna rivers to live a devotional life. Even larger numbers converge to immerse themselves in the Ganges on the various auspicious 'bathing days' that occur during the event. Throughout the day and night there are talks, dramas and discussions for these devotees. But given the numbers, the Mela attracts many other individuals and organisations. There are large shopping areas. There is a funfair. Many NGOs attend to raise awareness of issues from environmental pollution to child labour. Trades Unions hold mass meetings. And Hindu nationalist organisations also pitch camp. Of particular importance among them is the *Vishwa Hindu Parishad* (World Hindu Council—VHP), a religious organisation close to the *Bharatiya*

Janata Party (Indian people's party—BJP). Their audience consists primarily of the day visitors, a cross section of the Hindu population. Their aim is to draw on that identity, to define that identity and to politicise that identity.

One day in 2006, we walked into the VHP tent. It was a huge space, full of many exhibits. There were largely printed posters and charts, supposedly demonstrating the high birth rates and demographic threats posed by Christian and Muslim groups in various parts of the country. But one set of 16 posters caught our attention. They were very graphic. They were hand drawn and hung together. They clearly functioned as a set and worked together to tell a story. What is more, many of the posters had been daubed with sympathetic graffiti, showing that the audience were engaging with the message and also how they were engaging.

The most obvious thing about the series was the presence of the cow (depicted in 15 of the 16 posters) being subjected to various tortures and humiliations. In many posters the animal was shackled, in some cases stabbed, or scalded with boiling water or cut open, but most frequently, its throat was being cut. The global impression was clearly one of Hinduism—the cow has long been used as a symbol of Hindus and Hindu identity—in deadly danger from a merciless foe.

One of the posters struck us by being particularly graphic. It was set on the background of the Indian national flag and showed two figures, a Muslim Arab and a Congress politician (i.e., a representative of India's first political party and main rival of the Hindu nationalists), both identifiable by their dress. The former was holding a cow by its legs and pulling it onto the symbolic Indian wheel of law (*Ashoka Chakra*), which had been transformed into a knife-edged slaughter wheel. He was aided by the politician, the latter pushing as the former pulls. In other posters, the identity of the enemy varied but the complicity of Congress remained constant. Congress politicians were depicted as either ignoring, colluding or as actively benefitting from the acts of those who so cruelly attacked the symbol of the Hindu nation. They either failed to protect the cow or else, as in the *Ashoka Chakra* poster, actively took part in the slaughtering. Whatever the case, they were always guilty of treason.

Two years later, we came again across the same dramatic triad composed of the nation (represented by its sacred symbols or devoted servants), its enemies and its traitors. This time, it was in a speech given in Mumbai by the political leader of the BJP and the then Chief Minister of Gujarat, Narendra Modi. This speech was given shortly after the city had become the theatre of a series of train bombings on 11 July 2006 that left 189 people dead and several injured (for an account of the bombings, see Sayed & Hakim, 2016).[1] At one point in the speech, Modi asserted how he was defeating Islamic terrorism and then quoted an anecdote comparing the states of Gujarat and Assam, both with 'Muslim' neighbours (Pakistan and Bangladesh), the former run by Modi and the latter by a Congress-led coalition. He recalled his words to a local villager at a rally in Assam:

'look brother, Assam's neighbour is Bangladesh, and Gujarat's neighbour is Pakistan. My situation is the same as yours. They are your next-door neighbours, and these are my next-door neighbours'. And I said, 'but there is a slight difference. You are tormented because of them, they are tormented because of me'.

What makes this claim particularly powerful, of course, is the contrast that Modi makes between himself and his political rivals. He defeats the out-group enemy; the out-group enemy defeats them. Modi's words were met with cheers and claps from the audience. Some cried 'well said', while others whistled.

At other moments of the speech Modi's supporters went further. When he declared that the response to terrorists should be 'hard-hitting', the audience replied again with whistles and claps and with a cry of 'drop bombs on a Friday', which was widely applauded. Friday, of course, is the Muslim day of prayer. Bombs on a Friday imply an attack on the Muslim faith itself.

This chapter will be about the posters presented at the VHP tent and about Modi's speech as two concrete examples of how communal violence is mobilised for partisan ends in the political and religious arena of early twenty-first-century India. To this end, we shall start by sketching out this context in a little more detail and then show how the posters

---

[1] See http://www.thehindu.com/news/cities/mumbai/all-you-need-to-know-about-711/article7640887.ece.

and the speech function within it. We shall then broaden our focus and show how the very opposition between Hindus and Muslims so often portrayed as timeless, natural and inevitable is in fact none of these but rather arises out of and draws upon specific struggles rooted in India's colonial past.

6.1 The Contemporary Scene: Politics and Violence in Gujarat

In order to understand the role of religious violence and Hindu nationalism in contemporary Indian society, it is critical to understand Modi's and BJP's stronghold of Gujarat. And in order to understand the political and social context in Gujarat, it is critical to understand the February 2002 riots.

In January 2001, the parliament of the VHP declared that the construction of a temple would begin on 15 March 2002 on a highly contested location in the Northern Indian city of Ayodhya. This had been the site of the sixteenth-century Babri mosque, but, for the nationalists, the mosque itself was built on an earlier Hindu sacred site, birthplace of the god Ram. In 1992, a crowd of Hindu religious activists (*kar sevaks*) had stormed the site and destroyed the mosque. The 2001 declaration started a process whereby the VHP sought to mobilise *kar sevaks* once more, this time to prepare the ground for a new building (International Initiative for Justice in Gujarat, 2003).

On the 27 February 2002, one such group of volunteers was returning home to Gujarat on the Sabarmati Express train. At Godhra station they got into an altercation with Muslim tea vendors. Shortly after, the train was brought to a halt outside the station and two train carriages were set on fire. Somewhere in the region of 60 *kar sevaks* died. The details of the event are highly controversial (see Nussbaum, 2007), but for Hindu nationalists, the fire was deliberately started by a Muslim crowd.[2]

Over the following four days, there were attacks on Muslims in 19 districts of Gujarat. According to official figures 762 people were

---
[2] See http://www.rediff.com/news/2002/feb/27train3.htm Retrieved on 3 October 2016.

killed. Other estimates put the toll considerably higher, in the region of 2000–3000. Well over 100,000 people were displaced (Human Rights Watch, 2002; International Initiative for Justice in Gujarat, 2003). The violence was swift and extreme. Women-pregnant women in particular- far from being spared, seemed to have been deliberately targeted (Amnesty International, 2005; Human Rights Watch, 2003; Sarkar, 2002).

While most narratives present the Gujarat riots of 2002 as a response to the train burning, there is evidence that much had been prepared in advance. The Human Rights Watch report is blunt in its summary:

> The Gujarat government chose to characterize the violence as a "spontaneous reaction" to the incidents in Godhra ... (but) the attacks on Muslims are part of a concerted campaign of Hindu nationalist organizations to promote and exploit communal tensions to further the BJP's political rule—a movement that is supported at the local level by militant groups that operate with impunity and under the patronage of the state. (2002, p. 4)

The report then goes on to document the role of the police and of workers and officials from Hindu nationalist organisations in various acts of violence, such as the murder of the former member of parliament Ehsan Jafri and some 64 others in Gulbarg Society, a Muslim neighbourhood of Gujarat's largest city, Ahmedabad. There is also evidence which points to the organisation of violence prior to the 27 February. The attackers had stockpiled weapons such as Liquefied Petroleum Gas cylinders and were well resourced despite a general shortage. Muslim homes and Muslim organisations had been marked out in advance (and in some areas, Hindu houses were marked out with saffron symbols so as to be left alone). The VHP made clear that they had lists of local Muslims and, in some places, announced that certain areas would 'burn' months before they did (Human Rights Watch, 2002; International Initiative for Justice in Gujarat, 2003).

The nationalistic agitation that culminated in the Gujarat riots in 2002 was part of a broader movement that had shaken India over the previous two decades and had shifted the domestic balance of power. From the 1980s onwards, Hindu nationalist organisations like VHP and BJP attracted increasing support. Notably, the BJP rose from under 8 % of the national vote in 1984 to over 25 % in 1998. Moreover, from 1998 to 2004, they were in power at the centre. Additionally, the BJP was in power or else shared power in 14 different Indian states including, significantly, Uttar Pradesh (the site of Ayodhya) in 1992 and Gujarat (the site of Godhra) in 2002. Alongside the rise of BJP and allied organisations, there was a rise in communal violence: the Muslim death toll of the 1980s was quadruple than that of the 1970s (Ludden, 1996).

There are a number of explanations for the rise of BJP influence—and Hindu nationalist influence more generally. One factor seems to have been to do with changes in the political system which in turn have to do with broader social changes. Ludden (1996) suggests that the old system of political patronage, whereby local 'headmen' could deliver blocks of votes to the Congress party, began to break down. In this context, new ways of mobilising came to the fore, including attempts to mobilise groups on an ethnic basis. Not only did this provide a space for the BJP, VHP and others, but it also created a temptation for Congress and others to act likewise. The stage was set for what has been called a 'competitive populism', whereby different parties sought popular support through street politics. To invoke Ludden again:

> Using mass street mobilizations to topple governments became standard practice, and organized Hindu activists turned their violence against Muslims as part of their political strategy to dislodge the Congress. (1996, p. 19)

As we discussed in Chap. 4, there is little doubt that communal agitation was linked to electoral considerations. According to Wilkinson (2004, 2007), hostility was much more likely in close constituencies where it was critical to mobilise a majority constituency or in seats where parties did not rely on minority votes (and had no need to enter into coalitions with parties that do). Gujarat in 2002 was a clear case in point. The BJP, which was in power, had no support from Muslim voters in the state. For a variety of reasons, it was losing support in the

6 Riots, Religion and the Mobilisation of Communal Hatred... 161

period 1999–2002 and was in danger of losing the state election due for 2003. Wilkinson concludes that:

> At least some on the right seem to have calculated that communal tensions and violence would reap electoral dividends for the BJP in the forthcoming state elections. The result was that the state administration was at worst highly partisan and at best inexcusably hesitant in preventing anti-minority violence and in its willingness to call in central troops and paramilitary forces to do the job for them. (2007, p. 19)

In the Gujarat state elections shortly after the riots, which beforehand were thought to be hanging on a knife edge, the BJP swept the board. Overall, they won 126 seats with 49.8 % of the vote as against the Congress Party, which won only 51 seats with 39.3 % of the vote. What is more, a district by district breakdown of the vote shows that the BJP fared better in areas where there had been riots. As Kumar (2003) concludes, "the BJP may accept it or not, but the landslide victory for the party in constituencies affected by the communal riots do suggest that the polarisation between the Muslim and the Muslim voters did work largely in favour of the BJP" (p. 272).

Two simple points emerge from this description of the Gujarat context. The one is that antipathy is mobilised by portraying certain groups (notably Muslims) as a dangerous enemy. This has been a characteristic of Hindu nationalist organisations since their inception (Tambiah, 1996). The other point is that antipathy is mobilised in order to gain political advantage—polarising communities and validating the nationalists as defenders of embattled Hindus. But these conclusions raise further questions. *How* precisely is it that certain others are constituted as a dangerous enemy? *When* and *why* will this lead people to hate and destroy—and just why should invoking such antipathies be a means of garnering support? In order to move forward on these matters, let us turn now from a general account of twenty-first-century Hindu nationalism to an analysis of Hindu nationalist agitational materials. Specifically, let us look first at the VHP posters at the Magh Mela and then consider the key speech given by Modi just after the 2006 train bombings in Mumbai.

162 Identity, Violence and Power

6.2 How to Mobilise Intergroup Antagonism: An Analysis of VHP Posters

Amongst the set of 16 posters we came across in the VHP tent, it was possible to distinguish a number of different types. Let us now consider these in some detail, both how they differ and also how they work together in telling an overall story (see Rath, 2016).

The *first type* of poster (of which there is just one example) portrays India as a sacred Hindu territory. The poster depicts the God Krishna, also known as the divine cowherd, emerging from the Himalayas into an idealised landscape of rivers and plains. A headline proclaims that 'the essence of India is the cow (or gau)'.[3] The landscape is then made up of multiple holy sites all of which are labelled with derivations of the word 'Gau'. Some of these sites are generic, like Gopuram, the intricately carved towers at the entrance of South Indian temples. Some are specific places like the river Godavari which flows into the Bay of Bengal. A speech bubble from Krishna draws the elements together. It reads, "the term 'gau' is a symbol of sanctity, greatness and compassion in India. That is why so many holy places in India start with the term 'gau'."

In this way, India is conflated with 'Hindu', and Indianness is conflated with Hinduness (Hindutva). Certain groups are, by commission, subsumed into the fold—thus, there is an image of the 'Gautama' Buddha in the poster which represents Buddhism as part of Hinduism. Other groups, notably Muslims and Christians, are excluded by omission.

In addition, Hindu India is represented as inherently virtuous. It is a sacred space, a benign and bountiful space and a compassionate space. Anything toxic must therefore be an imposition from the outside. Moreover, like desecrating a temple, those who threaten the land are responsible for violating the sacred and destroying a site of virtue.

The *second type* of poster (of which there are three examples) depicts a threat to India through images of violence done to the cow. In one poster, the focus is on the threat itself. A cow is depicted tethered to a post, being sprayed with scalding water. The headline reads, 'Animals tortured before

---

[3] All original text is in Hindi, translations by the authors.

slaughter'. This is elaborated upon in smaller text: "The thirsty, hungry and nearly dead cow is thrashed and dragged to the machine. The animal is beaten incessantly with one leg shackled to the pulley. The boiling water is unleashed onto the cow, so that its blood spreads quickly in the body and softens the skin."

In the other two posters, the focus is on what is under threat. That is, a threat to the cow is not just a symbolic threat to Hindus (and not just an attack on a symbol of Hinduism). In the one image, a cow with its throat slit is accompanied by the words of a Hindu sage: "All spiritual activities carried out on the land where even a drop of cow's blood has been shed become fruitless." In the other, a cow is being stabbed in the back, its blood flowing over a giant Indian rupee coin. The text reads, "Murder of cattle is the murder of the country's finances: As the murder of cattle increased, there was a simultaneous increase in India's poverty, expenses and debts. India is the most debt-ridden country in the world."

In other words, the threat is to all aspects of Hindu well-being, spiritual and material (see Adcock, 2010 for a comparison with the arguments of the early cow protection movement). In these posters, the source of the threat is not made explicit although it is arguably implicit in some. Thus, the slit throat is a sign of ritualistic killing for halaal meat as practised by Muslims.

The *third type of poster*, by contrast, makes explicit just who is the source of threat to cows and to the (Hindu) community. This is the most frequent category, with nine examples. What is particularly striking here is the variety of sources that are identified. In some posters, Western corporations are responsible. For example, in one, a plutocratic figure holding a huge machete stands by the cow. The accompanying text reads, "International conspiracy to destroy India's natural food resources: American Cattle Corporation advising India to slaughter 80 % of its cows." In other posters, Arab corporations are named as responsible for large-scale killing in their mechanised slaughterhouses. And in yet others a generic Muslim figure is identified as the perpetrator.

Of this last type, two examples are particularly graphic. One contrasts the serene Hindu deity, Krishna, with two Muslim butchers. Krishna is feeding a cow on grounds in the shape of India. Of the two butchers, one sits on the cow as the other slits its throat. Both are grinning widely, clearly taking pleasure in what they do. The one says to the other, "She's the mother of the Hindus." The headline denotes that this is meant as a parable. It reads simply, "In the land of Gopal …" (another word for Krishna, derived from Gau). The word 'mother-fucker' has been scrawled as graffiti across the arms of the two butchers.

The other poster also depicts two Muslims standing over the prone body of a cow—its legs bound and its throat slit. This time, though, one of the figures (an attractive young boy) expresses concern, "Father, if it's really necessary to slaughter her, please speed it up. Look how the poor thing is writhing in pain. I feel for her and her pain." The father, a gross figure with a large paunch standing with a bloodied machete in his hand, replies, "Fool, stop talking like an infidel. If I do not torture her before I kill her then, according to Islam, her meat would become *haraam* (forbidden) instead of *halaal* (edible)." A graffiti artist has again scrawled the word 'mother-fucker' across his paunch.

In these posters, a peaceful, nurturant and virtuous India is beset by the lascivious, sadistic Muslim other. Moreover, such sadism is not incidental or accidental. It inheres in the very nature of Muslim culture. Those who do not torture willingly and eagerly are not true Muslims.

This takes us to a *fourth type of poster* (of which, again, there is just one example) which uses the historical figure of Shivaji to depict how enemies should be treated. Shivaji was a seventeenth-century ruler from the central Indian state of Maharashtra, who played a key part in the Hindu nationalist imagination. He is represented as "a zealous Hindu warrior fighting Muslim demons to create a Hindu nation-state" (Davis, 2004, p. 1047), and his memory is sufficiently sacred that the translator of a book (Laine, 2003) which simply reported historical controversies about Shivaji's parentage was attacked and publicly humiliated by a group of Shiv Sena activists (a particularly militant Hindu nationalist grouping whose name means 'Army of Shivaji').

In the poster, Shivaji stands between a cow and a Muslim butcher. With his sword he slices off the butcher's arm. Massive script at the top of the poster proclaims, "Cow-killer deserves to be slain". Lest anyone misses the historical reference, the rest of the script reads, "Brave founder of the Hindu kingdom, who chopped off the arm of the cow-murderer butcher". Note how, in contrast to the sadistic violence of Muslims,

Shivaji's violent act is depicted both as justified (the butcher deserves his fate) and as positive (it is brave).

Putting together the various elements that we have encountered thus far, they constitute a powerful and coherent narrative which weaves together many of the historical threads in Hindu nationalist thought. The starting point is a definition of the in-group in terms of Hindu nationhood. This then leads to multiple acts of exclusion: those who are either non-Indian or non-Hindu are constituted as an out-group. Muslims become strangers in their own land. Next, these others are depicted not only as alien but also as a serious threat. Because of their inherently vicious nature, they are driven to destroy the well-being and indeed the very identity of Hindu India.

We have seen how the Hindu Indian in-group is described verbally in terms of sanctity and compassion. Equally, in images, there is a contrast between the way that outsiders (specifically Muslims) are depicted as gross, salacious, physically repulsive and the way that Indians are portrayed as modest, ascetic and trim of body. In this way, the destruction of such outsiders can be seen not merely as an act of self-defence but as an act *in defence of virtue*. Violence is not just motivated (we must hate them because they harm us) but justified (and by destroying them, we are doing a good thing).

At first pass, it might seem paradoxical and contradictory to have a series of posters in which, on the one hand, Hindus are defined in terms of compassion and peacefulness, but, on the other, in which they are enjoined to kill Muslims. In the context of the entire logic, however, these two things are not contradictory. To the contrary, they actually entail each other. Drawing a narrow definition of in-group boundaries, thereby excluding sections of the population as out-groups, constituting these out-groups as a threat and constituting the in-group as virtuous: together these various elements lead irresistibly towards another, intergroup antipathy and violence (see Reicher, Haslam, & Rath, 2008). They flesh out the '*how*' of mobilising intergroup hatred.

But there is something more. A *fifth type of poster* depicts another actor in the drama. This is the Congress Party and the state that they created after independence in 1947. There are six of these posters. Sometimes Congress is represented on its own. In one instance, the symbols of the

Indian constitution are accompanied by the number 350,000 in large script, the images of slaughtered cows hanging out of each zero. The text reads, "Before independence, India had 300 slaughterhouses for meat export. In independent India, 36,031 slaughterhouses: large scale meat export. Everyday 350,000 animals are killed cruelly."

In another instance, the responsibility for this growing slaughter is spelled out. A Congress politician (as denoted by his Nehru cap and clothes) sits on a throne-like chair and addresses a poor peasant carrying a small bowl: "To fight an election, one pot of milk from your cowshed will not do. A suitcase full of notes is required. And that, I cannot get from you, I will only get it from slaughterhouses." At the bottom of the poster, the text reads, "The government has given the green signal to major mechanized slaughterhouses in the country."

In other posters of this type, Congress is depicted alongside one of the enemies that we have previously described. The Ashoka Chakra poster, to which we alluded near the start of this chapter, is one of them. At the top of this poster, large text proclaims, "Either change the national symbol or shut down mechanized slaughter-houses and stop meat export. In smaller writing, the message is elaborated: 'the "Ashoka Chakra" is in the middle of our tri-coloured national flag, which is a symbol of ahimsa (non-violence). Anyone who insults this is punished. But the Government of India by its cruel policies is insulting this symbol and committing crimes of treason." The graffiti on the image is equally explicit, if cruder. The politician is daubed with "You killing a cow, what? Has your wife run away with someone?" and "Send your daughter over to me". That is, he is accused of sexual inadequacy and threatened with sexual humiliation. In the case of the Muslim figure, the words "meet me and I will kill you" are inscribed, along with "I will kidnap your daughter, mother-fucker". In this case, humiliation is replaced by obliteration.

In another example, a corporate worker and a Muslim hold down and kill a cow; the text proclaims that "the constitution has allowed the slaughter of incapacitated animals". Or again, a fat grinning Muslim butcher holds aloft the dying calf whose throat he has slit while a farmer holding a hoe and a bunch of grass looks away. Here the text explains that "by naming the butcher's cruel act as 'farming' the government is insulting the holy ritual of farming and also the saint-like farmer" (note how, here, the contrast between the venal other and the virtuous Hindu is particularly explicit).

Thus, as well as showing us *how* intergroup hatred is mobilised, this analysis of VHP posters goes some way to showing us *why*. Why, that is, should invoking a communal threat be a means of garnering political support? The important point here is that by identifying a threat and proposing a response to that threat, a claim can be made to acting in the interests of the group and hence deserving to represent the group (see Haslam, Reicher, & Platow, 2011 for an analysis of how being seen to 'act for the group' is critical to effective leadership). But, equally importantly, by identifying a threat which ones rivals do not identify or counter, one can claim that they are not acting in the interests of the group and hence do not deserve to represent it. In many ways the use of 'threat' discourse is as much, if not more, about disqualifying rival contenders to influence as it is about achieving one's own influence. It is about demobilisation as much as mobilisation.

This might seem a strange claim to make about an organisation like the VHP which is not a political party, which does not stand for elections and which does not have leaders who personally need votes to achieve office. So, to investigate in more detail the 'why' of mobilising intergroup antagonism and to show how this can be used to bolster one's political influence, let us shift source from the VHP to the BJP politician Narendra Modi and let us also shift modality from poster to speech.

6.3 Why to Mobilise Intergroup Antagonism: An Analysis of a Modi's Speech

While attending the Dharm Sansad (religious parliament) of the VHP in 2008, we were handed a number of written documents and heard many speeches. We were also given a video containing just one speech—originally delivered by Modi (then the Chief Minister of Gujarat, since 2014, Prime Minister of India) on 17 July 2006 at Shanmukhanand Hall, Mumbai. The written text and speeches included a set of proposals from the President of the VHP, Ashok Singhal, on 'Reinstating the Hindu nation', 'Hindu Unity' and 'Societal health and fitness'; Praveen Togadia, General Secretary of the VHP, made a call to action and Kamlesh Bharti of the Matrushakti (Motherpower) spoke about the perils facing Hindu mothers. The only contribution by a party politician was Modi's post-Mumbai speech, 'a challenge to terrorism'.[4]

The first thing to note is that all the speeches, Modi's included, confirm what our analysis of the VHP posters told us about the 'how' of mobilising antagonism. That is, they contain the self-same elements which build up to the advocacy of violence as a defence of virtue. India is portrayed as a virtuous Hindu space under grievous threat from many corners, but particularly from a dangerous Muslim foe.

What distinguishes Modi is that his arguments are somewhat more coded, using terms which are intelligible to an in-group audience but which provide him with 'deniability' if accused of fomenting violence. For a politician who may need to enter into coalitions in domestic politics and into alliances in international politics, this is critical (cf. Jaffrelot, 2013; Wilkinson, 2007).

Thus, for instance, where others declare that "This is Bharat (India)—a Hindu Nation and it will remain a Hindu nation", Modi states more obliquely:

> I, today, on the soil of Mumbai, have come with a very heavy heart. I cannot imagine why, in a country like India, the innocent citizens of India are thrown into the throes of death. What is the fault of those youth? What is the fault of those mothers and sisters? Someone's brother is snatched away, someone's beloved son is snatched away. A sister's *sindoor* is wiped away.

The crucial word here is '*sindoor*'—the vermillion spot worn on the forehead uniquely by married *Hindu* women. Thus, Modi appears to talk in inclusive terms about the 'innocent citizens of India' and in generic terms about the mothers, sisters, brothers and sons of India. However, in speaking of a sister's sindoor, he indicates that his references to an Indian people are limited to those who are also Hindu.

---

[4] The speech is available at https://www.youtube.com/watch?v=wkqLkcztKXw.

Equally, other speakers are quite open in declaring that Muslims are a dangerous threat to the Hindu nation. Thus, Kamlesh Bharti of the women's 'Motherpower' (Matrushakti) wing of the VHP raises the spectre of demographic domination through conversion and intermarriage. She declares that if a Hindu woman marries a Muslim man, "her children will become Muslims, and they will be known as enemies of our Hindu nation". Modi is also clear about threats to the Hindu nation. He emphasises that as the Mumbai attacks demonstrate, there are threats to life and limb. There are also threats to the economy, and the drugs trade represents a threat to the health of the nation's youth.

But when it comes to identifying the source of this threat, he is decidedly more circumspect. Ostensibly, the source is terrorism: armed terrorism, financial terrorism, narco-terrorism. And while Modi stresses that the terrorists are Muslims ("the world faces danger from Jihadi terrorism"), he equally stresses that one should not conflate 'Muslim' with 'terrorist' ("every Muslim does not do jihad"). Nonetheless, this explicit distinction is constantly undermined by insinuations that there is something about Islam which tends towards terrorism and makes everyone into at least a potential terrorist.

For instance, Modi insists that "the terrorists aim to spread hatred in the country. It is the responsibility of the citizens of the country not to allow hatred to spread under any circumstances. Do not allow hatred to spread under any circumstances. This is their aim." Although he is speaking in Hindi, he uses the Urdu term for aim—*mansuba*. Hence the terrorist's promotion of hatred is Islamicised and contrasted to the (Hindu) citizen's opposition to terrorism.

Or again, Modi raises the case of a young woman, Ishrat Jehan, who was suspected (but not proved) to be a terrorist and was shot dead by the police in his home state, Gujarat. He then observes that "just a while ago, a TV reporter was saying that someone saw a girl planting the bomb. I do not know what the truth is. Girls have been used." In other words, perhaps not all Muslims are jihadis, but any Muslim might be—females as well as males, children as well as adults. From there, it is only a short step to imply that all are—and need to be treated as—suspect. However, Modi leaves it to the audience to complete this step, unlike others who take it for them.

Nonetheless, the major differences between Modi, the electoral politician, and the others come when we turn again from analysing from *how* antagonism is aroused to *why*. Modi spends much more time and is much more open in insisting that he, unlike his rivals, is of the people, with the people and, above all, acting for the people. Very near the start of his speech, Modi proclaims that:

> I have not come to see the colour of the blood of those friends and sisters who were martyred. They are all my brothers. What is his language? What is his community? What is his attire? What is his faith? These have no meaning for me. Each martyred brother is my Hindustani brother.

The force of this is not simply to constitute a unified and horizontal Hindu community, where language, class, caste and sect make no difference. It is to cast himself as part of this band of brothers—an exemplary in-group member.

Throughout the rest of the speech, Modi elaborates this claim, using, as evidence, his stance on terrorism. He stresses that he is one of the people, standing amongst them, not seeking to put himself above them. This is illustrated with an anecdote about airport security, his refusal to accept special treatment and his insistence on being screened ('welcomed') like everyone else:

> The police recognized me at the airport, and would usher me through. So I used to refuse and say 'No, I won't go'. First welcome me. They circle the metal-detector around, right? [He mimes the circular motion with his hands, associated with the traditional welcome of Hindu guests] I used to insist on the welcome and only then will I go. So that, I can proceed further. This is very holy work.

Closely linked to this, Modi also stresses that he acts for the group, never for himself (or for the enemies of the group), even if this is at own inconvenience or even his own danger. He insists, "Friends, I have promised, while there is life within me, I will search these merchants of death one by one and sort them out." He then describes how this brings him the hatred of the terrorists, their allies and their apologists. But he retorts, rhetorically and poetically:

> Only those are afraid who die for their own image
> I am that person who dies for India's image
> I do not care for my own image

Finally, Modi stresses that he does not just act for the group interest but that he is effective in advancing the group interest. He does this in various ways, notably by showing that he is prescient in identifying dangers to the group. He tells a complicated story about going to the USA in 1992 and explaining the dangers of terrorism, but being ignored—then going back in 2003 and having the dangers of terrorism explained back to him. More concretely, he outlines the tough anti-terrorist laws he passed in Gujarat while others ignored the threat.

But overall, Modi spends more time on showing how his rivals are not exemplary in-group members than showing how he is. Thus, the anecdote about airport security starts with the observation: "Sometimes, I am shocked, that these big leaders of ours, go to the airport, and if someone dares to check them, then their eyes turn red. How dare they check us? Do you not recognize us?" Such leaders clearly are not *of* the people.

Equally, when Modi draws a contrast between himself, as someone who works for India's image, and others, who are only concerned with their own, he clearly has Congress, the Communists and their allies in mind. They do not act in the group interest. They do not pursue terrorism and terrorists with sufficient energy. Indeed, he goes further: they actually collude with terrorists if it is to their advantage. Modi illustrates this claim with a number of examples. He claims that the Kerala Assembly, dominated by the Left and by Congress, let all terrorists out of jail because they wanted some as political candidates. He claims that in Tamil Nadu, Congress entered into an alliance with a Muslim party which has terrorist links. And he then tells a story involving the Congress-dominated United Progressive Alliance (UPA):

> Friends, the Bihar election. A supporting party of the UPA, in that election, they used to roam around the election polls with a certain person. Why did they roam? Because his face was like Bin Laden. He looks like Bin Laden!—and this they showed to garner votes in Bihar!

Further, Modi suggests that, even were they want to, his rivals (unlike him) would be unable to advance the group interest. He refers to the UPA Prime Minister Manmohan Singh as "a highly qualified doctorate who was leader of the World Bank", competent in economics, perhaps, but out of his depth when it comes to fighting terrorism. He is weak, talking tough at home, but forgetting his commitments once abroad. Indeed, Modi claims that the entire (non-BJP) political elite are weak and fearful. "When they meet me personally", he states, "all these leaders speak the same words that I am speaking. The ones that shout outside, when they come home, they pat my back." This is because as "the country's leaders, they are scared to speak out against terrorism".

In sum, where Modi stands for and stands up for Hindu India, Singh, his party and his parties allies do neither. This is all brought together in the closing words of the speech. Modi first expresses his wish that the 200 dead souls in Mumbai will inspire 100 crore Indians (a billion, since a crore is 10 million) to fight terrorism. Then he says,

> I do not expect this from the Government at Delhi. Because even if the soul tries, the soul will return broken hearted. That is why I am saying this to the 100 crore citizens of this country. The country's future has to be decided by the country's citizens. It is up to us to end this game played by the merchants of death. We must do it. We will have to do it together. And once again, I send my condolences to all the families who were affected.

By raising the threat to the nation to the status of a crisis of survival, the fact that it is not prioritised over all else by the existing government becomes, for Modi, a means of establishing his own right to lead. Modi and the BJP represent and defend the nation, defined as a Hindu nation. Singh, the Congress alliance and the Left, either knowingly or inadvertently, play into the hands of enemies who attack the nation in the name of Islam. Those who stand for the group should receive the group's support when they stand for election. That, at root, is the 'why' of invoking intergroup antagonism.

6.4 A Bloodied Chain of Events?[5]

All this talk of mobilising antagonism, and of the 'how' and the 'why' of such mobilisation, would suggest that it takes some effort to create hatred and to turn hatred into violence. And yet a cursory glance at history seems to suggest that such violence happens all too regularly. The Gujarat riot may well be the most significant outbreak of the recent times, but it is far from unique. In fact, it was just one incident in a long string of violent communal confrontations. Wilkinson (2005) estimates that there have been around 40,000 casualties in such riots since Independence in 1947—a figure that itself is dwarfed by the catastrophic death toll during the partitioning of India from Pakistan. It is estimated that up to 1,500,000 people may have died in that process (Godbole, 2006). Looking only at these numbers, it seems all too easy to believe that the subcontinent is inescapably bound together across space and time by a bloodied chain of violence.

Once we look for such a chain, the historic span can even be broadened well beyond partition. Pandey (2006) notes how the colonialist Government of India drew up lists of riots going back to the dawn of British rule and there is evidence that goes even further into the past. He remarks laconically that "the list of Hindu–Muslim riots in colonial and pre-colonial India lengthens all the time with lengthening research—as indeed it must if 'riots' are what one is looking for" (2006, p. 26).

Pandey's point is precisely that the representation of riots—and violence more generally—as an indistinguishable and endless chain of events makes it easier to see them as part of a natural order (or, rather, a natural *dis*order). He analyses how colonial academics and administrators reduced different events to a generic template of religious conflict and how this was then described as the result of timeless Hindu–Muslim hatreds deriving from the primitive and irrational religious fervour of both groups. To quote the Rev. James Kennedy, who was writing about his life and work in Northern India from 1839 to 1877:

---

[5] Thanks to Sammyh Khan whose thesis on Hindutva was invaluable in charting the history and ideology of the Hindu nationalist movement.

The antagonism [between Hindu and Muslim 'systems'], though generally latent, every now and then breaks out into fierce strife, which but for the interposition of Government would lead to civil war. (Cited in Pandey, 2006, p. 45)

What is revealing about this quotation is not just the representation of riots as all equivalent and the explanation of these riots in terms of age-old rivalries. It is also the political message. The colonial power disappears from the explanation of the conflict itself. It has nothing to do with creating the conditions for conflict. It has nothing to do with the incidents themselves. It simply arrives afterwards to restore order: never part of the problem, always the solution. To cite Pandey once more, "by the later nineteenth century, it is no longer the power of English science and commerce, but also the argument that the 'natives' are hopelessly divided, given to primitive passions and incapable of managing their own affairs, that legitimizes British power" (2006, p. 45).

While it is nearly always fanciful to project the categories and conflict of a particular place and time back into a timeless past, a number of authors point out that anything more than an entirely cursory look at history shows that it is particularly unconvincing to suggest that Hindus have always stood together in antagonism to Muslims. For what makes Hinduism distinctive is precisely its diversity and multiplicity. There are multiple sacred texts—the Vedas, the Upanishads, the Bhagavad Gita, the Puranas, to name but a few. There are multiple deities and multiple accounts of each of these deities. Different sects lay different emphases on these different sources, and as Jaffrelot (2013) suggests, rather than thinking in terms of a single 'ism'—Hinduism—it is better to think in terms of a conglomeration of sects (Thapar, 1989). As Shani (2007) says:

> The notion of a monolithic Hindu identity, no more than a homogenous Muslim identity, is inherently implausible. Hinduism has been the bearer of diverse theological interpretations. Hindus have been deeply divided as much by caste as by ritual observance and sectarian differences. (p. 3)

Indeed, Pandey (2006) notes that the term 'communalism', which we ourselves have used and which, nowadays, denotes hostility between

Hindus and Muslims, was earlier used to denote conflict between the upper Brahman caste and non-Brahmans. The debate around the communal question was centred as much on the so-called untouchables as on religious minorities. Pandey's argument is that the creation and consolidation of differences between Hindus and Muslims was very much a creation of British colonialism. In part, this was a product of their orientalist fantasies which saw primitive colonial subjects as locked into religious fervour and which then led them to impose forms of governance which treated people differently as a function of their religion.

In part, though, it also derived from indigenous reactions to colonialism. Jaffrelot (2013) relates how many of the Indian intelligentsia became fascinated by British success and by their achievements in scientific, technical, legal and social domains. Ram Mohan Roy, who in 1828 founded the *Brahmo Samaj* (community of worshippers of Brahma, the creator) was typical of these. He sought to unite and to revive indigenous society on the basis of a reformed set of Hindu beliefs, claiming that there was nothing inherently superior about Western Christian culture.

These ideas were further developed by Dayananda Saraswati and a new organisation, the *Arya Samaj* (noble community), which he founded in 1875. But the *Arya Samaj* also took Hindu revivalism in important new directions. Critically, it formed a link between culture, people and land. In Jaffrelot's (2013) terms, the noble people of the Vedas formed the autochthonous people of 'Bharat', the sacred land below the Himalayas. This incipient link between the original Indians and the Hindu text was fateful. If nothing else it suggested that those who were not 'people of the book' (even if there is some debate over which Hindu book this is) are not properly Indian.

But also, while Hindu revivalism had always been torn between admiring and fearing the British, Dayananda altered the balance increasingly towards fear and threat of the 'other'. The *Arya Samaj* became particularly concerned with the conversion of Hindus to Christianity and even invented reconversion ceremonies in order to combat it. But Dayananda and his organisation also began to alter the balance in another way—that is, in terms of defining the identity of the 'other' who is the source of threat. Whereas the British and their Christian religion had been and still remained a focus of concern, now Muslims began to loom larger in the revivalists' imagination. This is well illustrated by the cow protection movement, one of the most significant initiatives of the *Arya Samaj*. From its beginnings, it drew on the cow as a Hindu symbol and on cow slaughter as an attack on Hindus. As Adcock (2010) argues, Dayananda's pamphlet from 1881 out of which the movement arose, *The Ocean of Mercy*, centred on the notion that cows bring economic good, their milk sustains the physique and intellect and, hence, killing cows leads to disease, unhappiness, poverty and powerlessness.

When it came to those responsible for such attacks, the British certainly figured prominently. They both consumed beef directly (one of the demands of the movement was for an end to the supply of beef to the British Army) and their laws allowed for others to consume beef. These others were mainly Muslims. More specifically, the ritual slaughter of cows at the end of the festival of Eid-ul-Adha (a practice known as qurbani) became a focus of contention. Once again, hostility to Muslims and to the colonisers was intermixed. The first recourse of the cow protection societies was to call on the authorities to give legal protection to the cow as an object of religious worship. But once this failed, attacks on Muslim communities ensued, most notably in 1893 and again in 1917. Pandey (2006) translates some of the leaflets—patias—which circulated in order to mobilise such attacks:

> The religion of the cow is being destroyed. What crime has she committed that she should be killed by non-believers. Hindu brothers are entreated to watch over the cow in every village and every house. If they do not, the cow will sadly breathe its last and disappear from the village. If you see a Musalman with a cow, it is your duty ['religion'—the word *dharma* stands for both] to take it from him. It is also your duty ['religion'] to write and send on five patias. If you do not, you bear the sin of cow-slaughter. If you do, it is equivalent to the gift of five cows. (p. 283, notes in brackets in the original)

Other leaflets are yet more explicit, both about what should be done and about the implications of not doing it. One declares that "you must loot the houses of the Musalmans and kill the Musalmans". It asserts that "those who are Hindus have no choice" and says of anyone who demurs that "you do mount on your daughter, drink your wife's piss, and mount on your sister's daughter" (pp. 284–285). In other words, exclusion and violence are not simply the fate of the out-group, it is also the fate of dissident in-group members. The declaration that Hindus have no choice is not just an exhortation, it is a threat. Indeed one of the leaflets is explicitly aimed at those Hindus who shield Muslims in their houses. It tells "Hindu brothers" that "all of you must turn out with your weapons" (p. 284).

There is a point here that is so obvious that it almost seems superfluous to mention it. Although, perhaps that very obviousness thereby leads the point to be overlooked. That is, if Hindus were inherently inclined to hate Muslims, they would not need such exhortations and such dire threats to make them join in the violence. It becomes far simpler and more plausible to argue (as we did in Chap. 5) that the violence does not derive from preformed communal identities but rather serves to discipline people into communal groups and to cohere around communalist leaders. From this perspective, the argument that violence is natural is not simply an innocent mistake. Rather it is a deliberate device for covering one's tracks and denying one's complicity in inciting violence.

This amalgam of representation, explanation and politics in accounts of communal riots serves to link the colonial era to the closer past. At its meeting of mid-March 2002, the *Rashtriya Swayamsevak Sangh* (RSS—a volunteer paramilitary Hindu nationalist organisation deeply involved in the events of Ayodhya and Gujarat) adopted a resolution which stated that "the reaction to this murderous incident in Gujarat was natural and spontaneous. The entire Hindu society cutting across all divisions of party, caste and social status reacted" (cited in Varadarajan, 2002, p. 21). Or in the words of the VHP leader Pravin Togadia, "wherever there is Godhra, there will be Gujarat" (ibid., p. 23).

Togadia continued, "In Gujarat, for the first time there has been a Hindu awakening and Muslims have been turned into refugees. This is a welcome sign and Gujarat has shown the way to the country." That is, the murderous rioting was not only naturalised, as in colonial times, but actively celebrated. The difference between eras reflects the different relationships to the groups involved in conflict. Whereas the British portrayed themselves as neutral arbiters, holding the ring and keeping order between Hindus and Muslims, the RSS, Togadia and others in the Hindu nationalist fold represent themselves as champions of the aggrieved Hindu masses. So whereas the colonial narrative accords no precedence to one side or the other in the dynamics of conflict, and stereotypes both as equally violence-prone, the Hindu nationalists see the action as always having an origin in the perfidious Muslim 'other'. For Togadia and others, Godhra was an organised conspiracy, provoked by the Pakistani security services, whereas the subsequent riots were a spontaneous and natural reaction.

In both the colonialist and the contemporary cases, then, a primordialist or otherwise fatalistic account serves to remove responsibility for conflict from political actors. But whereas in the former case it justifies rule of the civilised west over the primitive east, in the latter case it justifies championing the innocent Hindu over the rapacious Muslim. In other words, the accounts themselves are far from neutral or innocent. They are not simply accounts of a political process, but they are an integral part of the political process in terms of creating and of legitimating particular types of rule.

6.5 Conclusion

In this chapter, we have examined the example of so-called communal violence in India, combining secondary sources with primary analyses of religious drawings and political discourse from the Hindu nationalistic movement. All elements analysed converge on one point: the notion that communal violence reflects ancient hatreds between Muslims and Hindus simply does not stack up (just as the idea of ancient hatreds fails to stack up in other sites we investigate in the book, notably the Balkans). Not least this is because people have not seen themselves in terms of such categories throughout history, and when they have, they have not always seen the relationship between the categories in terms of opposition or antagonism.

Where we find communal hatred and where we see instances of communal violence, it is because communal categories have been brought into being at a particular time and place. The riots we have described are not atavistic outbursts. Antagonism has been systematically propagated and violence has been systematically organised, identifying targets, providing weapons, ensuring that the forces who might prevent them either stand aside or else actually join in. In short, communal violence is deliberately mobilised. If this is clear, it is equally clear who is driving this mobilisation in contemporary India: the *Sangh Parivar* or family of Hindu nationalist organisations—some more crudely, some in more coded terms, but the different members of the family complementing each other.

This then leads to the question of why such ideas are being propagated. Both in the posters and in the speech that we have analysed, we meet a curious phenomenon. These different texts are ostensibly about the out-group threat. But in both, the source of that threat is variable—Muslims, Westerners, Arabs, corporations, on the one hand; armed terrorists, economic terrorists, narco-terrorists, on the other hand. But what remains constant in both is another actor, the in-group rival who, by omission or by commission, is responsible for allowing the threat to flourish.

So what appears to be about intergroup dynamics may be better understood in terms of intra-group dynamics. If there is a dire threat to the in-group, then clearly those who experience the threat, are concerned by the threat and are able to deal with the threat are those who are of the group, act for the group and deliver for the group (the three components of leadership and effective influence over group members—see Haslam, Reicher, & Platow, 2011), while those who do not experience the threat, are not concerned by the threat and do not deal with threat are not of the group, do not act for the group, do not deliver for the group and hence lose leadership and influence over group members. To put it slightly differently, invoking a threat which one's rivals do not recognise is a powerful way of shifting the balance of support within the group and hence of achieving both electoral power and the power of influence. This, of course, begs the question of why people should accept discourses of threat and of hatred.

Here, the role of violence in turning discourses of out-group threat into the lived experience of out-group threat becomes pivotal. In the case of the Gujarat riots, once Hindu nationalist groups had turned Muslim homes into sites of danger and co-opted their Hindu neighbours in the process, at the least by getting them to mark their own homes so they wouldn't be attacked, Muslims fled into their own enclaves in fear of 'Hindus' in general. The monolithic categories 'Hindu' and 'Muslim' and the antagonism (or, at least, mistrust) between them became a material reality. In line with the arguments we developed in Chap. 4, violence, far from reflecting ancient hatreds between groups, was a most effective means of creating and freezing such group relationships. And, as our argument went on in Chap. 5, it created the constituencies for the ideologues of antagonism to represent and to draw upon to build their power.

References

Adcock, C. S. (2010). Sacred cows and secular history: Cow protection debates in Colonial North India. *Comparative Studies of South Asia, Africa and the Middle East, 30*(2), 297–311.
Amnesty International. (2005). *Justice, the victim—Gujarat state fails to protect women from violence*. London: Amnesty International.
Davis, R. H. (2004). Review: Shivaji: Hindu King in Islamic India. *Journal of the American Academy of Religion, 72*, 1045–1050.
Godbole, M. (2006). Pandora's box no one wants to open. *Economic and Political Weekly, 41*(12), 1179–1184.
Haslam, S. A., Reicher, S. D., & Platow, M. J. (2011). *The new psychology of leadership: Identity, influence and power*. London: Psychology Press.
Human Rights Watch. (2002). We have no order to save you. *State Participation and Complicity in Communal Violence in Gujarat 14*(3) (C).
Human Rights Watch. (2003). *World Report: Events of 2002*.
Jaffrelot, C. (2013). Refining the moderation thesis. Two religious parties and Indian democracy: The Jana Sangh and the BJP between Hindutva radicalism and coalition politics. *Democratization, 20*(5), 876–894.
Kumar, S. (2003). Gujarat assembly elections 2002: Analysing the verdict. *Economic and Political Weekly, 38*(4), 270–275.
Laine, J. W. (2003). *Shivaji: Hindu king in Islamic India*. Oxford: Oxford University Press.
Ludden, D. (1996). *Contesting the nation: Religion, community, and the politics of democracy in India*. Pennsylvania: University of Pennsylvania Press.

Nussbaum, M. C. (2007). *The clash within: Democracy, religious violence and India's future*. Cambridge: Harvard University Press.

Pandey, G. (2006). *Routine violence: Nations, fragments, histories*. Standford, CA: Stanford University Press.

Rath, R. (2016). *Virtuous violence: A social identity approach to understanding the politics of prejudice in intergroup relations*. Unpublished Ph.D. Thesis, University of St. Andrews.

Reicher, S., Haslam, S. A., & Rath, R. (2008). Making a virtue of evil: A five-step social identity model of the development of collective hate. *Social and Personality Psychology Compass, 2*(3), 1313–1344. doi:10.1111/j.1751-9004.2008.00113.x.

Sarkar, T. (2002). Semiotics of terror: Muslim children and women in Hindu Rashtra. *Economic and Political Weekly, 37*(28), 2872–2876.

Sayed, N., & Hakim, S. (2016). *Six minutes of terror*. Gurgaon: Penguin Random House India.

Tambiah, S. J. (1996). *Leveling crowds: Ethnonationalist conflicts and collective violence in South Asia*. Berkeley: University of California Press.

Thapar, R. (1989). Imagined religious communities? Ancient history and the modern search for a Hindu identity. *Modern Asian Studies, 23*(02), 209–231.

The International Initiative for Justice in Gujarat. (2003). *An Interim Report* (p. 6). Retrieved from http://onlinevolunteers.org/gujarat/reports/iijg/interimreport.htm

Varadarajan, S. (2002). *Gujarat, the making of a tragedy*. India: Penguin Books India.

Wilkinson, S. I. (2004). *Votes and violence: Electoral competition and communal riots in India*. Cambridge: Cambridge University Press.

Wilkinson, S. I. (2005). Communal riots in India. *Economic and Political Weekly, 40*(44/45), 4768–4770.

Wilkinson, S. I. (2007). Explaining changing patterns of party-voter linkages in India. In H. Kitschelt & S. Wilkinson (Eds.), *Patrons, clients and policies* (pp. 110–140). Cambridge: Cambridge University Press.

7

Ethnic Violence in the Former Yugoslavia: From Myth to Reality (with Sandra Penic)

During the early post-Cold War era, to much of the Western public, the former Yugoslavia soon came to epitomise a representation of a world of ethnic rivalry and primitivism abruptly revealed by the lifting of the Iron Curtain. Tito's rule over Yugoslavia has sometimes been depicted as akin to the proverbial 'lid on a cauldron', eventually removed by Tito's death and the mounting weakness of the regime during the 1980s. International media depictions of war in the former Yugoslavia have certainly played a pre-eminent role in entrenching and popularising the notion that ethnic conflicts are somehow part of a natural course of events. These simple depictions contrast with the complexity that local populations experienced, especially during the early war period. Where the battles were fought in 1991 and 1992, things typically looked far less black and white.

There are many instances of collective behaviour that did not fit into the ethnic hatred narrative, and sometimes there was active resistance to ethnic categories of action imposed by politics and warfare. In Chap. 4 we already referred to the way the fighting parties in the trenches around Sarajevo only gradually came to understand themselves and their enemies as ethnically defined 'Serb' and 'Muslim' forces. But even once that was the case, there were still times when people transcended the ethnic trenches that separated them. Here is an example, narrated by a former Sarajevan soldier:

> The first years of the war I spent several months defending Sarajevo in a trench that was only 50 meters from the Serbian army trenches. Between us was an unmined, level meadow (…) After several nights of us listening to and watching the enemy trench, one morning a man's voice called out from the other side, and astonished us, 'Hey, you guys, let's play a round of soccer on the meadow! (…)
>
> We played soccer with them every day. If someone had seen us at that time they would have probably said we were insane. But looking back at that time from the vantage point of today it seems to me we were more sane than most people.

The quote is part of a much wider corpus of testimonies collected by Svetlana Broz (2005, 2014) during and after the war in Bosnia, which brings together a hundred cases where people defied members from 'their own' ethnic community to protect, support or cooperate with people from a different ethnic background. Gagnon (2004) reviewed broader evidence of collective behaviour that was not consistent with the ethnic conflict narrative and highlighted three such types: (a) *mass desertions*—more than 200,000 young Serbs preferred to hide or flee rather than to serve, when they were called to save their 'ethnic brothers' in Bosnia from what Serbian mass media propaganda portrayed as 'genocide', (b) *anti-immigrant sentiment* against incoming refugees from the same ethnic background, which was equally strong in Zagreb, Belgrade and Sarajevo; and (c) *intraethnic violence*, which was systematically used as a political weapon, notably between Serbs in Krajina and between Croats in Herzeg-Bosnia.

These observations led Gagnon to dismiss the notion of ethnic war and refer to it as a 'myth'. While we largely concur with Gagnon's refutation of ethnic conflict as a satisfying explanation for the tragedies that unfolded in the former Yugoslavia, our interest here lies more in understanding how the myth turned into reality. How did empirically unfounded, but politically instrumental, beliefs trigger social processes that eventually resulted in a situation where many people did experience ethnic conflict as real in its consequences?

Changes in the social acceptance of mixed marriage provide telling evidence concerning the scope of the phenomenon. In 1990-less than a year before the war started in Croatia, and then in Bosnia-a representative sample of adult residents of Yugoslavia were asked, in the Yugoslav Public Opinion Studies (YPOS), whether they could conceive of marrying into the various ethno-national communities that composed Yugoslavia. In our re-analyses of these data, we calculated for each republic or province the rate of majority members who expressed a positive attitude towards marrying someone from the main minority group, or *vice versa*. The first column of Table 7.1 shows findings for young adults in 1990. These findings reveal a strong norm of acceptance of mixed marriage in the most diversified parts of Yugoslavia: in Bosnia, Croatia and Vojvodina, a large majority stated their willingness to marry across ethnic boundaries.

Ten years after the end of war in Bosnia and Croatia, the same question was asked again to respondents from the same generation, as part of the TRACES project. This survey was conducted in 2006 among a representative sample of the cohort of people born between 1968 and 1974 across all countries of the former Yugoslavia (Spini, Elcheroth &

Table 7.1 Rates of acceptance of mixed marriage before and after the war, across eight political entities (sorted by decreasing level of pre-war ethnic diversity)

Would you be willing to marry into the group of … ? (% Yes)		
	18–25 in 1990 (%) (*Source*: YPOS)	32–38 in 2006 (%) (*Source*: TRACES)
Bosnia and Herzegovina	67	17
Vojvodina	95	65
Montenegro	38	59
Croatia	63	22
Macedonia	14	6
Kosovo	12	3
Serbia	41	39
Slovenia	59	49
(Former) Yugoslavia	42	27

Fasel, 2011). It is striking to see how in post-war Croatia and Bosnia, the acceptance of mixed marriage had collapsed. In Croatia, the rate of positive answers declined from 63 % to 22 %, in Bosnia from 67 % to 17 %. While mixed marriage seemed something normal to most young adults in before the war, the war itself transformed social norms. Only a tiny minority could still imagine marrying across ethnic lines a decade after the end of combat.

In the following pages, we will proceed in two steps. First, we will elaborate our portrait of Yugoslavia on the eve of war, present more findings that corroborate the notion of the 'myth' of ethnic conflict, but also try to understand the processes through which the myth became a social fact. That will bring us back to the question of how wartime social practices, and adaptation to wartime dilemmas, transform collective identity (see Chap. 4). Second, we will address how, when and why exclusive ethno-national identities and loyalties persist even after the guns have fallen silent. To that end, we will focus specifically on one of the new nation-states to emerge from the wars—Croatia. This will allow us to understand how the combination of triumphant nationalism and politicised threat was used to entrench the status quo and silence critical voices.

7.1 How Exclusive Ethno-national Identities Became Social Facts

Responses to another question asked in the 1990 YPOS are instructive about pre-war perceptions of social cleavages in the population. People were asked to choose from a list in order to indicate where the greatest intergroup inequalities lay in Yugoslavia. Only in Kosovo, which had already been the theatre of ethnic riots and repression in the early 1980s, did respondent put inequalities between 'people from different nationalities' (which in Yugoslav terminology meant people from different ethnic backgrounds) in first place. In all the other republics or provinces, ethnicity was only quoted as the fourth or fifth most important source of inequality, ranking behind differences between 'individual republics', 'political magnates and ordinary citizens', 'rich and poor' and, in the economically less endowed central and southern republics, between 'employed and unemployed' people. Thus, overall, people were more concerned with political, economic and social inequalities, and with inequality created by the federal system of distribution of wealth, than with ethnic inequalities (Table 7.2).

But did widespread dissatisfaction with the federal system lead to popular demands that it should be broken up? The YPOS data suggest that it didn't. In Slovenia, Croatia and Bosnia—which all declared independence in the following two years—the most frequent call was for more federalism, whereas only a relatively small minority supported the separatist option (see Table 7.3). In Macedonia and Montenegro, the most frequently expressed wish was actually to maintain the *status quo*. Ironically, it was only in Serbia, which would subsequently fight for the maintenance of the Yugoslav federation, where most people went for the break-up option.

These historic survey data hence appear to contradict the notion that there were strong bottom-up forces leading to the inevitable dissolution of the Yugoslav federation or to struggle between its constituent ethno-national communities. But the most interesting findings arise from a question where people were directly asked to assess the quality of relations between different national groups, across various contexts. In seven out of eight political entities, people described these relations as on average better than satisfactory, as far as their own places of work and living were concerned. (The exception was again Kosovo, where average answers were located between 'satisfactory' and 'bad'.) Strikingly, however, when the same people were asked about the quality of ethnic relations in their republic or province overall, their judgements were less favourable, and when they were asked about Yugoslavia as a whole, their answers even ranged between 'bad' and 'very bad' (Table 7.4).

There is thus a conundrum here. While everywhere except in Kosovo people viewed interethnic relations within their personal sphere of experience as positive, the same people were convinced that elsewhere these relations were far less rosy. This discrepancy raises the intriguing question as to which other sources people relied on to form an opinion about the

Table 7.2 Perceived sources of inter-group inequality in pre-war Yugoslavia

Where do you personally think most inequality in Yugoslavia exists? (% who chose cleavage among up to two different answers) (Source: YPOS 1990)

	Between individual republics (%)	Between political magnates and ordinary citizens (%)	Between rich and poor (%)	Between people of different nationalities (%)	Between employed and unemployed (%)	Between manufactural and non-manufactoral professions (%)	Between young and old (%)	Between males and females (%)	Between believers and atheists (%)
Bosnia–Herzegovina	41	33	24	23	26	12	8	7	4
Vojvodina	37	42	32	23	25	11	9	3	1
Montenegro	40	31	27	20	39	13	8	5	2
Croatia	28	37	34	27	16	15	8	4	5
Macedonia	33	35	31	22	30	13	9	4	1
Kosovo	27	31	12	66	22	4	2	4	1
Serbia	39	39	27	23	26	13	8	5	2
Slovenia	32	29	33	19	11	18	10	6	4
Yugoslavia	**35**	**35**	**28**	**27**	**24**	**13**	**8**	**5**	**3**

7 Ethnic Violence in the Former Yugoslavia: From Myth to Reality... 189

Table 7.3 Popular support for future institutional scenarios in pre-war Yugoslavia

In your opinion, what kind of state should Yugoslavia be in a near future?
(Source: YPOS 1990)

	More centralist (%)	*Status quo* (%)	More federalist (%)	Different sovereign states (%)
Bosnia–Herzegovina	3	37	43	16
Vojvodina	4	38	30	28
Montenegro	1	54	27	18
Croatia	1	20	63	16
Macedonia	3	54	31	12
Kosovo	2	10	49	40
Serbia	1	33	28	37
Slovenia	1	9	68	23
Yugoslavia	**2**	**31**	**43**	**24**

Table 7.4 Perceived ethnic conflict in pre-war Yugoslavia

In your opinion, what is the quality of relations between different nations…?
(average response on 4-point scale: 1-good, 2-satisfactory, 3-bad, 4-very bad)
(Source: YPOS 1990)

	…in your working organisation	…in the place where you live	…in your republic, province	…in Yugoslavia
Bosnia-Herzegovina	1.5	1.4	1.9	3.1
Vojvodina	1.3	1.2	1.7	3.4
Montenegro	1.5	1.5	2.1	3.4
Croatia	1.5	1.7	2.5	3.1
Macedonia	1.4	1.4	2.1	3.3
Kosovo	2.6	2.9	3.5	3.4
Serbia	1.3	1.3	2.5	3.5
Slovenia	1.5	1.6	1.9	3.3
Yugoslavia	**1.5**	**1.6**	**2.3**	**3.3**

state of interethnic relations, and what led them to lend more credit to alarming second-hand information than their own daily experience.

The findings shown in Table 7.1 already suggest that the discrepancy between what people experienced and what they believed about interethnic relations actually *prefigured* a dramatic social change—a violent process through which people's beliefs about ethnic tensions (and separation) became true. The findings reported in Table 7.5—which combines responses from the YPOS sample in 1990 and from the TRACES sample in 2006—provide insights into what happened to the sense of identity among those who were in their formative years when Yugoslavia broke up. The average response patterns show how Yugoslav identity become obsolete. Interestingly, to many in the former Yugoslavia, affiliation to Yugoslavia was seen as more important than any other (infra- or supranational) affiliations. That was still true in 1990 for young Bosnians, Vojvodinians, Montenegrins and Macedonians. While Slovenes considered affiliation with their republic, and Kosovars with their province, as more important than affiliation to Yugoslavia as a whole, mixed patterns emerge for the two largest republics: affiliation with Croatia or Serbia was seen in the corresponding populations as of equal importance to affiliation with Yugoslavia.

A completely different picture emerges from the 2006 data: by then, identification with the former Yugoslavia had lost its importance virtually everywhere. Only in Montenegro and Macedonia did it still pass the threshold of 'somewhat important' on average. While the obsolescence of Yugoslav identity was nearly ubiquitous, it was replaced by different types of identity in different contexts. In those republics which, after having declared war and (in the case of Croatia) fought for their independence, had achieved in 2006 the status of indisputable and internationally recognised nation-states, identification with the new nation clearly prevailed. That was the case in Croatia, Slovenia and Macedonia. In most other places, where the confusion of political transition, state dissolution and war had not yet been replaced by the certainties of a new triumphant nationalism, more complex patterns arose. These generally involved simultaneous identification at both the local ('the place and region where I live') and global ('Europe'/'the World') levels.

As part of an interdisciplinary research programme, we had aimed to document how war experiences in the 1990s transformed collective identities much more profoundly than the combination of a deep economic depression, institutional disintegration and aggressive mass propaganda in 1980s. The resulting findings have been compiled in an edited book

Table 7.5 Affiliation to different territorial entities, before and after the war

There are some types of affiliation that may be important for an individual. Please indicate the importance that you attribute to each.
(reversed average responses on a 5-point response scale: 5-very important, 4-quite important, 3-somewhat important, 2-of little importance, 1-not important)

(Sources: YPOS 1990, TRACES 2006)

		Place and region where I live	Republic/Province/country	(former) Yugoslavia	Europe	World
Bosnia and Herzegovina	18–25 in 1990	3.0	3.1	4.0	3.9	3.6
	32–38 in 2006	3.9	3.6	2.6	4.0	4.1
Vojvodina	18–25 in 1990	2.9	3.1	4.0	3.7	3.5
	32–38 in 2006	3.3	3.3	2.7	3.7	3.8
Montenegro	18–25 in 1990	3.1	3.5	4.2	3.1	2.9
	32–38 in 2006	4.0	3.2	3.5	4.2	4.2
Croatia	18–25 in 1990	2.8	3.2	2.9	3.3	3.3
	32–38 in 2006	3.9	4.1	1.5	3.1	3.1
Macedonia	18–25 in 1990	2.8	3.0	3.5	3.1	2.6
	32–38 in 2006	4.0	4.3	3.2	3.9	4.1
Kosovo	18–25 in 1990	3.4	3.9	3.3	4.0	3.6
	32–38 in 2006	4.4	4.5	1.7	4.3	4.1
Serbia	18–25 in 1990	2.8	3.3	3.6	3.3	3.2
	32–38 in 2006	3.4	3.4	2.5	3.8	4.0
Slovenia	18–25 in 1990	3.5	3.7	3.0	3.3	2.9
	32–38 in 2006	3.7	3.9	2.5	3.5	3.5
Former Yugoslavia	**18–25 in 1990**	**3.0**	**3.4**	**3.5**	**3.5**	**3.3**
	32–38 in 2006	**3.8**	**3.8**	**2.3**	**3.7**	**3.8**

(Spini, Elcheroth & Biruski, 2013). They provide concrete insights into the wartime dilemmas and constraints that left many people with a new sense that ethnic affiliations matter. The bulk of these findings are based on a survey completed in the spring of 2006 by a representative sample of more than 6000 adults from all over the former Yugoslavia. Respomdents completed life events calendars in which they reported retrospectively on their experiences during the war (Spini et al., 2011).

On the basis of these data, the sociologists Gauthier and Widmer (2014) were able to show how, for most people, the 'decision' to leave the most war-affected regions in Croatia, Bosnia and Kosovo was directly related to their religious affiliation. It is important to be precise here: these decisions were influenced by people's ties to particular religious categories that functioned as markers of ethnic identity and that made it possible to distinguish among Orthodox Serbs, Catholic Croats, Muslim Bosniaks and Albanians. They were not determined, however, by the actual importance of religious identity in people's lives: those who left did not believe more strongly or practise their religion more frequently. In another contribution, the demographers LeGoff and Giudici (2014) have shown how, while in 1990 one out of seven marriages was 'mixed' (and the norm of mixed marriage was actively supported by institutional policies), mixed unions had almost disappeared from the statistics by the early 2000s. This was a combined consequence of three different processes: separation, emigration and conversion (i.e., the re-labelling of the identity of one of the partners).

These findings reveal that most people, when they encountered the dilemma of remaining or leaving a war zone, and sometimes even their spouse or family, acted *as if* ethnic identity was critical: they assumed that those who might attack or else protect them would rely on markers of identity to differentiate between foes and friends (even if religion was not important to them in private). More generally, these findings provide a sense of how many people were led to make difficult choices in an ambiguous environment: to leave everything behind, or to stay and comply with the logic of combat. In this process, the cumulative consequences of invidious individual choices then changed the environment in which others made sense of the collective situation. As more and more people began to take account of their own ethnicity-and the way their ethnicity was perceived by others-in making decisions, so yet others were led to think and act in ethnic terms. The acts of friends and neighbours were as important in validating an ethnic frame as official propaganda. Once collective behaviour had created new social facts, old norms became obsolete, and new norms of ethnic separation began to stabilise and acquire prescriptive value.

7.2 Keeping the Myth Real: Ethnic Nationalism in Post-War Croatia[1]

On 15 April 2011, the Croat general Ante Gotovina was convicted by the International Criminal Tribunal for the former Yugoslavia (ICTY) and sentenced to 24 years of imprisonment. The verdict was based on war crimes and crimes against humanity committed ten years earlier, during so-called Operation Storm. For Serbs, Operation Storm was an act of ethnic cleansing which forced nearly 200,000 of their compatriots to flee. For Croats, it was a heroic battle which won the war and led to the creation of their own sovereign nation-state.

Gotovina's sentence provoked a massive outcry across Croatia. Nearly all of the mainstream Croatian media portrayed the sentence as unjust, and this attitude was shared by the overwhelming majority of Croats. According to a poll conducted immediately after the verdict, 95 % of Croats perceived the verdict as unjust and 88 % of them still saw Gotovina as a hero (Jutarnji List, 2011). A year later, the Appeals Chamber of the ICTY, by a tight majority of three to two, overturned the previous verdict and acquitted Gotovina on formal grounds. The verdict was perceived as highly controversial internationally and was criticised in unusually blunt terms by the two dissenting members of the Appeals Chamber. Judge Agius described the verdict as "confusing and extremely problematic", Judge Pocar as "contradicting any sense of justice" and "grotesque"

---

[1] This section is adapted from Penic, Elcheroth, and Reicher (2016). Readers interested in more methodological detail might refer to this more extensive presentation of the study.

(Clark, 2013). But in Croatia it was met with widespread celebrations, which left no space for dissenting voices. It was widely interpreted as a full exoneration not only of Gotovina as an individual, but of Croatian actions during the war as a whole. Even the most-read left-leaning newspaper in the country, *Jutarnji list*, reacted to the acquittal by devoting the entire front page of its website to the headline "The war is over: Croatia is innocent".

The impression arises that, when it comes to the 'Homeland War', two decades after the end of fighting public opinion in Croatia remains monolithic. It is as if the rally effect never stopped. How does such a near-unanimous political climate perpetuate itself? Where are the critical voices—or what has happened to them?

According to a flourishing psychosocial literature, "critical patriots" would normally tend to act as nations' moral consciousness (Roccas, Klar, & Liviatan, 2006; Schatz & Staub, 1997; Staub, 1997). Even when they are only a minority within a nation, as long as they are consistent and vocal, they still retain the ability to mobilise support for their claims and provoke social change. However, the data at hand show that in Croatia, at least among the generation who were young adults during the war, critical patriots are difficult to find.

These data are taken from a subset of the TRACES survey data already referred to above. From the larger data set, we focus here on subsamples from Croatia and, for comparative purposes, from Serbia. The most striking finding from this quantitative analysis concerns the differences between these two national subsamples.

First, there are differences in the *incidence* of different modes of attachment. In particular, critical attachment, while being the least frequent mode in both samples, is much rarer in Croatia than in Serbia. In order to estimate the proportion of the population in each country who adopted the different modes of identification, we performed a cluster analysis on a joint sample of Serb and Croat respondents with two entry variables: national attachment and glorification. *Attachment to the group* was measured with the Doosje, Ellemers and Spears (1995) identification scale, which includes four items (e.g., "I identify with other Croats/Serbs"; "I am glad to be a Croat/Serb"). *National glorification* was assessed with the following three items from a larger National Identity scale (Corkalo & Kamenov, 2003): "There are many more capable people in my nation than in others", "In all historical conflicts with other nations my nation was always right" and "A good member of my nation should not associate with our enemies".

Table 7.6 summarises the results of the analysis, which display three different types of profile: (a) high national attachment with high glorification: *glorifiers*; (b) high national attachment with low glorification: *critically attached*; (c) low/average on both attachment and glorification: *detached*. As can be seen from the table, the Serb sample is roughly evenly split between the glorifiers (estimated at 40.9 % in the corresponding population) and the detached (45.2 %), with a significant minority of the critically attached (13.9 %). By contrast, the Croats are dominated by the glorifiers (67.5 %), with a smaller group of the detached (25.8 %) and a tiny group of critically attached people (6.7 %)—less than half as large as in Serbia.

Second, there are differences in the *relationship* between modes of attachment and collective guilt. *Collective guilt acceptance* was measured through a five-item scale developed by Branscombe, Slugoski and Happen (2004). Typical items on the scale are "I feel regret for my group's harmful past actions toward other groups" and "I can easily feel guilty for the

Table 7.6 Estimate of the population share for three types of identification in Croatia and Serbia; with group means of attachment, glorification and collective guilt acceptance

	Croatia			Serbia		
	Detached	Critically attached	Glorifiers	Detached	Critically attached	Glorifiers
Population share	25.8 %	6.7 %	67.5 %	45.2 %	13.9 %	40.9 %
Attachment	3.66	5.96	6.05	3.31	5.95	6.00
	0.76	0.64	0.72	1.03	0.70	0.79
Glorification	3.08	1.82	3.72	2.56	1.74	3.42
	0.93	0.40	0.70	0.86	0.44	0.63
Collective guilt acceptance	3.42	2.72	3.06	3.24	3.89	3.10
	1.25	1.26	1.30	1.32	1.37	1.34

bad outcomes brought about by members of my group". In the Serbian sample, the findings match the pattern found in previous research. That is, the critically attached show the highest level of collective guilt acceptance. However, in the Croatian sample, the pattern is very different: levels of collective guilt acceptance amongst the critically attached are much lower than in Serbia, and the highest level of collective guilt acceptance is found amongst *detached* respondents (see Table 7.6). What counts in Croatia, it seems, is *whether* one is attached to the nation, not how one is attached.

7.2.1 Why Is There No Space for Critical Patriots in Post-War Croatia?

So why should there be such a difference between nations? What are the critical elements of context which produce these differences? Why, more specifically, is critical patriotism so scarce in Croatia and why aren't critical patriots willing to accept the war guilt of the nation?

Perhaps the most obvious answer would be because, from 1991 to 1995, the war was fought on Croatian but not on Serbian territory. As a consequence, the suffering was far greater for ordinary Croats than for Serbs. Indeed several Croatian regions suffered tremendous destruction and loss of life. However, while there is evidence that victims of war are particularly reluctant to blame their own group for past wrongdoings (Corkalo Biruski & Penic, 2014), the same is not true for the broader communities from whom these victims are drawn. Moreover, there is contrary evidence from comparative studies showing that in the communities and regions most affected by the war, the condemnation of war-related crimes and the call for institutional justice is at its strongest (Elcheroth, 2006; Elcheroth & Spini, 2009, 2014).[2] Thus, war experiences in and of themselves are

---

[2] Similarly, in the comparative data set which we used in this research (TRACES), collective guilt acceptance is higher among Bosniaks in Bosnia than Croats in Croatia, although the former group was on average more exposed to the war victimisation. In contrast, Macedonians show lower collective guilt acceptance than both of the previous groups, although they are on average less victimised.

not sufficient to explain the lack of critical attachment and actual criticism in Croatia. What matters more is how these experiences are collectively interpreted and remembered. That is, how are events of war drawn upon in order to render criticism illegitimate and to deny that a *critical* patriot can be a *genuine* patriot?

War was and still is understood in very different ways in the two countries. In Serbia, the conflict of the 1990s led to defeat, to economic isolation, to ideological confusion and to moral doubt. In Croatia, what came to be known as the *Homeland War* is seen as righteous, as liberating and as the foundation of the sovereign nation-state of Croatia. In 2000, the Croatian Parliament institutionalised this official version of the war when passing a 'Declaration on the Homeland War'. The second paragraph of this declaration states that "The Republic of Croatia led a just and legitimate, defensive and liberating war, and not a war of aggression or of occupation war against anyone, in which it defended its territory from the great Serbian aggressor within its internationally recognized borders". Equally, those who prosecuted the war—the generals, but more particularly Franjo Tudjman as Head of State—became viewed as the founding fathers of Croatia (Uzelac, 1998). Finally, in a mutually reinforcing spiral, these leaders used the authority that they derived from their part in the war in order to reinforce the righteous and liberating understanding of the conflict. Thus, Tudjman (1992a, b) referred to "a holy Homeland War" which was necessary for achievement of "the centuries old dream".

It is also clear that, in Croatia, the right to criticise was radically constrained during the 1990s. The penal code of 1997 allowed for the prosecution of journalists or others who insult the president, prime minister, supreme court president, president of the parliament or president of the constitutional court. Even if reports are true, authors can still be prosecuted for causing emotional anguish. This law has been frequently enforced: in its first year of operation alone, 937 lawsuits were taken out under this provision (Jergović 2003). At the same time hundreds of journalists were sacked from the state broadcaster, simply for being Serb or else not a supporter of the ruling party. An estimated three million books in public libraries were burnt because the authors were Serb, the publishers were Serb or the text was "ideologically inappropriate" (Kurspahić, 2003; Lešaja, 2012).

But while it is fairly straightforward to establish that glorification of the nation is deeply entrenched both in political discourse and in formal documents and also that any criticism of the nation—or indeed a failure to actively endorse the national past and national representatives—was subject to severe repression during the 1990s, it remains to be explained exactly how the interpretation of the 'Homeland war' is used to deny a space for critical attachment; how, therefore, any expression of criticism is rendered illegitimate; and how the repression of critics is justified. The problem with such an analysis is that we are largely dealing with an absence. It is hard to see how repressive processes operate when people self-police and refrain from expressing criticism. However, there are occasional exceptions when people did publicly criticise Croatia's part in the war and the actions of the leaders in that war. One prominent example of this is the television programme *Latinica*, broadcast on 12 December 2005. The programme became the focus of a parliamentary debate the following day, 13 December. Through an in-depth analysis of the reactions to these critics and the way in which their position is treated, we sought to examine how the public space for a critical stance towards the nation is denied in Croatia.

7.2.2 The December 2015 Days

Ante Gotovina made his first appearance at the ICTY on 12 December 2005. On the evening of the same day, the political programme *Latinica* of the Croatian state television channel (*Hrvatska televizija*, HTV) broadcast a series of five small documentaries titled 'Tudjman's legacy', which addressed in an unusually critical way sensitive issues related to the "founder of the Croatian nation's" role during the war and political transition. Six guests discussed the regime of Franjo Tudjman, the first Croatian president, whose term of office spanned the first decade of the new nation-state (1990–1999). The discussion was organised around a series of reports dealing with various aspects of Tudjman's rule: his policies towards Bosnia and Herzegovina and relations with the international community; interethnic intolerance, ethno-centrism and nationalism in his politics; irregularities during the privatisation process and the economic decline of Croatia during the 1990s.

The guests on the show divided into supporters and critics of Tudjman's regime. Critics of the regime were represented by Zrinka Vrabec Mojzes, editor of the independent radio station 101; Zlatko Zeljko, president of the NGO 'Juris Protecta'; and Prof. Milan Kangrga, philosopher. Supporters of the regime were represented by Nenad Ivankovic, journalist, who wrote a biography of Franjo Tudjman; Ivan Vekic, Minister of Internal Affairs from 1991 to 1992; and Eduard Bajlo, historian. They differed substantially in their perception of recent Croatian history. In particular they expressed different views of the 'Homeland War' and of whether the Croatian side had committed war crimes. Whereas the critics emphasised the direct responsibility of the Croatian political elite for planning and executing such crimes, the supporters systematically denied that this was the case. For them, the Homeland War was defensive, and while they acknowledged that some crimes might have occurred, they represented them as individual acts committed out of revenge or despair.

The following extract involves an exchange between Zrinka Vrabec Mojzes and Ivan Vekic.

Vekic:	I am attacked and defending myself during the whole show, just because I am a Croat and I fought in the war.
Vrabec Mojzes:	And we ... What are we?
Vekic:	I don't know, I am not interested in that. But I am defending myself the whole time.
Vrabec Mojzes:	Obviously you think that we are not Croats, because we are critical towards crimes committed by Croats.
Vekic:	I am defending myself because of Ustashas, Tudjman, war, everything ...
Vrabec Mojzes:	But please, tell me, what are we if you are a Croat?
Vekic:	I don't know.

Vrabec Mojzes: Well, imagine, we are Croats too.
Vekic: I am not interested in that.
Vrabec Mojzes: But we are citizens of the Republic of Croatia.

The obvious and striking aspect of this exchange is the way in which the critic, Vrabec Mojzes, claims Croatian nationhood based on her citizenship (a broader and more inclusive criterion than alternatives such as ethnic background), the way that she repeatedly demands recognition of that nationhood by her opponent, Vekic, and the way in which Vekic, on four consecutive occasions, refuses to grant such recognition. But perhaps more important is the way in which she identifies this refusal with her status as a critic. Indeed it is striking how Vrabec Mojzes collectivises the issue. She never addresses her personal status. She asks who are 'we' (the critics) if Vekic is Croat. She asks Vekic to imagine that 'we' (the critics) are Croats. She insists that 'we' (the critics) are Croatian citizens. Most explicitly she complains that 'we' are not viewed as Croats because "we are critical towards crimes committed by Croats".

This exchange shows that being a critic is linked to one's national status—or rather, being a critic is used to deny one's national status, and hence being a critical patriot becomes an impossible position. It sets up the question for our main analysis of whether criticism is commonly used to deny nationhood and *how* it is used to deny nationhood.

This broadcast immediately provoked a fierce debate amongst the Croatian public and vehement disapproval from many quarters. Eventually, the show was suspended for one month. The editor of the show and two journalists received a formal warning. In addition, the editor of the show, Denis Latin, as well as Zrinka Vrabec Mojzes, one of the critics on the show, were placed under police protection following numerous threats. But perhaps the most important reaction relates to what unfolded in the Croatian Parliament over the next two days.

On 13 December 2005, the sitting of the Croatian Parliament was initially scheduled to discuss a report on the affairs of Croatian Radio Television (HRT) in 2004. In the event, much of the discussion was devoted to the *Latinica* show of the day before. Several members of parliament demanded an official statement from the director general of the HRT (who was present at the sitting). He declared that the programme was unprofessional and that the competent HRT bodies would state their position on the matter. He also stated that those responsible for the programme would be sanctioned. Such was the interest in the discussion that it was not completed by the end of its allotted time and an extension of the sitting was agreed for the following day. Finally, the discussion finished with a rejection of the Report under consideration.

Our main analyses are based on a full transcript of a parliamentary debate held on 13 and 14 December 2005. We conducted a thematic analysis, which was focused on the representation of the critical voices on the *Latinica* program, and the ways that this representation linked to construals of the national community and the national interest. Three broad thematic fields (or *a priori* coding categories) were distinguished as a basis for coding the text: constructions of critical voices, constructions of the nation and constructions of the international context.

The results of our qualitative analysis are summarised in Table 7.7. By far the most common category of argument was "construction of critical voices", with 29 speakers and 62 individual statements (77 % of the total). Critics were portrayed as distorting national values, as alien to the nation, as hurting the nation and therefore as people who needed to be identified and silenced. Arguments concerning the definition of the ingroup were considerably less common (seven statements from six speakers representing 9 % of the total): they represented Croatia as Catholic, tolerant and united behind its leaders. Arguments concerning the international context were similarly sparse (11 statement from eight speakers representing 14 % of the total): here the focus was almost entirely on a Croatia surrounded by powerful enemies—particularly the International Tribunal sitting in judgement on General Gotovina at that moment—who are aided and abetted by the critics.

7.2.3 How Have Critical Patriots Been Silenced by the Political Majority?

Already, we can glimpse the outlines of an overall argument: critics are not truc (i.e., loyal) Croats, but rather destroy the unity of the nation and attack the nation at a moment when it is vulnerable to its international enemies.

Table 7.7 Summary of the results of the thematic coding of the parliamentary debate held on 13 and 14 December 2005

Category	Number of arguments	Number of speakers
A. Construction of critical voices	62	29
1. What are they doing? ("A bad job")	7	6
1.1. Critics ... are misrepresenting the role of the Homeland War.	3	3
1.2. Critics ... are misrepresenting our national past.	4	4
2. Who are they? ("Alien individuals")	29	18
2.1. Critics ... are immoral and unprofessional.	11	8
2.2. Critics ... are profiteers and opportunists.	3	3
2.3. Critics ... are small elite that abuses its power.	3	2
2.4. Critics ... do not have popular support.	4	4
2.5. Critics ... are not part of the nation.	8	8
3. What are their intentions? ("To hurt us")	18	10
3.1. Critics ... are attacking the combatants of the Homeland War.	6	4
3.2. Critics ... are insulting Croatian people.	5	5
3.3. Critics ... are attacking the foundation of the Croatian state.	3	3
3.4. Critics ... despise our independence.	4	4
4. How shall we treat them? ("To defend ourselves")	8	8
4.1. Find the culprits.	4	4
4.2. Changing media policies.	4	4
B. Underlying construction of the national community	7	6
5. Who are we? ("The virtuous majority")	7	6
5.1. We are Croatian catholic majority	2	1
5.2. We are tolerant and respectful of pluralism	2	2
5.3. We are united in national interests and loyal to our leaders	3	3
C. Underlying construction of the international context	11	8
6. What is at stake? ("Not to let internal opponents play into the hands of external enemies")	11	8
6.1. Critics are collaborating with the historical enemies.	3	3
6.2. Critics are helping International Tribunal to build accusations.	8	6

It is quite clear from a quantitative summary that critics are portrayed as non-Croatian and indeed anti-Croatian in both intent and effect. Let us now look more closely at the debate in order to see just how this representation is sustained.

7 Ethnic Violence in the Former Yugoslavia: From Myth to Reality...

The President of the Parliament opened the session with a call to criticise *Latinica*:

> Yesterday's show, gentlemen from HTV and 'Latinica', was one blasphemous forgery of the Croatian history. Obviously biased, against all the principles of the journalistic profession. (…) And the Croatian Parliament should certainly talk about it. (…) We should not allow that we, as the highest representative body, do not speak out firmly and strongly about this and that we should be bound by the alleged freedom of the media. It is not media freedom when the truth is falsified, it is not media freedom when the elementary historical facts are represented in a disgusting, careless way, which irritates a huge proportion of the Croatian people and Croatian citizens.
> (Vladimir Seks, President of the Croatian Parliament)

There are three elements worthy of note here. To start with, in the very first sentence of the debate, critical positions are represented as a "blasphemous forgery". The notion of blasphemy sets up certain readings of the Croatian past as sacred and hence as not amenable to alternatives. Anyone who challenges these readings is therefore attacking the nation. Equally—and this is the second element—anyone who does so is advancing a falsehood. Therefore, repressing such voices is not curtailing freedom, it is defending the truth. In this way, an attack on the critics does not compromise the claim to be a freedom-loving nation and parliament. Third, insofar as this is an attack on the nation and an attack on the truth, it is opposed by (freedom-loving) Croats. If Seks uses a relatively mild formulation to express this (the criticism "irritates") and if he qualifies its application (to "a huge proportion" of Croats), others are both harsher and less qualified. Thus, Zdenka Babic Petricevic of the ruling HDZ argues that criticism "hurts" all true Croatians and Ivan Vucic, another HDZ member, suggests that it "disgusts" them.

This opening argument was never challenged. Rather, it raised a number of issues which were addressed by other speakers throughout the debate. The first of these issues is who are the critics and why are they critical. Some of the interventions characterise them as lacking positive qualities. They are stupid: "the lowest educated journalists in Croatia" according to Independent member Slaven Letica. They are insignificant: the ruling party (HDZ) member Kresimir Cosic refers to one critic as "such an obscure person". They are vicious: Cosic also refers to critics more generally as "indoctrinated and full of hate".

This last comment raises the question of who they are indoctrinated by and who they hate. The answer is that they serve alien interests. They hate Croatia and Croats. For instance, in the next extract, the insinuation by the right-wing HSP member Pejo Trgovcevic is that *Latinica* is a foreign show:

> Shows like this astound the Croatian public, and we ask, together with the majority of the Croatian public, which television have we watched yesterday? Are these shows from Croatian television or some other Television?
> (Pejo Trgovcevic, HSP)

Indeed, even the title of the programme is challenged to insist upon this alien character. With a play on words, the show is equated to the Serbian rather than the Croatian language to exemplify its supposedly hostile stance disguised as a national programme:

> And I personally cannot stand Latinica because it is written in Cyrillic, and that's why it is as it is.
> (Zdenka Babic Petricevic, HDZ)

The next issue concerns the nature of the sacred: What is it precisely which cannot be questioned by any true Croat, and which distresses Croats if questioned? The answer lies in a double elision, the first element of which is the wartime leader and first president, Franjo Tudjman. Above, we noted how Kresimir Cosic referred to one critic as "obscure". But this obscurity was emphasised through a contrast with Tudjman's pre-eminence. Thus, Cosic marvelled at how *Latinica* could provide public space for "such an obscure person to speak neither more nor less than about the Father of the Nation". The term 'father of the nation' is, of course, redolent with significance. It denotes someone who has given birth to the nation, someone who has unquestioned authority over the nation, and someone with whom nationals have an intimate and highly significant relationship. This, in part, explains why Croats would be upset by criticisms of Tudjman for these are akin to insulting a beloved family member. This is powerfully expressed by the following speaker, who compounds the sense of outrage by invoking his daughter, a child, who cannot understand why anyone should attack the dear leader:

> [Instead of *Latinica*] We should have broadcast some of [Tudjman's] speeches, performances, so our children can see who that great man was, instead of it happening that my daughter asks me in the morning, excuse me for my voice, how come they are speaking like that about our Franjo. Then I had to explain to her who was speaking and why.
> (Franjo Arapovic, HDZ)

Importantly, though, criticism of Tudjman is not represented as criticism of Tudjman alone. It is rhetorically elided with criticism of Croatian soldiers. Equally, criticism of Croatian soldiers is elided with criticism of the Croatian people and of the nation as a whole. Both elements are apparent in the following extract:

> We can clearly conclude that HTV is working against Croatian defenders and damaging them, because they want to vilify them, the whole victorious Croatian army, and it's commander, late President Tudjman.
> (Josip Djakic, HDZ)

On the one hand, then, Tudjman is positioned as commander of the army, such that an attack on him is an attack on the army (and *vice versa*). On the other hand, the army are characterised as 'Croatian defenders' (an official term). They are an embodiment of national independence—the fight to achieve it and to preserve it. Putting both elisions together, Tudjman himself is constituted as the embodiment of national independence. He himself becomes sacred. He is rendered inviolate, and an attack on him becomes an attack not just on the father of the nation, but on the nation itself.

> We do not need to defend Dr. Franjo Tudjman, he defended us as a supreme commander of the armed forces and the democratic movement. He freed, defended and left us in the legacy a sovereign independent State of Croatia. And Mr. Latin and many little "Latins" in Croatia cannot bear that legacy.
> (Jagoda Majska Martincevic, HDZ)

The final issue concerns the reason why it is so important to silence the critics. In part, this may be self-evident: to the extent that they are seen as attacking the (national) ingroup, this is bad in and of itself. However, this is not the end of the story. On the one hand, these attacks were represented as doing real harm. Some of the media invoked the suicide of a soldier—a 'Croatian defender' and hence a symbol of the nation—on the evening that *Latinica* was broadcast. For example, one of the most popular daily journals 'Vecernji List' published this information on the front page under the title 'Killed himself because of "Latinica"'. The suicide was attributed to the programme and, in some instances, was actually seen as intended by the programme—that is, the aim of the critics was to weaken or even destroy the nation. This argument was immediately taken up by several speakers:

> Yesterday's TV show about which we spoke a lot today, achieved its goal. I just received a text message—after watching Latinica yesterday, a Croatian defender in Glina committed suicide using a bomb.
> (Ivo Loncar, Independent)

On the other hand, the nation was represented as particularly vulnerable due to the actions of foreign enemies, in part Serbia (according to Josip Djakic of the HDZ, Croatian Television was 'helping Serbian spies to write accusations' against Croatia), but more characteristically—and not surprisingly given Gotovina's trial—the ICTY. Such times would normally compel unity. According to Ivan Vucic of the HDZ, this was a moment when "Croatian people and Croatian defenders" were organising rallies in favour of the general, and when "only those who do not wish well to Croatian people" would be critical. And yet, this was precisely the moment when *Latinica* chose to air its criticisms, thus strengthening the hand of the enemy.

> We are judged by the international community, we are judged in the ICTY, and we are blaming Serbs. But we are wrong! Us Croats, it is our own fault. These editors who are preparing such programmes. That show will for sure be watched at the ICTY. And what is it saying? What evidence is that? These are the transcripts which the worst enemy couldn't deliver to someone, but fortunately, they are not true.
> (Ivan Vucic, HDZ)

All 18 categories of argument previously summarised in Table 7.7 come from members of the ruling coalition or from independents. Members of the opposition only took issue with two of these arguments: 'changing media policies' (4.2), and 'we are tolerant and respectful of pluralism' (5.2). This fitted into the two broad arguments deployed by the opposition. First, they systematically accused the ruling parties of undermining freedom of speech and media independence. Second, they argued that attacks on HTV and *Latinica* were a cover for achieving greater state control over HTV.

However, throughout the entire debate, not a single opposition member either addressed the criticisms voiced in *Latinica* or reacted to attacks on the critics. To put it more starkly, no one contested the notion that critics are a deviant anti-Croatian minority who harm the nation and its people. Nor did anyone question the regime of Franjo Tudjman or its responsibility for crimes committed during the Homeland War. Altogether, this parliamentary 'debate' was *de facto* a *monologue*. Indeed, on the second day of the parliamentary sitting, members of the opposition declined to participate in the debate any further and they left the Parliament. Doing so, they dramatically enacted and at the same time consecrated the absence of space for critical debate among the elected representatives of Croatian citizens: potentially critical voices withdrew rather than contributed to the debate. Their inability to participate can be put down to the fact that it was self-evident that to voice anything but support for the attack on critics would position them—along with the critics themselves—as anti-national, which is a death knell for politicians, at least in a democratic system (Reicher & Hopkins, 2001).

7.3 Conclusion

So how, then, has the myth of ethnic war not only become real in its consequences during the war, but been nourished and kept alive during the post-war period? How, in post-war Croatia, have critical voices been marginalised, and their legitimacy to speak as members of the nation challenged? To summarise our findings, three key elements were involved. The first was to sacralise certain events and individuals—specifically, the Homeland War and those, like Tudjman, who prosecuted it. These, then, are not just incidental aspects of the nation which could be good or bad. Rather they are essential to and foundational of the nation: the war created the nation; Tudjman is the 'father' of the nation. It follows that any attack on either suggests that the nation itself is essentially bad. Such representations are not limited to the Croatian political elite—they have been promoted by a range of public actors and institutions such as the Catholic Church (Perica, 2002), the media (Kurspahić, 2003) and the school system (Barunčić & Križe, 2006). Consequently, it becomes impossible to sustain a critical stance which rests on the claim that candid self-scrutiny serves to improve the nation (Hornsey, 2005).

The second element was to go from claiming that criticism was an attack on the nation to a claim that criticism was damaging the nation. In part, this involved attributing actual instances of harm (e.g., the suicide of a soldier/'national defender') to the criticisms. In part, it involved construing the nation as highly vulnerable due to external threats as concretised in the ICTY, and in the person of General Gotovina standing before the International Tribunal in The Hague. As a number of authors have pointed out, invoking powerful enemies is a particularly powerful way of demanding unity and outlawing criticism (see Chap. 5). That is, by invoking enemies who constitute a serious threat to the ingroup, unity is demanded and criticism is outlawed.

Thirdly, then, true Croats are represented as active loyalists: according to some majority parliamentary members quoted in our analysis, they don't simply support the nation in principle, they rally for the nation (or even organise rallies for the nation). Likewise, true Croats are necessarily hurt, irritated and disgusted by anyone who is *not* loyal at the nation's hour of need. The corollary is that anyone who criticises the nation (or even fails to be disgusted by such criticism) is not only denied nationhood, they are constituted as active enemies of the nation (they don't have the country's interests at heart, they knowingly provide ammunition for enemies such as the ICTY); their goal is the destruction of national icons (such as Croatian soldiers) and the nation itself. They have to be repressed.

We do not suggest that all these elements are necessary in order to marginalise critical patriotism or that these are the only ways by which criticism of the nation can be outlawed. We simply present them as some of the ways by which critics can be silenced, and as the ways that this was done in Croatia. This analysis, then, helps explain the very low numbers of critical patriots in Croatia. For those few who do adopt such a stance, it also makes sense of the lack of a relationship with willingness to accept that the nation has done specific wrongs in the past. It is one thing to eschew claiming that one's nation is better than others; it is quite another to overtly express criticisms of the things it has done when one sees what does happen to those who do actually put their heads above the parapet.

But there may be another reason for the lack of a relationship between mode of attachment and acceptance of national guilt. We have already noted how speakers stress the isolation of the critics, how they are atypical of most Croats (certainly of 'true Croats') and how most people are opposed to them. More tentatively, we have suggested that this helps to explain why the opposition failed to address the criticisms and eventually withdrew from the debate—thus entrenching the impression that no one supports the critics. Even without overt repression, or even the threat of repression, this may itself be sufficient to silence those who identify with their nation but do not think it to be flawless. As we have argued in Chap. 3, people's stances in the world are determined by their assumptions about the interpretations that are shared with relevant others. If we assume that certain interpretations cannot be shared, we are likely to engage in self-censorship. Where we believe that the critical questioning of our nation's role in past conflicts will be rejected as disloyal by fellow nationals, we will be unlikely to voice any such criticisms. In this way, critical attachment becomes dissociated from the expression of criticism and of acceptance of guilt for our past deeds.

Another way of saying this is that, if it is impossible for a critical patriot to be a genuine patriot then, to continue as a patriot, one must censor one's criticisms. But there is another option. That is, to continue as a critic, one must discard one's patriotism. This would explain another feature of the findings from the representative cohort sample, that is, the only people to accept national guilt in Croatia (unlike Serbia) are those who are explicitly dis-identified from the nation.

The process whereby those who will not renounce their criticisms are led to renounce their nationhood is well expressed by two famous Croatian intellectuals: the writer Dubravka Ugresic and the philosopher Boris Buden. After becoming a target of the nationalistic media and Croatian public because of their critical attitudes about Croatian nationalism during the 1990s, both of them left the country. Ugrešić (2007) explained that "(T)hey excluded me from their literary and other ranks ... I became a literary representative of a place that no longer wanted me. I, too, no longer wanted the place that no longer wanted me. I am no fan of unrequited love". Buden (2000) was yet more explicit about the interconnections between being excluded and discarding identity: "I am not anymore a Croatian intellectual ... I have experienced a definitive exclusion, or separation, cutting of the umbilical cord that connected me with the Croatian identity".

What is most striking about the dialogue between regime supporters and regime critics in the TV show we analysed is that the latter did not *choose* to dis-identify with Croatia. They did not aim to become 'anti-Croats'. It was not a position that reflected their internal beliefs and desires. On the contrary, they struggled to be recognised as fully fledged members of the national community. The position of outsiders was imposed upon them because that which they would have chosen—critical attachment—was simply not available. This serves to underline a point that has been imminent throughout our discussion. That is, the relative incidence of critical patriots and national glorifiers in Croatia cannot be understood as a matter of individual differences (which is how differences in the mode of national identification are normally approached—see, for example, Kosterman and Feschbach, 1998; Mummendy, Klink and Brown, 2001; Staub, 1997). Rather, they reflect differences in the social availability of certain ideological configurations of belief.

The struggle for the recognition of critical attachment as a legitimate mode of identification thus unfolds at two different levels: (a) at a micro-level, where people negotiate their version of identification with relevant others through a myriad of individual decisions to express a particular voice or keep silent; and (b) at a macro-level, where elites use their control over institutional policies, party lines and/or mass media to systematically provide opportunities or, in contrast, discourage people from giving voice to a particular version of identity.

As we have seen from the parliamentary reaction to one television programme, when critical patriots raise their voice, they are met with extreme reactions. These reactions were overwhelmingly focused on the *delegitimisation* of these critical voices, by portraying them as disloyal, anti-national, aberrant and even dangerous for the nation. In such a political climate, where critical voices are denied social recognition as Croats and the right to speak as Croats, critics will have little opportunity to participate in public debates on the nation's past even if they want to. Most prefer to keep silent. This then perpetuates a vicious spiral in which the illusion of a monolithic public opinion becomes ever more entrenched and the possibility of changing it becomes ever more remote.

References

Barunčić, J., & Križe, Z. (2006). Domovinski rat u udžbenicima iz povijesti. *Casopis Za Suvremenu Povijest, 38*(2), 373–716.

Branscombe, N. R., Slugoski, B., & Kappen, D. M. (2004). The measurement of collective guilt: What it is and what it is not. In N. R. Branscombe & B. Doosje (Eds.), *Collective guilt: International perspectives* (pp. 16–34). New York: Cambridge University Press.

Broz, S. (2005). Facing the crime-vengeance, justice and understanding. *Yearbook of the Balkan Human Rights Network, 01*, 174–186.

Broz, S. (2014). When nobody stood up and everybody is guilty: A puzzle of individual responsibility and collective guilt. In D. Spini, G. Elcheroth, & D. Corkalo Biruski (Eds.), *War, community, and social change. Collective experiences in the former Yugoslavia* (pp. 155–162). Berlin & New York: Springer.

Buden, B. (2000). Interview in Vreme. Retrieved from http://www.ex-yupress.com/vreme/vreme100.html

Clark, J. N. (2013). The ICTY's Acquittal of Croatian Generals Gotovina and Markac. *Journal of International Criminal Justice, 11*(2), 399–423. doi:10.1093/jicj/mqt009.

Corkalo, D., & Kamenov, Z. (2003). National Identity and social distance: Does in-group loyalty lead to outgroup hostility? *Review of Psychology, 10*(2), 85–94.

Corkalo Biruski, D., & Penic, S. (2014). Traumatised selves: Does war trauma facilitate in-group bonding and out-group distancing? In D. Spini, G. Elcheroth, & D. Corkalo Biruski (Eds.), *War, community, and social change: Collective experiences in the former Yugoslavia* (pp. 137–154). Berlin & New York: Springer.

Doosje, B., Ellemers, N., & Spears, R. (1995). Perceived variability as a function of group status and identification. *Journal of Experimental Social Psychology, 31*, 410–436.

Elcheroth, G. (2006). Individual-level and community-level effects of war trauma on social representations related to humanitarian law. *European Journal of Social Psychology, 36*(6), 907–930.

Elcheroth, G., & Spini, D. (2009). Public support for the prosecution of human rights violations in the former Yugoslavia. *Peace and Conflict: Journal of Peace Psychology, 15*(2), 189–214.

Elcheroth, G., & Spini, D. (2014). Beyond collective denial: Public reactions to human rights violations and the struggle over the moral continuity of communities. In D. Spini, G. Elcheroth, & D. Corkalo Biruski (Eds.), *War, community, and social change. Collective experiences in the former Yugoslavia* (pp. 205–226). Berlin & New York: Springer.

Gagnon, V. (2004). *The myth of ethnic war: Serbia and Croatia in the 1990's.* Ithaca, NY: Cornell University Press.

Gauthier, J.-A., & Widmer, E. (2014). The destruction of multiethnic locations: Markers of identity and the determinants of residential trajectories. In D. Spini, G. Elcheroth, & D. Corkalo Biruski (Eds.), *War, community, and social change. Collective experiences in the former Yugoslavia* (pp. 85–98). Berlin & New York: Springer.

Hornsey, M. J. (2005). Why being right is not enough: Predicting defensiveness in the face of group criticism. *European Review of Social Psychology, 16*(1), 301–334.

Jergović, M. (2003). Zakonske promjene i tisak u Hrvatskoj od 1990. do 2002. *Politicka Misao, XL*(1), 92–108.

Jutarnji List. (2011, April 16). Samo 23% Hrvata za ulazak u EU! Čak 95% smatra presudu nepravednom [Only 23% of Croats to join the EU! As many as 95% considered the verdict unjust.]. Retrieved from http://www.jutarnji.hr/istrazivanje-nakon-presude-gotovini--samo-23--hrvata-za-ulazak-u-eu/939458/

Kosterman, R., & Feshbach, S. (1989). Toward a measure of patriotic and nationalistic attitudes. *Political Psychology, 10*(2), 257–274.

Kurspahić, K. (2003). *Prime time crime: Balkan media in war and peace*. Washington, DC: US Institute of Peace Press.

Le Goff, J.-M., & Giudici, F. (2014). The demise of mixed marriage? In D. Spini, G. Elcheroth, & D. Corkalo Biruski (Eds.), *War, community, and social change. Collective experiences in the former Yugoslavia* (pp. 63–84). Berlin & New York: Springer.

Lešaja, A. (2012). *Knjigocid—Uništavanje knjiga u Hrvatskoj tijekom 90-ih*. Zagreb: Profil/SNV.

Mummendey, A., Klink, A., & Brown, R. (2001). Nationalism and patriotism: National identification and out-group rejection. *British Journal of Social Psychology, 40*(2), 159–172.

Perica, V. (2002). *Balkan idols: Religion and nationalism in Yugoslav states*. New York: Oxford University Press.

Penic, S., Elcheroth, G., & Reicher, S. (2016). Can patriots be critical after a nationalist war? The struggle between recognition and marginalisation of dissenting voices. *Political Psychology, 37*(4), 481–496.

Reicher, S., & Hopkins, N. (2001). *Self and nation*. London: Sage.

Roccas, S., Klar, Y., & Liviatan, I. (2006). The paradox of group-based guilt: Modes of national identification, conflict vehemence, and reactions to the in-group's moral violations. *Journal of Personality and Social Psychology, 91*(4), 698–711.

Schatz, R. T., & Staub, E. (1997). Manifestations of blind and constructive patriotism: Personality correlates and individual–group relations. In D. Bar-Tal & E. Staub (Eds.), *Patriotism: In the lives of individuals and nations* (pp. 229–245). New York: Nelson-Hall.

Spini, D., Elcheroth, G., & Biruski, D. C. (2013). *War, community, and social change: Collective experiences in the former Yugoslavia*. New York: Springer Science & Business Media.

Spini, D., Elcheroth, G., & Fasel, R. (2011). *TRACES: Methodological and technical report* (No. 4). LIVES Working Papers.

Staub, E. (1997). Blind versus constructive patriotism: Moving from embeddedness in the group to critical loyalty and action. In D. Bar-Tal & E. Staub (Eds.), *Patriotism: In the lives of individuals and nations* (pp. 213–228). New York: Nelson-Hall.

Tudjman, F. (1992a). *Croatian Army achieved its historical duty*. Presented at the Speech given on October 29th 1992, Dubrovnik. Retrieved from http://www.slobodanpraljak.com/MATERIJALI/RATNI%20DOKUMENTI/TUDJMAN%20GOVORI%20I%20INTERVJUI%201990.-1998/Tablica-Tudjman-intervjui.htm

Tudjman, F. (1992b). *The centuries-old dream achieved!*. Presented at the Speech given on May 30th 1992. Retrieved from http://www.slobodanpraljak.com/ MATERIJALI/RATNI%20DOKUMENTI/TUDJMAN%20 GOVORI%20I%20INTERVJUI%201990.-1998/Tablica-Tudjman-intervjui.htm

Ugrešić, D. (2007). *Nobody's home*. London: Telegram/Saqi.

Uzelac, G. (1998). Franjo Tudjman's nationalist ideology. *East European Quarterly, XXXI*(4), 449–472.

8

British Warriors and Scottish Voters: When 'Rallying the Nation' Backfires

The 'Invasion of Iraq' commonly denotes the period between 20 March 2003 (when a military coalition formed predominantly of the USA and its most important ally, the UK, entered Iraqi soil) and 1 May 2003 (the day when US President Bush declared the end of major combat operations in a televised address from an aircraft carrier). In Britain the invasion provoked a massive national rally effect. When it started, it looked as if the anti-war mobilisation, which had been very strong during the preceding weeks, had lost its impact overnight.

In a retrospective survey conducted by Lewis (2004) among a representative sample of British adults in summer 2003, more than a third of respondents admitted that they had changed their stance on the war once it had started. This way, a minority of supporters mutated into an overwhelming national majority. Interestingly, when those who shifted from an anti-war to a pro-war position were asked why they changed their mind, the most frequent answer was "to support our troops". Lewis' analyses of the new mass media context created during the invasion elucidate the mechanisms by which people's desire to be perceived as loyal supporters of British troops "may have been compounded by the fear of being seen as part of an isolated, unpatriotic minority" (p. 301). As he points out, the 'embedded' war reporters programme designed by US and UK Ministries of Defence facilitated new forms of daily frontline journalism. These not only fostered concrete identification with coalition troops and their day-to-day activities—while 'enemy' troops remain largely abstract and dehumanised. They also shift general media attention away from the broader political and moral issues raised by the war, towards issues of military strategy and progress.

This conclusion has subsequently been corroborated in a detailed content analysis of televised images broadcast by the BCC during the early invasion phase (Lipson, 2009). While most camera shots showing coalition troops were close enough to read the facial expressions and emotions of individual soldiers, camera shots showing Iraqis were typically taken in anonymous group or crowd situations and most of them displayed males moving, running or behaving violently together.

The rallying effect of the war did not occur homogenously across Britain, however. There were pockets of resistance—even at the moment when triumphalist voices were at their loudest and the national rally effect was at its peak. By coincidence, on the same day that the world saw a triumphant Bush in front of a large 'Mission Accomplished' banner, Scotland's citizens went to the polls to elect their representatives for the second session of the devolved parliament in Edinburgh, created four years before. The parties which had campaigned against the war during the invasion scored well in these elections: in the regional vote, where people vote for party lists rather than individual candidates, the three anti-war parties—the Scottish National Party, Scottish Socialist Party and Scottish Greens—polled a total of 34.5 % of the vote, an increase of 1.6 %.

The greater level of anti-war sentiment in Scotland than in the rest of the UK was even more apparent in later opinion polls. The British General Election Studies of 2005 provide the opportunity to compare the lasting effects of anti-war mobilisation in Scotland with the rest of Britain, two years after the invasion. According to our analyses of this data set, 42 % of Scots declared themselves "angry" and 43 % "disgusted" by the war in Iraq, compared with only 36 %, for both emotions, in the remaining population. Scots were more likely to strongly disapprove of British involvement in Iraq and to judge that the Labour government handled the situation in Iraq badly. Furthermore, the Scottish respondents mentioned Iraq almost twice as often as the most important issue of the election campaign. In contrast to what was observed in England and Wales, the Scottish working class expressed critical stances on the war as frequently as members of the middle or upper classes. That is, in Scotland (and only in Scotland) anti-war mobilisation completely overcame class cleavages.

But there is a second reason why the Scottish reaction to Iraq's invasion is worthy of an analysis in its own right. When Billig (1995) commented on the two previous major rally events in British history—in 1982 during the Falklands War and in 1991 during the First Gulf War—his main point was that the apparent ease and speed with which national leaders in Britain (and elsewhere) mobilised support for war would not have been possible without steady, daily and unspectacular rehearsals around the national flag during the years and decades beforehand. Leaders who only started arguing about national identity and the national interest on actual entry to war would have little chance of engaging their population. Equally, dissidents who sought to invoke national values in opposition would have little chance of being heard above the drumbeat of war unless their arguments were already familiar. In particular, if the seeds of critical patriotism (see Chap. 7) have not been planted well before, it is unlikely that it will flourish in the harsh climate created when wars start.

But, interestingly, Billig's argument can easily be turned on its head: if a familiar and agreed view of national identity facilitates its use in creating a new consensus when wars start, so a contested view of national identity opens the way to challenging such a consensus. In other words, hegemonic support for war is less likely, and polemical debates more likely, when critics can draw on well-recognised alternative understandings of nationhood in order to advance their case.

From this perspective, the Scottish context provides opportunities for those who oppose British war policies. This is due to a pervasive tension between two co-existent, but potentially antagonistic, forms of 'banal' nationalism. From the Scottish public's point of view, there is indeed permanent ambiguity as to whether to salute the British Union Jack or the Scottish Saltire. Should people trust to the categories of the

Football World Cup (where Scots have their own team) or to those of the Olympic (where they compete for Great Britain); should they adopt the perspective of the British or Scottish editions of the same TV channels when watching the daily news? Interestingly, Rutland, Cinnirella and Simpson (2008) showed that, among Scottish students, identification with both Scotland and Britain is remarkably stable across different situations. This insensitivity to immediate contextual influences is related to "the fact that Scottish and British self-categories are chronically accessible" (p. 268). Furthermore, as shown by Sindic and Reicher (2009), in combination with particular understandings of intergroup relations, social identification with Scotland anchors specific political claims, like separatism.

In short, nationhood is more troubled and contested in Scotland than in the rest of the UK and that may account for the greater opposition to the Iraq war. This troubled sense of nationhood is reflected at the structural level in the shifting constitutional settlement between Scotland and England. Since the creation of a devolved Scottish Parliament in 1999, there has been an ongoing debate as to whether the devolved settlement is adequate, whether the parliament should have greater powers or whether there should be full independence. Furthermore, if the issue of how Scottishness relates to Britishness is at the top of the political agenda, it is equally salient at a psychological level. This makes Scotland a particularly promising place in which to examine how national categories are construed and how these are used to argue for or against war.

In this chapter, we will present systematic analyses of how the Iraq invasion of 2003 was understood in Scotland by both elites and by the overall population. The first part includes all the contributions to four Scottish parliamentary debates about the Gulf War which occurred between January 2003 and June 2004—a total of 106 speeches. Using a combination of qualitative thematic analysis and quantitative, multiple correspondence analysis (MCA) we examine (a) the definitions of identity that were invoked to support pro- and anti-war positions, and the extent to which they were rooted in the broader political culture; (b) consistencies and differences between different contributors to the debate, in relation to their party's position on Scottish nationalism; and (c) shifts in argument and in categorical structure over the course of events—especially between the pre- and post-invasion debates.

In the second part, we turn from elite discourse to popular understandings of the war, to analyse the constituency context of the political speeches. This part is based on data from the Scottish Social Attitudes (SSA) survey of 2003. We analyse how anti-war and pro-war respondents express their own nationhood and how the translation of individual anti-war positions into electoral support for the anti-war separatist parties relates to their exposure to mass media sources.[1]

8.1 Mobilising for or Against the Invasion

Two major debates concerning the possible war in Iraq occurred in the Scottish parliament before the invasion. The first was on 16 January 2003, when there was still considerable uncertainty regarding whether there would be a war and who would participate. The second debate took place on 13 March 2003, six days before the first air strikes on Baghdad. At this point, war (and British combat involvement in the war) was seen as all but inevitable by most observers. We also analysed the first two substantial parliamentary debates that took place after the invasion—the one on 20 November 2003 (when George Bush visited the UK), the other on 2 June 2004 (when the war crimes at Abu Ghraib had become public). The full transcripts of these four debates, which are published in the official records of the parliament, constituted the raw corpus of data for our analyses.

To prepare this corpus for both qualitative and quantitative analyses, we conducted two-step hierarchical thematic coding. The first step was aimed at identifying discrete arguments used within the corpus. These were organised into a 2 × 2 grid. The first dimension concerned whether the argument is about the categorisation of actors (who is against whom) or else the morality of events (whether, and in what way, the war is

---

[1] Another version of this study has previously been published in Elcheroth and Reicher (2014). The present version has been simplified for the presentation of the quantitative material, but significantly enriched with qualitative material as compared to the article version.

justified or not). The second dimension concerned whether the argument addressed the domestic significance of the war ('home front' arguments) or its international significance ('external front' arguments).

In a second step the resulting coding categories were reduced to create a set of *general arguments*. Thematic coding resulted in two types of outcome. First, it produced the structured inventories of arguments that are summarised in Tables 8.1 and 8.2 and which serve as a grid for qualitative analyses. These inventories provide an overall template for interpreting the grand-narrative structures spun by war supporters and opponents. Second, the coding resulted in a content analytical database in which the 106 parliamentary interventions (each representing the entire rhetorical contribution of one Member of the Scottish Parliament, MSP, to one of the four debates) are treated as cases, and arguments are treated as variables. Two external variables were added to this database: the date of the debate and the party affiliation of the speaker. This database is suitable to conduct MCA at the level of parliamentary interventions, based on the joint occurrences of general arguments invoked by the same speaker within the same debate.

The findings show first that there is a clear antinomic structure to the debate: each argument in favour of the invasion can be matched with an argument against it. The notion that war is a necessary act of self-defence is countered by the argument that it is unnecessary aggression; the notion that war will relieve suffering is countered by the argument that it will destroy lives; the notion that war will promote a democratic world order is countered by the argument that it will destabilise this order (see Table 8.1). Altogether, while pro-war speeches refer to a narrative of liberation and unity, anti-war rhetoric builds upon a narrative of aggression and division.

Table 8.2 presents the range of categorical arguments. The way categorical and moral arguments relate to each other and the way in which this relationship changes across the debates is the focus of an MCA, the outcome of which is reported in Fig. 8.1.

The two dimensions arising from this analysis are easily interpretable. The horizontal dimension represents pro- versus anti-war positions. The vertical dimension represents the time of the debate, from before to after the invasion. For ease of interpretation, we have divided the figure into

8 British Warriors and Scottish Voters: When 'Rallying the Nation'

Table 8.1 A structured inventory of moral arguments: generic moral judgements and nested concrete arguments invoked by the 'external front' and the 'home front' as well as frequencies before and after the invasion

External front	Before	After		External front	Before	After
Self-defence and containment	33 %	4 %	vs.	**Undermining a peaceful settlement of the crisis**	19 %	5 %
WMDs in the hands of a tyrant	13	1		No immediate threat	8	2
Military threat helps diplomacy	8			All other means not exhausted	14	
Humanitarian intervention	16 %	22 %	vs.	**Disproportionate killing**	23 %	29 %
Rescue a suffering people	10	4		Humanitarian disaster	8	6
More lives saved than lost		2		Selective morality	19	5
Promoting a democratic world order	27 %	52 %	vs.	**Destabilising the international order**	47 %	29 %
Democracy and peace-building	7	10		Violation of national sovereignty	6	6
Institutional backing for war	10	2		Undermining the UN and the rule of international law	40	
War against terror		2		Stimulating terrorism	8	5
Home front				**Home front**		
National loyalty first	25 %	22 %	vs.	**Bypassing democratic accountability**	10 %	37 %
The troops and their commander-in-chief need our support	4			No public mandate for war	9	
Opponents undermine our nation's leadership	8	4		Beware of blind support	2	11
No time for debate, too late to step back	4			Political deception	1	
Misjudgement is not deception		2		Perversion of democracy		3

Table 8.2 A structured inventory of categorical arguments: generic social cleavages and nested concrete arguments invoked by the 'external front' and the 'home front' as well as frequencies before and after the invasion

External front	Before	After
All vs. Saddam	6 %	6 %
Coalition for the Iraqi people	5	3
US-UK vs. Iraq	20 %	16 %
War against the Iraqi people	17	3
Army of occupation		5
Western powers vs. the Arab world	4 %	10 %
Clash of civilisations in the making	3	5
Home front		
Democrats vs. autocrats	8 %	6 %
Democracy unites us	7	3
Scotland vs. the rest of the UK	20 %	6 %
Vulnerable Scotland	5	
Shame on the UK	4	
Scotland's voice against the war	8	
The union and the impediment to a moral policy		3
Communities vs. elites	13 %	34 %
Virtuous troops led by immoral politicians	2	4
Undemocratic warlords	9	7
Tough towards the weak, weak towards the powerful		3
International capitalism, the grounds for violence		3
People of the world vs. US and UK state powers	29 %	22 %
US unilateral superpower policies	14	6
Fatal alliance with the US	10	5

two parts so we can see separately how moral and categorical arguments respectively map onto this space.

As can be seen, the pro-war 'liberation' morality is associated with an opposition between the world's democrats and (isolated) autocrats, which is subsequently resolved into the whole (democratic) world against a single tyrannical figure, Saddam Hussein. The anti-war 'aggression' morality is associated with a division of the world into dominant and subordinate groups: at the start of the debate, English war-mongers dragging the Scots into conflict; later, social elites against ordinary people; or a hegemonic USA/British West against Eastern/Arabic peoples.

To summarise, the pro-war discourse draws upon the 'new world order' narrative which has been prevalent since the first Gulf War and which in turn draws upon anti-Nazi narratives: the entire civilised world against

8 British Warriors and Scottish Voters: When 'Rallying the Nation' 223

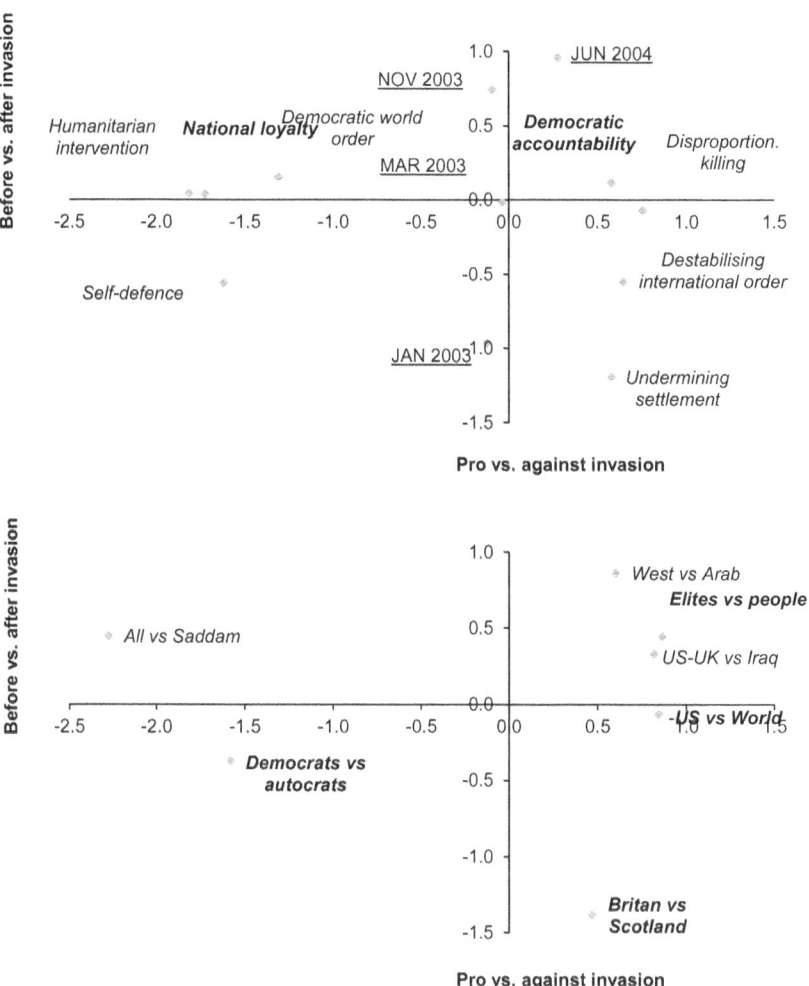

Fig. 8.1 Moral principle positions and the timing of debates (*above*) as well as social cleavage positions (*below*) according to their coordinates along two dimensions defined by an MCA of their joint occurrences within parliamentary interventions. Arguments related to the 'home front' appear in *bold*.

one mad dictator. The anti-war discourse draws upon the notion of a more aggressive England imposing its will upon the communal Scots within the political structures of the UK—a narrative which has become commonplace within Scottish political discourse (Reicher & Hopkins, 2001).

In other words, both the anti-camp and the pro-camp are anchored in familiar mainstream constructions.

There are two further aspects of the findings which speak to the relationships between the constructions of the one camp and those of the other, and also the relationships between constructions within the same camp.

First, as well as showing differences in structure between pro- and anti-war speakers, our data also point to differences in the amount of *rhetorical effort* they devote to different tasks. Opponents of the war spend more time than supporters in sustaining their categorical constructions. They generate more arguments in favour of these definitions and also more instances of each argument. Thus, 86 % of the category arguments made before the invasion—and 88 % afterwards—are made by anti-war speakers. Moreover, the ratio of categorical arguments to moral arguments is 4.33:1 for those against the war and 0.44:1 for those in favour of the war.

Second, further analyses were conducted to assess the *collective consistency* across contributions stemming from those in the same political party or else sharing the same broad political outlook. To this end, all 106 interventions were located along the two aforementioned dimensions (pro- versus anti-war and time) and identified by the party affiliation of the speaker. The contrast between separatist and unionist parties shown in Fig. 8.2 is striking. Every single intervention by a speaker from one of the three parties having Scottish independence on their agenda (Scottish National Party, Scottish Socialist Party and Scottish Green Party) takes an anti-war stance. Not one intervention deviates from the message that an independent Scotland goes hand in hand with opposition to the invasion of Iraq. In contrast, the unionist camp is profoundly divided in the debates, both between and within parties. The gap across the three parties is substantial; while conservative members are the strongest supporters of the invasion, most liberal democrats lean towards an anti-war position. Furthermore, members of the ruling Labour Party cover the full spectrum of these positions in the debate, from the purest pro-invasion stance (on the left of the graph) to a marked anti-invasion view (on the right).

8 British Warriors and Scottish Voters: When 'Rallying the Nation'

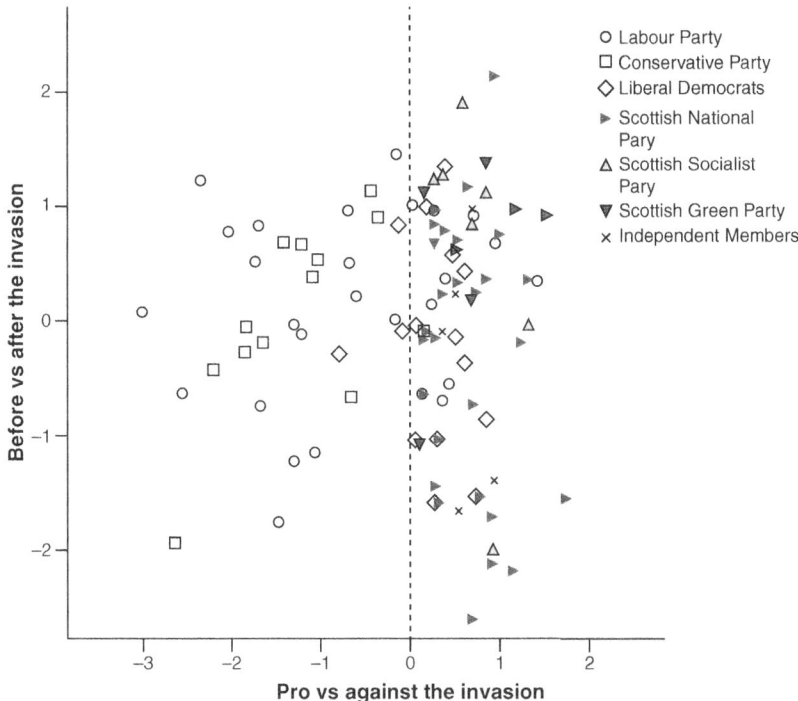

Fig. 8.2 The positions of individual interventions (marked by party affiliation) according to their coordinates along two dimensions defined by the MCA (see Fig. 8.1) of the joint occurrences of moral principles, social cleavages and the timing of debates. Interventions from members of separatist parties appear as filled *grey* triangles.

One of the clearest things to emerge from the MCA (see Fig. 8.1) is the shift in category constructions that occurs from before the invasion to when the invasion is imminent and after the invasion. More precisely, there is a clear evolution in the anti-war camp where, pre-invasion, the argument is organised around the Scotland—England division. Later, it shifts to a series of other divisions, all based on the opposition between the powerless and the powerful. In order to gain more insight into the meaning of these shifts, it is helpful to consider a set of extracts from the parliamentary debates. These are chosen from our coding categories in order to exemplify differences both between pro- and anti-war camps and also between the pre-invasion and post-invasion phases.

Let us start with an instructive plea for support. In Extract 1, a conservative MSP pledges his loyalty to the Labour government's war policies on the grounds that they are acting-or, rather, asking the military to act-on behalf of the nation.

> Extract 1: The troops and their commander in chief need our support
> I am associated with 603 City of Edinburgh squadron of the Royal Auxiliary Air Force. It is now public knowledge that many of its reservists and countless others have been called up. It is my conviction that if the Government, with the support of the House of Commons, asks our armed services to act on behalf of the nation, it must be given our total support.
> (James Douglas-Hamilton, Conservative Party, 13 March 2003a)

This top-down logic, where a leader's decision to go to war is to be supported by a loyal public, is typically reversed in the anti-war rhetoric. Extract 2 provides a good example of putting the demands and desires of the democratic public first. The fact that the "vast majority" is against a war fought by "Britain and America acting alone" then becomes in itself a moral argument against the war. The interesting detail lies in the way the democratic public is defined by the SNP speaker here: referring twice to 'the people of Scotland', she leaves no doubt as to the fact that the *Scottish* public has a natural right to confer democratic legitimacy to political decisions, even in the realm of foreign policies (contrary to its formal rights granted by the UK constitution).

> Extract 2: No public mandate for war
> We know from polling evidence that the people of Scotland want this debate and they want it to take place in Scotland. The vast majority are opposed to Britain and America acting alone and 68 per cent of the people of Scotland believe that Westminster should consult the Scottish Parliament before launching an attack on Iraq. Fat chance—Blair is not even going to consult the House of Commons, much less the Scottish Parliament. That is, unfortunately, what Johann Lamont and her colleagues have to accept. I wish that my Westminster colleagues had had the opportunity to vote on

the matter at Westminster, but thus far they have not. So much for democracy.
(Roseanna Cunningham, Scottish National Party, 16 January 2003b)

Obviously, war supporters put much effort into presenting opposition to the prime minister's policies, rather than these policies themselves, as the problem and the source of internal division. Often, as in Extract 3, the message is that to "undermine" the prime minister's policies can have grave consequences. The dangerous arena of "international relations" does not allow for divisiveness, because the stakes are "complex" and even "life threatening". But sometimes, as in Extract 4, opponents counter that the costs of blind support can be higher than the costs of disobedience, and that followership has no moral value in itself. This point is anchored here in both universal lessons learnt from world history—the "Nuremberg trial"—and the distinctive legacy of local history. The "declaration of Arbroath" is a fourteenth-century declaration of Scottish independence which includes a claim that the designated king is entitled to rule over Scotland by virtue of his concrete merits for the Scottish people, and not just by divine right.

Extract 3: Opponents undermine our nation's leadership
International relations are complex—they are life enhancing, but they are also life threatening. When we speak in Parliament, we should consider all the implications of our actions. When our Prime Minister has recognised public concern and has moved to ask the UN to give Saddam Hussein one last chance, we should not undermine his efforts to secure not just peace and justice in Iraq, but stability and strength in the United Nations.
(Jack McConnell, Labour Party, 13 March 2003)

Extract 4: No blind support
Do we have to follow our leaders once they have established a policy? The Nuremberg trial showed that people do not have to do that. Much closer to home, the declaration of Arbroath set out the Scottish view of leadership: Robert the Bruce was a great man who had saved us from the English but, if he went wrong, he was out and we got another leader. We do not have to follow Mr Bush and Mr Blair as they drive our collective car over a precipice.
(Donald Gorrie, Liberal Democrats, 13 March 2003)

In Extract 5, a conservative MSP presents democracy as a strong and binding force among similar-minded people.

> Extract 5: Democracy unites us
> In a democracy such as ours, all are free to express their thoughts and to live without fear of persecution. Indeed, that is a reason why thousands of asylum seekers—many of whom come from Iraq—have sought shelter on our shores. Oh, if only the situation were the same in their homelands. My platform is based on an acceptance that no democratically elected leader of our nation would act in any way that was detrimental to the principles and objectives of the democracy that we enjoy in the UK and to the overall well-being of our people. Furthermore, I do not believe that such a leader would act against what he considers to be the wider international interest
> (Phill Gallie, Conservative Party, 16 January 2003)

Given that a broad consensus of democratic values is generally assumed, this creates a highly inclusive category. The implication is that only isolated individuals who challenge or undermine these values are on the other side. The conservative speaker refers to democracy in the UK in order to locate the nation in an international context and simultaneously makes a domestic argument. The international argument concerns superiority; the fact that many people seek shelter in the UK is presented as evidence of the widely shared aspiration to live in a democracy. The domestic argument concerns legitimacy: to know that a leader has been "democratically elected" is sufficient to assume that he will faithfully represent the national interest and the "wider international interest".

Extract 6 is a subtle variant of the democratic unity argument. The Labour speaker begins by acknowledging "a variety of views" and "division in the debate"; however, beneath these differences are similar motives: "many people" are "deeply troubled" by the war. In this way, the speaker portrays a democratic community of people that openly discusses different stances precisely because they share each other's concerns. This closely tied community includes the speaker, his "party", "constituency", "friends" and "home".

Extract 6: Democracy unites us
Like many people throughout Scotland and the United Kingdom, I am deeply troubled by the current international situation. We know that there is a variety of views (…) The division in the debate is reflected in what I am told by people in my party or my constituency or by my friends and in what I am told in my own home. It is ironic that the one division that does not exist, which some would like to see, is a division between the peoples of Scotland and England on the issue. Indeed, as I reflect on our troubled world and on the divisions that our international community faces, I wonder how much more irrelevant it can be to have a party that is based entirely on the desire to seek further division within our country.
(Johann Lamont, Labour Party, 13 March 2003)

Given this background of sincere debate on grave issues among people of good faith, the division "between the peoples of Scotland and England" can be portrayed as futile and instrumental. This argument implies that the purity of democratic debate leaves no room for collective aspirations along communal or national lines because they are an artefact of party politics for those who "desire to seek further division within our country" (which, in this case, represents the UK and not Scotland).

Such a perspective can be confronted with the rhetoric of those who argue that, on the contrary, there is an authentic division between Scotland and the rest of the UK. The core of this argument, exemplified in Extracts 7 and 8, is that the war reveals objective and chronic inequalities that disadvantage the people of Scotland. In Extract 7, the nationalist speaker refers to the disproportionate contribution of Scottish troops in the war effort:

Extract 7: Vulnerable Scotland
As was the case in the Gulf war, the likelihood is that around one third of the front-line troops will be from Scottish regiments. As far as our citizens are concerned, we have to remember that it is those troops and their families who will bear the brunt of any war in Iraq.
(Kay Ullrich, Scottish National Party, 16 January 2003)

Before the war, anti-war arguments almost exclusively referred to the categorical opposition between British war-mongers acting against Scottish interests. Once the war starts, this shifts to a variety of oppositions such as the USA against Iraq or, more generically, elites against ordinary people. This shift may reflect the fact that the objective community of fate created between Scottish and (mainly) English troops at war have made anti-British rhetoric a high-risk operation for Scottish politicians. Aware that their constituencies might resent them for creating division among the troops who are fighting and risking their lives together, the MSPs have become attentive to include *all* of the troops in their concerns and hence to shift the precise terms in which they oppose the powerful to the powerless.

To deepen this point, consider the following account from an anti-war MSP, during the Scottish parliamentary debate of 16 January 2003:

> Extract 8: Vulnerable Scotland
> As a Glasgow MSP, I could not in conscience contribute to the drumbeats of war that are being stirred up in Westminster by those Dukes of Plaza-Toro who, as usual, will be 4,000 or 5,000 miles behind the front line ... The other month I was on a train when a 19-year-old man recognised me as being one of the MSPs who work in his area. He was going to Glencorse barracks ... I saw him go off into the morning mist and I thought, "Aye—same as in the first and second world wars. Scots troops in first."
> (Dorothy-Grace Elder, Independent Member, 16 January 2003)

In the ballad by William Gilbert, it is written of the Duke of Plaza Toro that "In enterprise of martial kind/When there was any fighting/He led his regiment from behind"; hence, the extract perfectly depicts the war in terms of cowardly war-mongers, who constitute the British Westminster parliament, exploiting (as always) ordinary Scots. It corroborates and populates our characterisation of the counterhegemonic discourse of the anti-war camp. When the protagonist of this true story goes alone "off into the morning mist" to his barrack and towards an uncertain future, he appears to incarnate the fate of generations of Scots: "Aye—same as in the first and second world wars. Scots troops in first". Once this background settled, it is possible to discern an implicit point about many Scots in what is explicitly said here only about a single Scot: he did not enlist because he wanted 'war', but simply a 'home' and to 'learn a trade'. The army offered him a promise of social mobility. The implication seems to be that social and economic disadvantage that young Scots have been and are still facing explains why, over a century, Scottish troops have fought and suffered in disproportionate numbers in Britain's wars: military subjugation reflects and prolongs economic subjugation of Scotland within the UK.

It is then instructive to contrast Extract 8 with Extract 9. During the debate of 13 March 2003, just as troops were about to go into action and at the point (as can be seen from Fig. 8.2) when the Scottish—English division begins to be supplanted by other constructions of the powerless versus the powerful, MSP Margaret Ewing, from the Scottish National Party, stated:

> Extract 9: Virtuous troops led by immoral politicians
> "our forces are an integral part of our communities. They are not aliens. They do not live separately from us. They are our friends and neighbours. They live next door. Their children go to our schools. They go to our hospitals (…) I take offence at those people (…) who say that anyone who votes against an immediate rush to war is in some way not supporting the troops. I would be more convinced if I saw the Government and the Ministry of Defence giving our troops the support that they deserve while they are out there, because some of the stories that come home are horrendous. As legislators, we have a duty and a responsibility to all our service personnel to give them a legal mandate that is agreed internationally without reservations"
> (Margaret Ewing, Scottish National Party, 13 March 2003)

At one level, this is very similar to the previous construction. Much work is put into constituting the troops as ordinary people like you and me in terms of who they are, where they live, what they do. Equally, there is a clear contrast with the pro-war politicians who do not support the troops and whose war is against the troops' (and hence our) interests. In this sense, there is a clear continuity between extracts. But there is one obvious difference. There is no mention of Scotland or England or Britain. The troops are not referred to as Scottish troops; they are troops in general. Concern is not for some troops as Scots, but for all troops as ordinary people. The government is not referred to as the Westminster government but as the government full stop. Opposition is not to an *alien* administration but to a *powerful* administration. So, this illustrates how, as the invasion becomes imminent, it is important to be seen as supporting all troops and not just the Scots amongst them, but also how the transition to this 'governments versus ordinary people' version of the counterhegemonic narrative has been set up by the previous use of 'Scots versus English'.

Extract 10 is even more explicit in its way of opposing national leadership, on the one hand, and the national community, including the armed forces, on the other. In this rhetoric, Tony Blair does not represent the interest and opinion of any wider public, not even of the 'grassroots' of his own party. His trivial and selfish motive of fighting for 'his political life' is contrasted to the grave and shared stakes of all those who are to endanger their *real* lives (as well as the lives of others) in Iraq.

> Extract 10: Undemocratic warlords
> It is tragic, therefore, that at this critical time we have a Prime Minister who is so belligerent and arrogant that he is prepared to defy grass-roots opinion in his own party, the majority of public opinion in this country and even the United Nations. It would be a supreme irony if his attempt to bring about regime change in Iraq were to bring about regime change in this country. According to some of the media, Tony Blair may be fighting for his political life. So what? The lives of innocent men, women and children in Iraq and the lives of our armed forces are far more important than any politician's career.
> (Dennis Canavan, Independent Member, 13 March 2003)

A final set of arguments takes the cleavage between the people and a narrow elite to an international level. From this perspective, the tragedy of the UK becomes that its leadership is more connected to the attitude of foreign elites than to the interests of the overall public. Many interventions denounce the arrogance of US elites and their superpower policies, often together with the submissive policies of the UK leadership. Extract 11 is a case in point.

> Extract 11: Fatal alliance with the US
> It is a measure of Mr Blair's closeness to Mr Bush that on Monday Mr Blair said that if what he described as "justified" military action were to be blocked by one member of the Security Council, he would be free to

commit the United Kingdom to war. That is Mr Blair talking in Mr Bush's language, and duplicating Mr Bush's attitude to the United Nations. Mr Bush is in the driving seat and Mr Blair is in the rear passenger seat.
(Colin Campbell, Scottish National Party, 16 January 2003)

While in the previous quote the argument was that Blair does not represent the national ingroup, here it is claimed that he works for a national outgroup. The image of him sitting "in the rear passenger seat" in Bush's car expresses the idea that the head of government himself has lost control, and that alien interests now dictate British war policies—obviously, a threatening prospect to all who are forced to embark on the trip.

8.2 The Invasion of Iraq and the Scottish Voters

The second set of findings are based on secondary analyses of the SSA survey, conducted in 2003 by the Scottish Centre for Social Research amongst a representative sample of the Scottish resident population aged 18 and above. Most interviews were conducted in May 2003, although some occurred up to September of that year.

A first analysis tested whether the way that respondents express their national identities is related to their stance on the war. In the survey, four items addressed the two dimensions of national identification which are of interest here: level of identification (Scottish versus British) and quality of identification (attachment versus pride). The precise wordings were "How closely attached do you feel to Scotland/Britain as a whole?" and "How proud are you of being Scottish/British?" War opponents were defined as respondents who (strongly) agreed with the statement "Britain was wrong to go to war with Iraq".

The findings reveal a clear and distinctive pattern of national identification among war opponents: attachment to Scotland net of pride (and net of identification to Britain) substantially increases the likelihood of holding an anti-war stance. An observed exponential logistic regression coefficient of 1.39 (the 95 % confidence interval ranged from 1.09 to 1.76) means that the odds of opposing the war increase by more than one and a third for every one-point increase in attachment to Scotland (on a 4-point scale), when other responses are held constant. By contrast, the net effects of Scottish pride (0.68, confidence interval: 0.53–0.88) and British attachment (0.81, confidence interval: 0.67–0.98) on anti-war stances were both *negative*, while British pride was not significantly related to stances on the war (0.88, confidence interval: 0.75–1.05).

Further logistic regression models addressed how personal opinions on the war interact with exposure to newspapers holding a certain stance on the war. The only media addressed by the SSA are daily newspapers. To record readership, respondents were asked to indicate up to three newspapers that they read either "normally" or "regularly". For the purposes of this study, we coded the resulting list of newspapers according to their editorial positions on the war in Iraq during the invasion phase (i.e., a systematic anti-war stance versus any other stance). To obtain a reliable coding, we first conducted secondary analyses of the 'Iraq War Press Coverage' database, which provided day-to-day content-analytical data of the major British print media during the invasion phase. These analyses clearly show that the three primary pro-war arguments (threat, humanitarian intervention and regime change) were challenged much more systematically in three newspapers (i.e., *Daily Mirror*, *The Guardian* and *The Independent*) than in all the other newspapers within the sample. Robertson's (2004) content analysis complemented this by including papers that are only available in Scotland and were not included in the Iraq War Press Coverage database. Robertson showed that *The Herald* distinguished itself among Scottish dailies by articulating a clear anti-war position from the start of the invasion. Respondents were defined as readers of anti-war newspapers if they reported reading at least one of the four aforementioned newspapers. Similarly, respondents were defined as readers of other newspapers if they claimed to be regular readers of one of the remaining newspapers (i.e., *Daily Express*, *Daily Mail*, *Daily Star*, *The Sun*, *Daily Telegraph*, *Financial Times*, *The Scotsman*, *The Aberdeen Press and Journal*, *The Courier*). The positions of these latter newspapers ranged between ambivalent and clearly pro-war during the invasion period.

Most importantly, we were interested in explaining separatist votes with regard to the interplay between personal opinions and newspaper exposure. The upper portion of Table 8.3 shows that the overall odds of voting for a separatist opposition party were exactly one and a half

Table 8.3 Multivariate predictors of the separatist opposition (above) versus the Labour majority (below) vote: partial logistic regression coefficients

	Model 1	Model 2	Model 3	Model 4
		Separatist vote		
War opponents	1.50**	1.43*	1.23	1.13
	(1.13–1.98)	(1.08–1.91)	(0.90–1.67)	(0.82–1.55)
Readers of anti-war newspapers	–	2.08***	1.09	1.15
		(1.39–3.10)	(0.56–2.14)	(0.58–2.29)
War opponents x Readers of anti-war newspapers	–	–	3.00*	2.81*
			(1.28–7.08)	(1.17–6.75)
Attached to Scotland	–	–	–	1.50**
				(1.11–2.03)
Proud of being Scottish	–	–	–	1.22
				(0.90–1.67)
Attached to Britain	–	–	–	0.91
				(0.73–1.15)
Proud of being British	–	–	–	0.57***
				(0.46–0.70)
		Labour vote		
War opponents	0.86	0.88	0.42**	0.43*
	(0.65–1.14)	(0.68–1.17)	(0.26–0.69)	(0.26–0.71)
Readers of other newspapers	–	1.29	0.82	0.76
		(0.97–1.73)	(0.57–1.19)	(0.52–1.10)
War opponents x Readers of other newspapers	–	–	3.06***	3.22***
			(1.68–5.58)	(1.76–5.89)
Attached to Scotland	–	–	–	0.96
				(0.72–1.27)
Proud of being Scottish	–	–	–	1.17
				(0.86–1.60)
Attached to Britain	–	–	–	1.25
				(0.99–1.56)
Proud of being British	–	–	–	1.09
				(0.89–1.34)

Note: Values significantly higher than 1 indicate a positive relationship between predictor and outcome variables, values significantly lower than 1 a negative relationship, stars indicate p-values (*$p < 0.05$, **$p < 0.01$, ***$p < 0.001$) and numbers inserted in brackets provide the boundaries of the 95 % confidence interval of the logistic regression coefficient

times higher for war opponents than for those who supported the war or who had no clear opinion (Model 1). The second model shows that the strength of this association does not substantially differ after controlling for the effect of reading an anti-war newspaper. That is, the effect of personal opinion regarding the war is *not mediated* by the type of newspaper read. However, the strong interaction effect introduced in Model 3 shows that personal opinion is *moderated* by newspaper exposure. Only amongst the readership of an anti-war newspaper did personal opinions against the war translate into separatist votes. Finally, Model 4 shows that this pattern holds after controlling for multi-dimensional national identification, although Scottish attachment and British pride are correlated with separatist voting (in opposite directions). To conclude, these analyses highlight the fact that the newspapers which disseminated anti-war positions played an important role in the mobilisation of war opponents in favour of separatist parties. By contrast, further outcomes (not shown here) suggested that reading newspapers that disseminated pro-war or ambivalent positions did not affect the relationship between anti-war opinions and separatist voting.

The lower portion of Table 8.3 displays equivalent models for voting for the Labour Party in power. Again, the most significant outcome is the strong interaction of personal opinion on the war and media exposure. In this case, reading a newspaper with a supportive or ambivalent stance regarding the war made the critical difference. War opponents who did not read such a newspaper were significantly less likely to vote for the Labour Party. Among the readership of these newspapers, however, the effect became insignificant and was even reversed. Hence, newspapers that disseminated pro-war positions appeared to play a role in the demobilisation of war opponents and in all likelihood limited further electoral losses for the ruling Labour Party.

8.3 Elite Constructions and Popular Understandings of War and Nation

To summarise the findings from the first part of our study, it is clear that the discourse of the pro- and anti-war camps was constructed around opposed versions of the groups and identities involved in the conflict. The pro-war camp referred to a narrative of liberation in which war was necessary to defend 'ourselves' and to alleviate the sufferings of others. The anti-war camp proposed a narrative of aggression in which war was imposed on 'us' by others and was to our detriment. In other words, for those in favour, this was 'our war', based on our values and advancing our interest. For those against, this was 'their war', violating our values and to the detriment of our interest.

These findings further highlight how the arguments of both the pro- and anti-war camp are rooted in well-established common sense ways of viewing the world. Those for the war use a notion of the civilised world fighting an evil dictator which has become particularly powerful since World War II, which was certainly central to narratives about the first Gulf War (Herrera & Reicher, 1998) and which is widely disseminated within and beyond the UK. Those against the war initially rooted their opposition in the notion of Scotland's domination by England within the UK (and the UK parliament which endorsed the war), and later on, this set up alternative ways of construing 'our' domination by the masters of war. The significance of this 'Scottish versus English' construction is not only its familiarity and ubiquity (especially during a Scottish election campaign) but also the fact that it is relatively conventional. Thus, the anti-war position in Scotland can be anchored in a mainstream view of the world, and the nature of the debate is marked by the availability of a respectable way of saying 'it's not our war'.

But it isn't just that such a construction is available. Looking at the argumentative context of the debate, we see, first, how much effort anti-war speakers devote to setting up a category system that is congruent with their stance on the war. Some four out of five of their arguments were devoted to who is against whom in the conflict (in contrast to about one out of three arguments only within the pro-war camp). Perhaps this is due to the fact that the 'official version' supported by the ruling parties in both Westminster and the Scottish Parliament, by their publicity machines and by the majority of the media takes for granted that this is 'our war'. In order to challenge their influence, great efforts are necessary to expose and establish an alternative perspective.

Second, we see that these efforts were collective and that they were conducted with great consistency. Every single intervention from a member of a separatist party rooted their argument in the idea that this was 'not our war'. In the first debate, this stance predominantly translated into 'England's war not Scotland's'. Then, in subsequent debates, they all drew on this to sustain other versions of 'it's their war'. No separatist MSP stepped out of the line, which created a stark contrast to the political cacophony displayed by unionist MSPs in general, and by members of the ruling Labour Party in particular.

This takes us to the importance of the changing course of events. While the separatists were consistent, they certainly weren't inflexible. As events changed, as the possibility of war became the near certainty of war and then as troops entered into the firing line, so the precise nature of the anti-war categories changed. Scottish-English gave way to other versions of a bellicose and dominant 'them' imposing war upon 'us'. The important thing about theses shifts, we have argued, is that the earlier division contrasts Scottish soldiers and their families to English (or Welsh or Northern Irish) troops and their families. The latter includes all British (and indeed allied) troops and their families as the 'poor bloody infantry' who are as ever traduced by their leaders in war. In making the shift, anti-war proponents cannot be accused of fostering divisions amongst the troops and thereby endangering them all. They cannot be dismissed as talking irresponsibly and ignoring the new realities of war. By being both consistent (in terms of their overall construction) and flexible (in terms of the precise categories they use), these oppositional politicians apply what have been classically shown to be the optimal conditions for contesting the dominant viewpoint (Mugny, 1982).

Turning now to the second part of the findings, focusing on popular opinion, there are two key findings that we wish to stress. The first is that being anti-war is clearly related to seeing oneself as Scottish. However, it is not just that anti-war respondents feel Scottish, but that they do so without necessarily feeling *pride* in Scotland. This pattern is akin to what some have dubbed 'critical attachment' or 'constructive patriotism' (see Chap. 7). Often, however, critical attachment or patriotism is seen as an individual orientation to the nation. Here we suggest that it is more a matter of assimilating a prevalent discourse in Scotland, where being critical is part of what it means to be Scottish (see Reicher & Hopkins, 2001). Rather than promoting a stance of 'my country right or wrong', the anti-war elites advance a notion of Scots as a less bellicose people who will challenge anything and anybody that violates their values—and hence who challenge the official drive to war. Hence, we can see a correspondence between the anti-war discourse of elites and the understandings of anti-war sections of the population.

The second key finding concerns the role of the press in the relationship between private opinion and political behaviour (in this case voting for anti-war and pro-separatism candidates). From a classic perspective of social influence or cognitive consistency one would expect that this relationship is in terms of mediation, that is, that those who are anti-war are led to read papers that are in tune with their stance and this in turn engages them so as to vote for anti-war/separatist parties, or else that those who read anti-war papers develop anti-war opinions that in turn make them into anti-war/separatist voters.

However, contrary to this common wisdom, we have found no evidence of a mediational relationship. Rather, and less intuitively perhaps, our findings clearly support a *moderational* relationship. Only those with anti-war opinions who *also* read anti-war papers are more likely to vote for anti-war/separatist parties. Equally, those with anti-war opinions who read pro-war papers (or papers that are ambivalent about the war) are not less likely to vote for the Labour Party—the party of government which pursued the war. These findings might appear counterintuitive. However, they are consistent with the position we advocated in Chap. 3 (and with, notably, Paluck's analysis of the role of the mass media in facilitating social behaviours of conformity or opposition to authorities). That is, the impact of the media lies not so much in changing personal beliefs or deeply ingrained opinions, as in changing the perception of social norms. It is by telling us that our opinions are *shared* by others—that they are normative—that the media affects what we do.

8.4 Conclusion

To summarise, in this chapter we have shown the work done by political elites in rooting their accounts of identity in various dimensions of context. We have shown in particular how those challenging the *status quo* are able to draw on a chronically available understanding of Scottish and British interests as opposed, and how they spend more effort than those defending the *status quo* in creating an explicit, consistent and flexible definition of the Scottish interest as anti-war. We have also shown that opposition to the war amongst the population at large is linked to a similar understanding of Scottishness as characterised by a critical and questioning relationship to authority.

In the light of these findings, it is possible to account for the convergence between the structure of elite discourse and of popular understandings—which was more evident for the anti-war separatist camps than for the ruling majority—in several ways. While top-down theorists might interpret it as a consequence of effective political mobilisation (opinions communicated by elites shape mass opinion and behaviour), advocates of bottom-up approaches would rather emphasise that elites adapt their rhetoric opportunistically to what their audiences want to hear. In all likelihood, there is a note of truth in both positions: on the one hand, we have shown how elite discourse is effective to the extent that it is rooted in pre-existing, widely shared, popular understandings; on the other we have shown how elites adapt these understandings to the present context in order to drive forward their own specific agendas.

References

Billig, M. (1995). *Banal nationalism*. London: Sage Publications Ltd.
Elcheroth, G., & Reicher, S. (2014). "Not our war, not our country": Contents and contexts of Scotish political rhetoric and popular understandings during the invasion of Iraq. *British Journal of Social Psychology, 53*(1), 112–133.
Herrera, M., & Reicher, S. (1998). Making sides and taking sides: An analysis of salient images and category constructions for pro- and anti-Gulf War respondents. *European Journal of Social Psychology, 28*(6), 981–993.
Lewis, J. (2004). Television, public opinion and the war in Iraq: The case of Britain. *International Journal of Public Opinion Research, 16*(3), 295–310.
Lipson, M. (2009). "If it wasn't rolling, it never happened": The role or visual elements in television news. In L. Harman & L. Lombardo (Eds.), *Evaluation and stance in war news: A linguistic analysis of American, British and Italian television news reporting of the 2003 Iraqi War* (pp. 140–169). London: Continuum.
Mugny, G. (1982). *The power of minorities*. London: Academic Press.
Reicher, S., & Hopkins, N. (2001). *Self and nation*. London: Sage.

Robertson, J. W. (2004). People's watchdogs or government poodles? Scotland's national broadsheets and the second Iraq war. *European Journal of Communication, 19*(4), 457–482.

Rutland, A., Cinnirella, M., & Simpson, R. (2008). Stability and variability in national and European self-identification. *European Psychologist, 13*(4), 267–276.

Sindic, D., & Reicher, S. D. (2009). "Our way of life is worth defending": Testing a model of attitudes towards superordinate group membership through a study of Scots' attitudes towards Britain. *European Journal of Social Psychology, 39*(1), 114–129.

Conclusion

Old Issues and New Questions

We began this book with a plea for perplexity: our expressed intention was to disrupt old certainties and to raise new questions both about the nature of identity, violence and power and about the relationship between them. We can now summarise such new questions as have arisen from our analysis of the literature and from our own case studies. We can also consider the extent to which we have progressed from new questions to new answers.

Our starting point lay in the observation that both scholarly and popular debates about collective violence still tend to be organised along an opposition between 'primordialist' and 'instrumentalist' positions. Primordialists assume an inbuilt tension between people of different descent, culture or faith and presuppose that people who share certain bonds will stand together against outsiders. To quote the American satirist Tom Lehrer from his ironic song 'National Brotherhood Week': "Oh, the white folks hate the black folks/And the black folks hate the white folks/To hate all but the right folks/Is an old established rule". Instrumentalists, by contrast, stress how identities are manipulated, histories rewritten, group boundaries redrawn and new enemies created, when it serves the political agenda of powerful elites. Here a more weighty literary analogy can be made to George Orwell's dystopian masterpiece *1984*. As popularly understood, this encapsulates the power of propaganda in the way that, in a moment, the people of Oceania can be led to forget their hatred of East Asians and transfer all animosity to the Eurasians.

However, our concern was less with the difference between these two positions than with the things that they have in common. Put simply, both provide a linear account of how we arrive at the same outcome: collective violence. There is some dispute as to the ordering of variables in this account: does identity come first and power only matters to the extent that it affects the exercise of identity-based animosities, or does power come first and identity only matters as a tool in the hands of leaders? Or rather, to use a motoring metaphor, primordialists contend that violence is the destination, identity is the driver, and power is the vehicle. Instrumentalists also regard violence as the destination, but the remaining two terms are shifted around: power drives, identity is driven.

Throughout this book, we have been highlighting how such conceptualisations constrain and construct the nature of the debate. They limit our curiosity and thereby limit our knowledge. There is far more to discuss than which of identity and power is the driver and which is the vehicle. There are so many more issues, so many more uncertainties and so many more questions.

To start with, we need to interrogate the terms of the debate. In different ways, primordialists and instrumentalists take the nature of identity as a given in any particular dispute—the primordialists because they tend to assume that people always see each other in terms of the same categories whatever the situation, the instrumentalists because they tend to assume that people will accept whatever categories are presented to them by elites and are incapable of dissenting, let alone resisting. Yet, this misses the basic point that, in many cases, the nature of the categories to a dispute is contested and indeed much of the dispute (and certainly its outcome) is about precisely what these categories are.

For instance, to invoke a significant moment in recent world history, was the first Gulf War of 1991 about warmongers pursuing their interests regardless of the cost to the rest of the population or was it about the democratic world facing up to a dictator? Opposition or support for the war hinged on how people saw the categories involved (Herrera & Reicher, 1998). More generally, the answer to the well-worn question 'which side are you on' depends on how one draws the sides.

In the same way as we need to problematise the 'identity' term in our models, we also need to question 'power' and 'violence'. Power is not just a thing that is either there or not, which groups possess in order to implement their urges or else elites have in order to sway groups. Indeed, in part at least, power is something that comes about by constituting groups and leading people to act together as group members. That is, state leaders consolidate their power by getting people to see themselves and to act together as members of a national community whose boundaries coincide with the boundaries of the state. By contrast, the power of, say, union leaders depends on people acting together as members of different classes within the nation. As for violence, the issue here is even more critical, albeit conceptually somewhat different. As long as violence is treated as the terminus of our enquiries, it will always remain somewhat opaque to us, because we lack a criterion beyond violence to differentiate the features of violence. We cannot ask what to include under the rubric of violence: does it simply involve ongoing physical and mental harm to others, does it include the threat of future harm, does it involve the possibility of past harm reoccurring? Nor can we ask what it is about violence which produces other outcomes. Is it harm alone or fear of harm or indeed something else? But all this changes once we regard violence as more than an end point, as more than a mere product of prior processes, and as something that itself produces new outcomes.

This takes us on to a further set of issues relating not to identity, violence and power as separate terms, but to the dynamics that exist between them. To reiterate, the conventional approach is to identity/violence and power violence in linear terms such that once we get to violence we have got to the punchline of our narrative. But that is to end the story just before we can learn something important from it. It terminates analysis at its most critical juncture. For when violence breaks out (or people believe in the imminent possibility of violence), no destination has been reached. Rather, the nature of the journey and the means by which it is undertaken are affected, as are the chances of reaching different destinations.

Violence is of interest not only in terms of what came before but also because of the way it affects what lies beyond.

In other words, if we are to advance our understanding of collective conflict and violence we need to address how violence not only arises and escalates out of identity and power processes but how it also transforms collective identities, how it shapes ongoing power struggles and how it reshuffles our possible futures. That was the aim of the second part of our text.

Towards Triangularity

A central aspect of our analysis has been to conceptualise terms in ways that are much more relational and communicational than is conventional. This starts with identity. Much research proceeds by asking people to what extent they see themselves as a man or woman, as white or black, as Scottish or Swiss, or whatever. If they choose to tick the appropriate boxes on our questionnaires, we accept what they say and classify them as 'high identifiers'. No one else is there to gainsay them.

But this is a strangely utopian world. In real life, we might well make claims to certain identities, but then discover that what sounds entirely reasonable to us sounds strange to others. If the first author of this book, born in Luxemburg and living in Lausanne, defines himself as Swiss, his claim might passed unchallenged at an international conference, but his Swiss neighbours are likely to question how it goes together with the colour of his passport, with the intonation of his French, or with his inability to stand straight on a pair of skis. If the second author, born in England and living in St. Andrews, claims Scottishness in an unmistakable English accent, will he be embraced by others as a fellow Scot? Would he dare walk into a local pub wearing a kilt knowing that he could be met with derision? Identity, then, is about more than self-perceptions and self-definitions. Identities involve the ways we are positioned and the ways we act in the world, which are as much about the ways others treat us as the ways we see ourselves. Indeed, they are about the way we anticipate that others will see and treat us and the way we constrain our own claims as a result.

In suchlike ways, we become aware of ourselves and begin to tailor our actions and cognitions to the way we believe we will be treated. What we know of what others think of us is therefore critical and hence communication becomes central to the construction of identity.

Similar constructions apply to issues of power. Our own ability to act depends upon how others respond to us. Will they support us, in which case we are able, together, to achieve what would have been impossible alone. Do they ignore us, or do they oppose us, in which case we are unlikely to be able to achieve very much.

Thus, when we anticipate the opposition of others and when we therefore anticipate that our acts will achieve little beyond earning the opprobrium of others, we are likely to say nothing and do nothing whatever our beliefs or inclinations. This can then entail a spiral of silence (as defined by Noelle-Neumann, 1984/1993) whereby others see no signs of support for similar views and hence say nothing themselves. Eventually, action becomes difficult for everyone, as no one knows where the others stand.

Such a sense of *epistemic isolation* has been of central importance to our argument. The ability to speak and act—especially when it comes to challenging a powerful status quo—depends upon knowing we will not be alone. Hence one of the ways in which the powerful can maintain this status quo is by disrupting the ability of people to communicate their opposition. Earlier, we cited how Orwell's *1984* is understood to illustrate the supposed ability of elites to manipulate identities through recounting how the people of Oceania are led to turn against the people of Eurasia. But when we look at Orwell's argument in more detail, we see that he well understood how domination is maintained less by affecting people's own views than by restricting their knowledge of the views of others:

> *The Party said that Oceania had never been in alliance with Eurasia. He, Winston Smith, knew that Oceania had been in alliance with Eurasia as short a time as four years ago. But where did that knowledge exist? Only in his own consciousness, which in any case must soon be annihilated. And if all others accepted the lie which the Party imposed—if all records told the same tale— then the lie passed into history and became truth.* (Orwell, 1949[1])

---

[1] For the full text, see http://www.george-orwell.org/1984/2.html.

Now, if both identity and power are, at least in part, constituted through the ways that others relate to us, and through our ability to gain knowledge of how they relate to us, then anything which changes such relations/knowledge of relations will serve to reconfigure identity and power. This is how violence enters our account. For we argue that violence is a particularly potent means of changing relations and communications between people.

Consider, for instance, the case where Hindu extremists have rampaged through a street, attacking all the Muslims and leaving alone those houses marked as Hindu, or the case where Serb vigilantes have gone into a village, compelled local Serbs to divulge the location of the Croats amongst them and then assaulted those so identified. After that, how can things be the same again? The mere possibility that your neighbour may identify you as a Muslim/Croat—with the terrible consequences that ensue in a climate of violence—means that you are led to act with the presumption that you may be viewed as such and also to see them as a Hindu/Serb—even if you had never done so before. And, as you are distanced from them and communication with them becomes difficult, the possibility of breaching these presumptions fades further.

In effect, violence radically alters the contingencies of acting on the basis of different self-definitions, and the implicit risk calculus they superpose on social relations. If you act towards your erstwhile neighbour as still your neighbour, and if you get it right, you will perhaps receive a measure of companionship and support. But if you get it wrong, you and your family may be killed in your beds. Even if the odds of getting it wrong remain low in comparison with getting it right, the perceived costs or benefits associated with either scenario can prevail over the odds. In other words, the peculiarity of a violent environment resides in the fact that it leads people to *bet on the unlikely*, and to align their behaviour with the worst-case scenario. What is more, even if individuals opt for bravery and decide to show solidarity with the new, ethnically defined, other—treat them as what they have been so far, a simple neighbour— members of their new (ethnic) ingroup might not let them do so, for fear of supporting an enemy in their midst.

On the one hand, then, our argument involves a reconceptualisation of violence as a driving force and not just as a product of prior forces, and an analysis of the ways in which violence produces its effects. To restate our case: violence serves to enforce new solidarities and silence dissent. If 'we' are under attack from 'them' we cannot interact or listen to 'them' and we must speak and act as one to prevail.

By the same token, however, our argument serves as a reconceptualisation of the relationship between violence, identity and power. We have shown that violence is not a terminus but a way station at a crossroads and that it feeds into identity and power as much as it derives from them. In sum, we call for an analytic framework which gives up the neat parsimony of a linear conceptual model—where identity conflicts/power struggles lead to violence through influencing the use of power/the manipulation of identity—and which trades it in for the increased realism of a dynamic triangular model. In such a model there is no set starting point or end point. The three nodes—identity, violence and power—alternate their analytic status and each potentially functions as a cause, a mediator or an outcome at different moments in time, or at different steps of the analysis.

Trading parsimony for realism? Given the importance of parsimony as a principle for evaluating analytic models, that is certainly a risky trade. It becomes profitable only when more contextualisation sheds light on critical processes that a more parsimonious analysis would have overlooked—and that takes us to the third part of our text, the case studies.

Learning from the World

Our three studies addressed three very different areas of conflict: firstly, Hindu nationalism and communalist tensions in India; secondly, war and ethnic violence in the former Yugoslavia; thirdly, mobilisations against the invasion of Iraq in Scotland. The first and the most obvious point to be made from all three analyses concerns the contested nature of social categories and the centrality of such contestation to the nature of the conflict. In the Indian case, the contestation concerns both what categories are involved, and how those categories should be defined. Or rather, by redefining the meaning of the core category 'India', the nature of the intergroup relations in which Indians are involved is changed. Thus, by construing the country as an essentially Hindu nation (as symbolised by the cow), Hindu nationalists not only exclude Muslims from the national category but constitute them as a threat both symbolically (they kill cows) and practically (they undermine the economy).

In the former Yugoslavia we see even more starkly the ways in which categories are contested and categories change. The major issue in the region is how diverse and cosmopolitan populations became frozen into ethnic categories. How come people who married across ethnic boundaries, who prioritised class above ethnicity, who often were ignorant of the ethnic origins of even close friends came to act and see the world through an ethnic prism? To refer to ethnic categories as if they were timeless, sheds no light on the process. Indeed to treat ethnic categories as timeless is part of the process.

Finally, in Scotland, the question of whether to support the Iraq invasion or not depended on whether it was regarded as 'our war' and that in turn depended upon how people defined who 'we' was. Was the conflict one in which British democracy stood together against an evil dictator with all the echoes of a united Britain in the Second World War? Or was it one in which English imperialism was having its last throw—an imperialism in which, it was claimed, Scotland shared no part and indeed had been more a victim that a contributor to it in the past? On such matters popular support for the war—and hence the political ability to prosecute the war—depended.

But, each of the three case studies also tells something more about the nature and dynamics of identity, violence and power. The Indian case tells us how violence is not simply a product and alerts us to the multiple ways in which identity, violence and power influence, and are influenced by, each other. When we first went into the tent of the *Vishwa Hindu Parishad* in Allahabad and came across the vile depictions of Muslims—so reminiscent of Nazi anti-Semitic caricatures—it seemed to us that the key issue was indeed to explain why such celebrations of intergroup violence were possible. But the more we analysed the images, we saw how the outgroup target varied while the overall message stayed the same: 'our political rivals expose you to threat while we defend you'. Increasingly it became clear that the invocation of intergroup violence was a means of altering relations of power and influence within the Hindu community itself. It was a means of saying that Hindu *Nationalists* represent interests of all Hindus, while others don't. In this instance violence was a tool designed to help substantiate the claim that 'we are of you, we understand your experience, we act for you'—the key claims of effective leadership (Haslam, Reicher, & Platow, 2011).

But if influence and power are outputs of invoking violence, this is not to deny that the exercise of power is also an input to violent social relations. Indeed, we saw how the Gujarat riots of 2002 are a classic example of authorities condoning violence and failing to intervene against it. As we have stressed, our aim is not to substitute one linear model of identity-violence-power for another, but rather to discard linearity in its entirety, to examine the ways in which each term relates to others in different ways at different points in time. Hindu nationalists both use power to enable violence to occur and use this violence to consolidate power. As we write, with the *Bharatiya Janata Party* (Indian people's party—BJP) in government and Narendra Modi in office as Prime Minister, it is a depressingly effective strategy.

Moving now to the former Yugoslavia, we see even more clearly and in more detail how violence becomes a driving force, specifically in reconfiguring identities. The figures are quite stark. Ethnic and religious identity became entrenched only in the aftermath of violent conflict. Likewise, forms of cross-ethnic solidarity, which were widespread in 1990, had all but disappeared by 2006. To recap, perhaps the most dramatic of all our figures concerns support for 'mixed' marriages (the most intense of solidarities). Over the period, this fell from 63% to 22% in Croatia and from 67% to 17% in Bosnia among young adults.

The point here, though, is that not only did war change social categories but also those categories stayed changed after the war was over. It is not only present violence but also the shadow of past violence that configures identity and power. That is particularly clear in our analysis of post-war Croatia, as are the reasons. On the one hand, past violence can always be invoked to support the narrative of a nation under siege, always vulnerable, always under potential attack, where survival depends upon further enforced solidarity. Those who criticise Croatia succour its enemies and pain its defenders.

On the other hand, where violence forges a new identity (in this case Croatian nationhood) then to question that violence or those who carried out that violence is not to criticise a contingent aspect of the group, but its very existence. It is impossible to both claim loyalty to the group and to oppose the conditions of its formation. So individual critics are left with one of two choices: either they stay silent or they place themselves in exile. Either choice contributes to the epistemic isolation of other critics and renders dissent ever more improbable.

Moving once more, this time to Scotland, we gain further insights into the ways that particular constructions of identity gain purchase—and also when they fail to gain purchase. For the first and most obvious point here is that the 'official version' in support of the Gulf war, one supported both by the UK government and by the devolved Scottish government, gained only limited support. Between a third and a half of the Scottish electorate declared themselves 'angry' or else 'disgusted' by the invasion. What is more, an analysis of political debates suggests that this opposition is bound up with a rejection of the 'official' identity narrative. As we argue above, supporters of the war characterised it as a defence of British democratic values against a foreign dictator; opponents (at least initially) characterised it as an assertion of English imperialism against a weaker foe.

So why did the dominant version fail, and why particularly in Scotland? Three factors emerge as particularly important. The first is the way that the oppositional narrative resonates with other familiar narratives. Ever since the Thatcherite deindustrialisation of the 1980s hit Scotland's traditional heavy industries particularly hard, there has been a strong sense of Scotland as a victim of English domination. Scotland could be characterised as a victim of English colonialism (sometimes dubbed 'the wretched of the north' in clear reference to Fanon's, 1961/2004, classic anti-colonial text). The anti-war position was easily assimilated to this familiar story.

Second, the opposition showed considerable rhetorical skill—witcraft, to use Billig's (1987) term—in expounding their position. They devoted particular attention to establishing an alternative construction of identities to the mainstream and, unlike the mainstream, they were both consistent (speaking with one voice) and yet flexible in adapting their 'Goliath versus David' construction to new circumstances once the war had started. Consistency combined with flexibility constitutes the ideal characteristics for minority influence (Mugny, 1982).

Third, there was a lively anti-war media in Scotland to let people know that, if they opposed the war, they were not alone. Unlike the epistemic isolation which curtailed dissent in Croatia, epistemic validation was available in the Scottish context and where those against the war were exposed to such validation (by reading the anti-war media) they were willing to give political expression to their views.

So, bringing the case studies together, they underline not only the contingent nature of identity, but also the inadequacy of a linear approach to identity-violence-power. They sustain the need to treat violence as not just a product but as productive of identity/power; They show how violence functions by altering epistemic relations between actors; and they highlight the role of epistemic isolation in sustaining dominant narratives, and hence the importance of maintaining and creating epistemic fluidity in order to enable opposition. But there is one more key element which we need to add to this list and which, like the contestation of social categories, is evident in all three of the case studies.

That extra element is a fresh look at the dynamics of mobilisation, which has been imminent throughout our discussions. Indeed, mobilisation occurs at multiple levels. To start with, insofar as categories are not naturally given, particular categorical constructions are actively promoted by leaders and active choices are made by followers as to whether to accept or reject them.

Next, those categories create new constituencies (and destroy old ones) which deliver the social power to impact the social fabric. In India, the consolidation of a Hindu constituency has provided a route to state power for the Hindu nationalist BJP. In Croatia, the occlusion of cleavages based on political and economic inequality diffused the opposition to Tudjman for a critical period and gave time for the old apparatchiks to become new oligarchs. In Scotland, the formation of a nationalist constituency that feels ill-served by the UK's Westminster Parliament lies behind the relentless rise of Scottish nationalism to the extent that, as we write in 2016, parties supporting independence now have an absolute stranglehold on the electoral landscape.

These successes illustrate the fact that the processes we describe do not just create new constituencies, but consolidate particular individuals and parties in leadership positions for those constituencies. By invoking, facilitating or permitting violent confrontations with Muslims, Modi and the BJP were able to position themselves as defenders of the Hindus. Through association with the struggle which founded an independent Croatian state, Tudjman's position was rendered inviolate and critics of his regime, or of his policies of privatisation of public goods, were excluded from the nation. Through dissociation from violence that is seen as imposed on the Scottish people, Alex Salmond became the only First Minister of Scotland with an absolute majority of seats in the devolved Scottish Parliament.

Learning from Perplexity

Having summarised what we have learnt from our studies of specific case studies, let us now conclude by considering the general lessons that emerge from our overall analysis. We divide these into conceptual, methodological, and practical implications.

Conceptually, we have sought to challenge models which are based on identifying root causes and predicting outcomes. But why bother with analysis if we cannot foretell the future? To borrow from a longstanding critique of economics, aren't we like the forecaster who cannot tell you what the weather will be like tomorrow, who probably cannot tell you whether it will rain today, but who can explain why you needed an umbrella yesterday?

Our intellectual and practical cases are intermeshed. The reasons for rejecting the root cause and prediction approach stem from our critique of linear approaches to identity, violence and power. As we have stressed, it is more helpful to view these as elements in an interconnected system where each can be a precursor or an outcome, a moderator or a mediator to the others. Moreover, just as each element may impact the others, so it may itself be impacted and change in the process. As a result, the route through which one got into a particular configuration of elements is not necessarily the best way out. It may not even be a possible way out since, as one moves through the terrain of identity, violence and power, the terrain itself is changed. Therefore, instead of undertaking the futile enterprise of identifying root causes of a conflict, it is generally more productive to look for a variety of factors that can play the role of *levers for change*, whether or not these factors were drivers in the historic process that brought about a current crisis or stalemate. For example, electoral settings that create a political incentive to mobilise ethnic hatred will always add an additional burden to a society that has already been the theatre of ethnic violence (whether or not there has been a causal relation between elections and violence in the past); humanitarian interventions that contain the human consequences of a conflict are always likely to affect—ideally, to broaden—future options for handling a conflict (because it will necessarily make a difference for the subsequent dynamic which magnitude of violence has being reached).

The triangular dynamics between identity, violence and power also heighten the need for a representational and a mobilisational view of understanding and action. Issues of identity and power are not given 'out there' in the world such that we read them off in ways that are pre-given by our cognitive architecture. Rather, we are confronted with an inherently opaque world and we are offered ways of making sense of it by our peers, by the media and by our leaders. Sense making is a slippery and non-deterministic process. In dealing with identity and power (and hence violence) it is made all the more slippery and unpredictable by the fact that we are dealing not only with our own understandings of the world but also with our understandings of how others understand the world.

So if we cannot identify root causes and we cannot predict futures, what can we do? At the outset, we argued that we can precisely puncture certainties—often self-fulfilling—by pointing out the contingent nature of identity, violence and power and the dynamics between them. Indeed, by opening uncertainties we allow new possibilities and new choices about the future. Hindus are not doomed to riot against Muslims, Croats are not doomed to build their nation as a fortress against Serbs and Scots are not doomed to side with the English to colonise the world. To argue as if they are is to buy in to the arguments of those who seek to essentialise these options by any means. It is, effectively, to reward them for their use of violence. Therefore, the importance of chipping away at certainties should not be underestimated.

But now, at the end of our book, perhaps we can go a little further. While we still cannot predict outcomes, we can at least identify some of the levers by which different configurations of identity, violence and power may be brought about. That is, even if one cannot definitively say what the outcome of a particular sense-making process will be, the dynamic triangular model developed in this book points to specific processes through which certain representations outweigh others, or new alternatives open up. It invites analysts of social change or activists of social justice to look more closely at what people think others think— and at which new channels of communication must open in order to make available the understandings of others. In the same way that our model opens new questions, so it identifies new sites where efforts might be more profitably applied in order to produce a less oppressive and less violent world.

One direct implication concerns the relationship between generality and specificity. In moving away from linear and predictive models, we argue that the relationship between the elements of our model can take many forms and can be dealt with in many different ways. The most propitious explanation and the most effective response therefore depend upon examining how a general analysis (e.g., of the involved psychological processes) plays out in specific contexts. Analyses of violence must therefore always be situated rather than abstracted. This, then, takes us on to the methodological lessons that we draw from this book.

On the one hand, it should be apparent, both from the evidence adduced in our theoretical chapters and from our own empirical chapters, that we are firm advocates of methodological pluralism. Different approaches are necessary to ask different questions. For instance, survey methods and statistical analyses are helpful in identifying general patterns and their change across time, while close textual analysis helps us identify the rhetoric constructions of identity and power which sustain those patterns (driving change and/or flourishing when changes occurs). So, our argument is to retain the broad nature of our methodological tool kit and not to throw anything out.

On the other hand, we appeal for this tool kit to be made even broader by including an approach that is much too rarely applied in social psychological analyses: the *case history study*. Moreover, we don't relegate case studies to the background—as something which we perform in order to inform subsequent and supposedly more definitive social psychological studies. We see them as a full-fledged component of a research design in their own right.

Case studies are the means par excellence by which we can examine in their full richness how psychological processes manifest themselves in specific social contexts and how they manifest themselves differently in different social contexts. They expose our models to the harsh discipline of the real world. They tell us whether our models are actually useful in making sense of the phenomena we purport to explain, they let us know whether the variables we manipulate in our experiments and the constructs we include in our questionnaires are actually relevant or important to these phenomena and they alert us to errors of commission and omission in our thinking. They allow us to develop as well as test out existing models. It is therefore rare to conduct a case study and not be forced to adjust these models a little bit at least. Case studies, in other words, help us learn from the world—and not just declare to the world that our hypotheses were right.

Case history studies are particularly valuable for examining relatively rare and unpredictable phenomena such as those that concern us here. Studying the critical processes through which the fluidity of collective identity is temporality suspended or violently disrupted is highly challenging. Such events are a rare species indeed. The challenge is made even greater by the fact that (by definition) turning points constitute transient phenomena whose occurrence only becomes obvious *in retrospect*—when the opportunity to make direct observations has already passed. As a consequence, social psychologists need to enrich their methodological expertise with the kind of instruments that historians resort to in order to reconstitute past events: archival materials, testimonies and other oral histories, retrospective surveys, secondary sources and so on. What is more, we need not only to study the past but also to study how the legacy of the past shapes the path from the present into the future; that is, how collective memories shape present options (as well as how present agendas reshape collective memories).

Finally, case studies alert us to the contingency of social processes. As we look in detail, we see the roles of human agency and of chance at critical junctures. We see particular *moments of fluidity* where very small differences could have radically altered the trajectory of events (even if, later, much larger differences would have made no difference at all). We are left with the sense that things didn't have to turn out like that. People were not doomed to end up as they did. In this particular sense, our fate is of human making.

That, ultimately, is our key practical message. The notion that 'that's just the way things are' is a clarion call to passivity, to accepting the status quo and hence to ensuring that the status quo endures. 'Boys will be boys' allows us to live with gendered violence. 'Groups will be groups' allows us to live with ethnic, religious and other forms of collective violence. Moreover, even if we ourselves reject these siren words, the belief that others believe them is equally pernicious and equally effective in demobilising dissent. Ultimately, then, the most significant service we can provide is to show that identity, power and violence are not set or pre-ordained and to show it in a way that we know others have been shown it too.

In short, this book feeds into a vision of social psychological research that takes the study of turning points in conflicts seriously, that orients to fundamental shifts in collective identities whenever and wherever these occur, that rejects the notion that we are trapped in deterministic causal webs and that uses turning points—however sombre the places to which they take us—as inspiration for a fresh look at human nature. This fresh look allows us to see human beings neither as programmed to hate nor as programmed to obey. It suggests instead that what makes us human is our capacity to come together, to struggle and to make our own histories both for the better and for the worse.

References

Billig, M. (1987). *Arguing and thinking: A rhetorical approach to social psychology.* Cambridge: Cambridge University Press.

Haslam, S. A., Reicher, S. D., & Platow, M. J. (2011). *The new psychology of leadership: Identity, influence and power.* London: Psychology Press.

Herrera, M., & Reicher, S. (1998). Making sides and taking sides: An analysis of salient images and category constructions for pro- and anti-Gulf War respondents. *European Journal of Social Psychology, 28*(6), 981–993.

Mugny, G. (1982). *The power of minorities*. London: Academic Press.

Noelle-Neumann, E. (1984/1993). *The spiral of silence: Public opinion—Our social skin* (2nd ed.). Chicago and London: The University of Chicago Press.

Orwell, G. (1949). *Nineteen eighty-four*. London: Secker & Warburg.

Index

A

accountability, 26–33
ancient hatreds, 3–35
anti-war protest, 215–20, 224
apartheid, 32, 88, 109
Arendt, Hannah, 50–3
authoritarian personality, 41

B

Balkan Ghosts, 30
banal nationalism
    and mobilisation, 217
    in Croatia, 112
banality of evil, 50–3
Billig, Michael, 17, 21, 79, 111, 112, 217
Brubaker, Rogers, 8, 147
Burgundian, 18

C

case histories, 149, 247–57
clash of civilizations, 5, 6, 8, 11
Cold War
    emergency rehearsal, 115
collective agency, 85–8
collective guilt, 195, 196, 196n2
collective memory, 18, 42, 106–12, 124, 143–8, 164
colonialism
    divide-and-rule, 145
    in India, 148
    in Rwanda, 49, 82, 145
communication
    implicit, 79
conformity bias, 43–8
critical junctures, 129–50
critical media, 9, 81

Note: Page numbers followed by "n" denote notes.

© The Author(s) 2017
G. Elcheroth, S. Reicher, *Identity, Violence and Power*,
DOI 10.1057/978-1-137-31728-5

critical patriotism
  in Croatia, 196
  in Scotland, 217
  in Serbia, 196
Croatia
  Homeland war, 194, 197, 199, 202, 207, 208
  Tudjman's legacy, 198

D

Davies, James C., 116, 117
de Villepin, Dominique, 5, 6
democracy, 221, 222, 227–9
devolution, 218
disobedience, 50, 59, 227
dissent
  delegitimisation, 211
  repression, 8, 123, 136, 186, 198, 209
  self-censorship, 81, 209
diversionary war hypothesis
  in interstate war, 135
  in intrastate violence, 121, 136

E

elections, 135, 137, 139, 140, 161, 167, 216
epistemic isolation
  and discrimination, 77, 78, 80
  and epistemic coordination, 77–80
  and media repression, 123, 136, 186, 198, 209
  in extermination camps, 55, 56, 64
  in the Milgram experiment, 58n1
ethnic
  competition theory, 20, 22
  conflict, 8, 11, 18, 24, 73, 75, 135, 147, 183–6, 189
  groups, 10, 18, 27, 32, 117, 124
  segregation, 30–3
evolutionism, 10, 11, 47, 76, 88, 116, 117, 146, 225

F

fatalism, 19, 31, 33–5
Former Yugoslavia
  ethnic relationships, 19–21, 28, 43, 62–4, 67, 77, 85–7, 89, 92, 101, 121
  mixed marriage, 185, 186, 192
  myth of ethnic war, 207
  Yugoslav identity, 190

G

Gagnon, Valère, 134, 184
genocide
  Rwanda, 49, 82, 145
Guisan, Henri, 106–8

H

Hindu nationalism
  Arya Samaj, 175, 176
  Indian Peoples Party (BJP), ix, 156–61, 167, 172, 251, 253, 254
  revivalism, 175
  Sangh Parivar, 179
  World Hindu council (VHP), 155–69, 177
Hobsbawm, Eric, 101, 118
humanitarian aid, 103
Huntington, Samuel, 5, 8, 11–13, 17, 20, 31, 116

I

identity
  and performance, 73–95
  and social practice, 99, 108, 124, 129
  demystification, 88–91
  entrepreneurs, 134
  manipulation, 90
  markers of, 10, 76, 88, 89, 104, 192
institutional facts, 86
instrumentalism, 93, 147, 185, 229
International Criminal Tribunal for the former Yugoslavia, 193
invasion of Iraq, 5, 93, 133, 215, 224, 233–6
Israeli-Palestinian conflict, 92, 142–3

K

kinship, 9–11, 13, 20, 32, 33

L

leadership, 8, 27–9, 34, 35, 39, 45, 65, 107, 122, 129–50

M

Macek, Ivana, 102, 103, 105
mass media influence, 81, 82, 84, 90, 93, 94, 184, 211, 215, 219, 239
Milgram, Stanley, 40–5, 48, 52, 53, 58–64
Milosevic, Slobodan, 40, 132, 133, 140, 141
Minorities at Risk, 121, 136

mobilisation, 88–94, 108, 117, 119, 120, 123, 132, 138–41, 155–80, 195–205, 219–33, 236–9, 253–4
Modi, Narenda, 157, 158, 161, 167–72

N

nationalism
  in Scotland, 218
  national identification, 210, 233

O

obedience, 40–4, 48, 53–60

P

Paluck, Elisabeth, 82, 239
parliamentary debates, 218, 219, 225
perplexity, v–viii, xvi–xvii, 254–8
persecuting society, 146
Peterson, Roger, 27
Pluralistic Memories Project, xx–xxi
power struggles, 10, 129–43
prediction, x–xiv, 6, 115, 254–5
primordialism, 3–26
prisons, 55

R

rally effects
  in Serbia, 132
  in the UK, 133
realistic conflict theory, 13–6, 21
resilience, 53, 102–4, 217–8, 229–33

resistance
  in extermination camps, 55, 56, 64
  in Robben Island, 55, 65
riots
  Gujarat, 159, 173, 179
  India, 25, 155–80
root causes of conflict, 101, 115–23

S
Sarajevo
  siege, 100, 105
  trenches, 104, 105, 183, 184
self-fulfilling prophecies, 141–2
self-sustaining conflicts, 121
Sherif, Muzafar, 14, 15, 21, 22
social dominance theory, 46–8
social identity theory, 21, 24, 77
social representation theory
  meta-representations, 80–2
  shared knowledge, 77–80
Stanford Prison Experiment, 43, 48, 54, 57
system justification theory, 46, 48

T
Tajfel, Henri, 21–3, 77
terrorist threat
  in US, 144
trial
  Abu Ghraib, 48, 49

Eichmann, 50–3, 56, 57
Gacacas, 49
Gotovina, 206
Karadzic, 28
Lasva Valley, 29, 105
turning points, 76, 100, 257

U
Underground, 109

V
violence, 3, 4, 6–8, 17–20, 24–35, 48, 73, 99–125

W
war against terror, 221
Wilkinson, Steve, 25, 138, 139, 160, 161, 168, 173
World War I
  outbreak, 40, 119

Y
Yugoslav Public Opinion Studies (YPOS), 185–91

Z
Zimbardo, Phil, 43–6, 48, 49, 54, 58

The manufacturer's authorised representative in the EU is Springer Nature Customer Service Centre GmbH, Europaplatz 3, 69115 Heidelberg, Germany. If you have any concerns regarding our products, please contact ProductSafety@springernature.com

Printed and bound by CPI Group (UK) Ltd, Croydon, CR0 4YY

23/03/2026

02076734-0003